THE SUBLIME SAVAGE

A study of James Macpherson
and
The Poems of Ossian

James Macpherson 1736–96 (by Reynolds)

I dined with Dempster, having engaged to meet Dr Blair and Mr Macpherson at his house. The Sublime Savage (as I call Macpherson) was very outrageous today, throwing out wild sallies against all established opinions. We were very merry. He and I and Blair walked into town together. I brought on the subject of reserve and dignity of behaviour. Macpherson cursed at it, and Blair said he did not like it. It was unnatural, and did not show the weakness of humanity. In my opinion, however, it is a noble quality.

James Boswell, *London Journal*, 1762–3.

THE SUBLIME SAVAGE

A Study of James Macpherson
and
The Poems of Ossian

FIONA J. STAFFORD

EDINBURGH UNIVERSITY PRESS

© Fiona J. Stafford 1988
Edinburgh University Press
22 George Square, Edinburgh

Set in Linotron Palatino and
printed in Great Britain by
Redwood Burn Limited,
Trowbridge, Wilts

British Library Cataloguing
  in Publication Data
Stafford, Fiona J.
The sublime savage: a study of James
Macpherson and the poems of Ossian.
1. Poetry in English. Macpherson, James.
Ossianic poems
I. Title
821'.6

ISBN 0 85224 569 5
     0 85224 609 9 Pbk

Contents

	List of illustrations	vi
	Acknowledgements	vii
	Abbreviations	viii
	Prologue	1
1.	Macpherson's Childhood in the Scottish Highlands	6
2.	Macpherson at the University of Aberdeen, 1752–1755	24
3.	Macpherson's Early Poetry	40
4.	*The Highlander*	61
5.	*The Death of Oscur*	77
6.	*Fragments of Ancient Poetry*	96
7.	The Highland Tours	113
8.	*Fingal*	133
9.	Macpherson's Vision of Celtic Scotland	151
10.	The Response to *Ossian*	163
	Epilogue	181
	Surviving Gaelic Manuscripts collected by Macpherson	184
	Works by James Macpherson, including major editions of Ossian	185
	Index	188

List of Illustrations

1. James Macpherson 1736–96 (by Reynolds)
2. Map of Scotland
3. Map of Badenoch area
4. Map of the North-West Highlands and Islands showing places visited by Macpherson
5. Weird Scene, Moonlight, 1803 (by Cotman)
6. Title page of Fingal
7. Trenmor and Inibaca (by Angelica Kauffman)
8. Ossian Evoking Spirits on the Banks of the Lora (by Gerard)
9. Apotheosis of Napoleon's Generals (by Girodet)
10. The Dream of Ossian (by Ingres)

Acknowledgements

Before mentioning the numerous individuals who have contributed to this book, I would like to express my gratitude to the staff of the following institutions: The Bodleian, Taylorian and English Faculty Libraries in Oxford, The National Library of Scotland, the Scottish Records Office, The School of Scottish Studies and Edinburgh University Library in Edinburgh, Aberdeen University Library, The Macpherson Museum in Newtonmore, The Public Records Office, the India Office Library and the British Museum in London.

For permission to reproduce the illustrations, I am indebted to The Trustees of the British Museum, The National Portrait Gallery, London; The Collection of Lord Hume of the Hirsel KT; Musée National de Malmaison, Rueil-Malmaison, France; Musée Ingres de Montauban, France. The maps are the work of Malcolm Sparkes.

Many people have helped me with my research and I would like to express warm thanks to all of them, including those who prefer to remain anonymous. Special thanks must go to Mr W. D. Macpherson for his invaluable help, and also to Dr Alan G. Macpherson and Mr Ronald Black for information and advice. For constructive criticism, I am also grateful to Dr Howard Gaskill, Dr Roger Lonsdale, Professor David Daiches and Professor Thomas Crawford. I would like to thank Col and Mrs R. T. S. Macpherson for inviting me to Balavil to see James Macpherson's country mansion and I am also indebted, in various ways, to Sir William Macpherson of Cluny, Mr Alan Bell, Mr A. I. S. Macpherson, Mr Jack Richmond MBE, Jay Macpherson, Dr Malcolm Chapman, Mr Harry Ritchie and Ms Veronica Watts. Professor Marilyn Butler and Dr J. D. Fleeman, too, have always been generous with their time and knowledge.

My chief debts, however, are to Dr Roy Park, who has guided my work with ceaseless enthusiasm, and to my parents, whose contributions are too varied and extensive to list. I would also like to thank my husband, Malcolm, for providing the maps and so much more: this book is dedicated to him.

Finally, I would like to thank the British Academy and Lincoln College, Oxford, for the Research Fellowship which has enabled me to complete this book.

Abbreviations

Texts
Fingal   J. Macpherson, *Fingal, an Ancient Epic Poem in Six Books; together with several Other Poems composed by Ossian, the Son of Fingal* (London 1762)
Fragments   J. Macpherson, *Fragments of Ancient Poetry, collected in the Highlands of Scotland, and translated from the Galic or Erse Language* (Edinburgh 1760)
Ossian   Refers to the collected edition, including both *Fingal* and *Temora*, but not *Fragments*.
Temora   J. Macpherson, *Temora, an Ancient Epic Poem in Eight Books: together with several Other Poems composed by Ossian, the Son of Fingal* (London 1763)

Manuscript Collections
ADV MS   National Library of Scotland (MS from the Advocates Library)
BL MS   The British Library
Bod MS   The Bodleian Library
EUL MS   Edinburgh University Library
IO MS   The India Office Library
PROB   The Public Record Office (Probate)
SRO   The Scottish Record Office

Journals
BNYPL   *Bulletin of the New York Public Library*
CD   *Creag Dhubh* (Journal of the Clan Macpherson Association)
MLR   *Modern Language Review*
SGS   *Scottish Gaelic Studies*
SHR   *Scottish Historical Review*
SLN   *Scottish Literary News*
SR   *Scottish Review*
SS   *Scottish Studies*
SSL   *Studies in Scottish Literature*
TGSG   *Transactions of the Gaelic Society of Glasgow*
TGSI   *Transactions of the Gaelic Society of Inverness*

Prologue

> I shall conclude this general account with some remarks on four of the principal works of poetry in the world, at different periods of history – Homer, the Bible, Dante, and let me add, Ossian.
> William Hazlitt, 'On Poetry in General', 1818[1]

To the modern reader, Hazlitt's addition of *Ossian* to his short-list of the world's greatest poetry seems bizarre. Few people today have even heard of *The Poems of Ossian*, and fewer still have read them (indeed, Macpherson's obscurity is more or less sealed by the lack of twentieth-century editions). Those who do know something of *Ossian* tend to dismiss it with a smile and a vague reference to literary forgeries – wasn't it something to do with Chatterton? Surely Macpherson was a fraud and, therefore, unworthy of any serious attention? And yet Hazlitt was by no means dull. He rated *Ossian* among the best in the world.

Whatever we may think of Hazlitt's judgement in this instance, there is no doubt that Macpherson's *Ossian* aroused enormous enthusiasm in the late eighteenth and early nineteenth centuries. Its immediate appeal to readers of the 1760s can be seen in the effusive letter Andrew Erskine sent to James Boswell, after discovering the delights of *Fingal*:

> It is quite impossible to express my admiration of his Poems; at particular passages I felt my whole frame trembling with ecstacy; but if I was to describe all my thoughts, you would think me absolutely mad. The beautiful wildness of his fancy is inexpressibly agreeable to the imagination.[2]

For Erskine, Macpherson's translations of the third-century Celtic bard, Ossian, were the supreme expression of sublimity and sensibility in poetry: the question of authenticity was not an issue.

Erskine's response is typical of readers of the late eighteenth century, when the vogue for *Ossian* spread rapidly from Britain to Europe and America. During the century following the appearance of *Fragments of Ancient Poetry*, 1760, Macpherson's work was translated into twenty-six different languages. *Ossian* provided inspiration for readers as diverse as Burns and Buonaparte, Ingres and Angelica Kauffmann, Madame de Staël and Mendelssohn. All the major English Romantic poets came under Macpherson's spell, while on the Continent, Goethe's young Werther created a cult of melancholic, blue-coated Ossian readers. *The Poems of Ossian* were turned into plays, paintings and musical works, as artists all over the world turned to Macpherson for fresh subjects.

Although a number of works have been written on Macpherson's influence abroad, *Ossian* continues to be virtually ignored by twentieth-century critics of English and Scottish literature. In a recent article, urging a reconsideration of Macpherson's achievement, Andrew Hook commented, 'Scottish cultural historians just cannot go on dismissing Macpherson because of the largely irrelevant fraudulence issue.'[3] The 'fraudulence issue', however, persists in damaging Macpherson's reputation, as it has for the past two centuries. Within weeks of Macpherson's first publication, doubts were raised about the authenticity of the Gaelic material and the controversy has raged fitfully ever since. Had Macpherson really translated ancient Gaelic poetry collected in the Scottish Highlands? Or had he invented Ossian and the stories of the Celtic heroes in order to dupe the English reading public?

The debate over whether Macpherson was a scholarly editor or a charlatan was at its most heated in the two decades following his publications. The most famous of the attacks came in 1775, when Johnson published his *Journey to the Western Islands of Scotland*:

> I suppose my opinion of the poems of Ossian is already discovered. I believe they never existed in any other form than that which we have seen. The editor, or author, never could shew the original; nor can it be shewn by any other; to revenge reasonable incredulity, by refusing evidence, is a degree of insolence, with which the world is not yet acquainted; and stubborn audacity is the last refuge of guilt.[4]

Although much of Johnson's attack was unfounded, the moral indignation and authoritative delivery set the tone for the ensuing controversy. Johnson's remarks were followed by Malcolm Laing's debunking edition of *The Poems of Ossian*, 1805, in which eight years' efforts to prove Macpherson's work 'full of falsehood', were presented triumphantly to a bewildered public.[5] Even in the most recent contribution to the long-running debate, Hugh Trevor-Roper adopted a similarly judgmental attitude, presenting his case with a prejudice surpassing anything displayed by Johnson.[6]

The combative atmosphere of the *Ossian* controversy has distorted numerous views over the years. Critics have tended to be either 'for' or 'against' Macpherson and, therefore, highly selective in their presentations of evidence. The question of fraudulence has always loomed over any discussion of Macpherson's work, to the exclusion of more constructive approaches. Those who admired *Ossian* have devoted their energies to finding arguments for its authenticity, while those who disliked either the text or Macpherson himself, marshalled evidence to prove the poems a fake. Anyone coming to the controversy for the first time is likely to emerge exhausted and quite baffled about whether Macpherson created any or all of *The Poems of Ossian*? Did he actually translate many or any Gaelic poems? And if he did, were they ancient or modern? In manuscript or orally recited? Short, lyrical pieces? Or ballads? Or rambling epics?

During the course of the long debate, however, there have been a number of objective studies by scholars well qualified to assess Macpherson's treatment of his sources. The first, which appeared in 1805, contained an invaluable mass of letters and testimonies, collected by the Highland Society of Scotland during the major investigation that followed Macpherson's death in 1796.[7] The *Report*, edited by Henry Mackenzie, concluded that Macpherson had based his work on the popular ballads of the Highlands, incorporating some traditional plots and passages of accurate translation in long poems spun from his own imagination. The Committee's conclusions have been confirmed by all the most distinguished scholars who have since addressed themselves to the question, although it was not until 1952 that the Gaelic poems used by Macpherson were identified exactly, by D. S. Thomson.[8]

Although the Ossianic controversy has long been settled, a degree of confusion still attends Macpherson. The entry in the *Oxford History of English Literature* is a good example of the contemporary attitude to Macpherson. John Butt's account of *Ossian* is refreshingly free of Johnsonian moralising, but on the question of Gaelic, he remarks tentatively, 'Macpherson certainly knew some Gaelic'[9]. In fact, Macpherson was a native Gaelic speaker and continued to use a colloquial form of Gaelic in correspondence with fellow Highlanders long after he left Inverness-shire for London. One of the main problems with Macpherson criticism is the way in which it has tended to divide into two separate fields: those of Gaelic scholarship and English literature. The Gaelic scholars have generally attacked Macpherson for falsifying his sources, without showing any interest in the circumstances or the motives which led to the translations. *The Poems of Ossian* was published as an English text, but English literary critics, unfamiliar with the Gaelic tradition, have felt uncertain about dealing with it at all.

One of the chief difficulties is the lack of information available. The texts needed to understand Macpherson's work, such as the *Report* of 1805, J. F. Campbell's *Leabhar na Féinne*, (The Songs of the Fiana), 1872, or D. S. Thomson's *The Gaelic Sources of Macpherson's Ossian*, 1952, are neither easy to acquire, nor particularly inviting to the non-specialist (Campbell, for example, published all the surviving collections of heroic Gaelic ballads untranslated, so that readers could compare the various versions of a poem). Biographical information, so vital to any interpretation of Macpherson, is also scarce. Apart from the scattered references in eighteenth-century writings, the only biography is Bailey Saunders' *The Life and Letters of James Macpherson*, 1894, which has been out of print for nearly a century. J. N. M. Maclean's biographical thesis on 'The early Political Careers of James 'Fingal' Macpherson (1736–1796) and Sir John Macpherson, Bart. (1744–1821)', 1967, was so biased against the Macphersons that much of the material is distorted to the point of inaccuracy. But in order to understand *The Poems of Ossian*, some knowledge of James Macpherson's background and character is essential.

Macpherson's *Ossian* was by no means the work of a confidence trickster, bent on achieving fame and fortune through a clever hoax. Neither was it what it purported to be – a literal translation of Gaelic poems which had survived unaltered since the third century. Rather than sitting in judgement, however, it is perhaps more fruitful to consider Macpherson's motivation. Why should a young man of twenty-two be drawn to the character of an old Celtic bard? And what attracted Macpherson to the Gaelic poetry in the first place? Why did he think it would interest English speakers? And why didn't he produce straightforward, literal translations of the Highland poems? Above all, what was it about *The Poems of Ossian* that caused such a furore during the latter half of the eighteenth century and the Romantic period?

Although *Ossian* is a crucial text for literary historians interested in the origins of the Romantic Movement, it is also important as a work representative of the 1760s. Andrew Erskine saw *Fingal* as a 'criterion, to discover the taste of the present age',[10] and there can be few works which embody more fully the conflicting attitudes of the mid eighteenth century. Ossian was heralded as an Original Genius, and yet his simple effusions were polished enough to suit the refined tastes of the eighteenth-century aesthete. The work was presented as a classical epic and yet offered an alternative to the tired models of Greece and Rome. Macpherson opened a world of stormy mountain scenery, full of the grandeur and terror demanded by the new taste for the Sublime. At the same time, the appearance of antiquity gave a reassuring sense of permanence. *The Poems of Ossian* offered an imaginative escape to any one who found the prevailing climate of the Enlightenment somewhat lacking. As such, it is worth more than a passing smile.

NOTES
1. *The Complete Works of William Hazlitt*, ed. P. P. Howe, 21 vols, (London 1930–1934), V, 15.

Prologue

2. Erskine to Boswell, 10 January 1762, *Boswell's Correspondence with the Honourable Andrew Erskine*, ed. G. Birkbeck Hill, (London 1879), 39.
3. '"Ossian" Macpherson as Image Maker', *SR*, xxxvi, 1984, 39.
4. *A Journey to the Western Islands of Scotland*, 1775; ed. J. D. Fleeman, (Oxford 1985), 98.
5. *The Poems of Ossian, &c, Containing the Poetical Works of James Macpherson Esq, in prose and rhyme: with notes and illustrations by Malcolm Laing, Esq*, 2 vols (Edinburgh 1805), hereafter referred to as Laing, ed.
6. 'The Ossian Forgeries: Wrong but Romantic', *The Spectator*, 16 March 1985, 14–15.
7. H. Mackenzie (ed), *Report of the Committee of the Highland Society of Scotland, appointed to Inquire into the Nature and Authenticity of the Poems of Ossian*, (Edinburgh 1805), hereafter referred to as *Report*.
8. D. S. Thomson, *The Gaelic Sources of Macpherson's Ossian*, (Edinburgh 1952).
9. J. Butt, *The Mid-Eighteenth Century*, ed. G. Carnall, (Oxford 1979), 107.
10. Erskine to Boswell, 20 January 1762, op. cit. 43.

Macpherson's Childhood in the Scottish Highlands

> We were once ferried over the Spey by an old grey-haired Celt
> . . . who had, fifty years before, done the same duty for Macpherson. The poet was a great man from London and the court, bedizened with rings, gold seals, and furs; but he looked with a moistened eye on the turf school-house in which he had once taught English, and on the hills on which he had run in his youth. They were then his own property, and he told the ferryman, with strong emotion, and no doubt with Highland pride, that he would make every poor Highlander on his estate a comfortable and a happy man!
> R. Carruthers, *The Highland Notebook*, 1843[1]

As the Inverness train pulls out of the station at Kingussie, it passes a stone obelisk from which the face of an eighteenth-century gentleman is gradually wearing away. To most passengers, the monument is meaningless. James Macpherson is no longer a household name, and the idea that the man on the stone left instructions in his will for such a memorial to be built seems nothing but a piece of eighteenth-century folly. And yet, when Macpherson died in 1796, his body was taken from Badenoch on a journey lasting eighteen days, to be buried in Westminster Abbey. The news that the world famous author, James Macpherson, was dead, hit the national press.

Although Macpherson's statue, with its broken nose, is showing signs of age, a more lasting monument survives on the hill above. Balavil House (named Belleville by its original owner) was built by the Adam brothers as a Highland retreat for Macpherson, for times when the pressures of Parliament and London society became too intense. Balavil appears to have been more impressive than even Macpherson had intended, as he admitted in a letter to his friend Sir John Macpherson, the Governor General of India: 'I am involved in stones and mortar at Raits, and I partly repent of the magnitude of my Castle. The truth is that Adam's plan did not appear so large in my eyes on paper as on the hill, on which the House is rising. But I have gone too far to stop with any credit to myself.'[2] The elegant Georgian mansion overlooking the Spey valley is an appropriate memorial to the complicated character of its first occupant. Although the foundations are sunk deep in Highland soil, the house itself is a neoclassical edifice, designed according to the architectural canons of the late eighteenth century. Such a mixture of Highland materials and Lowland aesthetics is typical of Macpherson. *The Poems of Ossian* were the product of a similar taste, while Macpherson's own life shows a constant struggle to reconcile the conflicting loyalties to North and South.

Although Balavil may appear to have more in common with Bath or Edinburgh New Town than with the Highlands, Macpherson was by no means a wealthy stranger who bought up estates in the 1780s for their picturesque value. From the windows of the house, he could gaze across the Spey to a small farm at Invertromie, where he had been born on 27 October, 1736. Despite his own description of London as 'the city where I lived and passed the greatest and best part of my life'[3], Macpherson retained a strong affection for his native land throughout his life. Even in London, as a successful man about town, Macpherson continued to use his influence to obtain commissions for fellow members of the Clan, while his dinner parties frequently included recitations of Gaelic poetry. In Boswell's witty descriptions of his friend's behaviour, too, the joke is always upon the image of the Highlander in the capital city of England.[4] Although Macpherson left Scotland at the age of twenty-five, his character, attitudes and, indeed, his success were largely dependent on his early experiences of Highland life. *The Poems of Ossian* were rooted in Macpherson's native culture and in order to understand the English text, some knowledge of the Highlands in the eighteenth century is essential.

Any attempt to reconstruct an image of Highland life two centuries ago is limited by the difficulty of obtaining information. When Macpherson was a child there were still two distinct cultures in Scotland, divided by location, language and tradition. Although the division was gradually dissolving, the mutual suspicion between the Highlanders and Lowlanders was strong. In 1741, the SSPCK (Society in Scotland for Propagating Christian Knowledge) reported that the Highlands were the home of 'Ignorance, Popish and even Heathenish Superstition, Profaneness, Idleness, Theft, and many other Disorders'.[5] The Highland attitude to outsiders was hardly less prejudiced : according to the poet and essayist, Anne Grant, whose husband was the Minister at Laggan, ten miles west of Kingussie, the locals defined a Lowlander in the following terms:

> One who had neither ear for music, nor taste for poetry; – no pride of ancestry; – no heart for attachment; – no soul for honour: One who merely studied comfort and conveniency, and was more anxious for the absence of positive evil, than the presence of relative good . . . in short . . . what all highlanders cordially hated, – a cold, selfish, formal character.[6]

In the eyes of the Highlander, the rest of the country was filled with weak, materialistic people who were interested in nothing but their own advancement. Outside the Highlands, Northern Scotland was regarded as a wild, remote region, peopled by barbarians who should either be tamed or firmly ignored.[7]

Much of the prejudice against the Highlands stemmed from ignorance. The hostility of the landscape discouraged all but the most determined travellers, and it is significant that what is perhaps the fullest account of the region in the early eighteenth-century was written by a man who was not visiting the Highlands through choice. Edward Burt was employed in the Central Highlands in the 1720s–30s to execute General Wade's plans to build strategic military roads. His invaluable observations on the area were later published as *Letters from a Gentleman in the North of Scotland to his Friend in London*.

Burt's account of his journey makes it easy to understand why outsiders were reluctant to visit the Highland region, with the frequent references to snow and violent winds, to bogs and precipices, to the lack of roads and to the 'seeming sameness in all the rocky places'[8]. Crossing rivers sounds particularly hazardous :

> there was a river in my way so dangerous that I was set upon the shoulders of four Highlanders, my horse not being to be trusted to in such roughness, depth, and rapidity; and I really thought sometimes we should all have gone together.[9]

In addition to the dangerous terrain, there was also a strong likelihood of being robbed. The previous owner of Macpherson's estate, for example, Mackintosh of Borlum, was renowned for lurking in a souterrain above the road and ambushing travellers as they passed.[10] The physical dangers were also aggravated by the problem of Gaelic: not only was the landscape terrifying, but the natives spoke a foreign language. Even the houses, clothes and food were totally different from the rest of the country and to visitors, the Highlands seemed a primitive country, where strangely clad savages lived in huts. As a result, very few travellers ventured into the Highlands, and the descriptions that survive tend to be unsympathetic reports by men who were sent there for military reasons.

If there are few first-hand accounts from visitors in the early part of the century, however, there are even fewer descriptions from natives of the region. People who spend their whole lives in the same area are seldom aware of the distinguishing characteristics of their own society.[11] Only the educated Highlander who had travelled outside Northern Scotland would be in a position to write objectively about his home, while retaining the insights of the native. According to Anne Grant, however, the very fact of being educated altered the Highlander's attitude, especially towards traditional customs:

> the illiberal, ignorant, and bigotted prejudice, with which the

lowlanders formerly regarded this insulated, and, in a manner, concealed people, whom they only knew as rude warriors or valiant robbers – these prejudices I say, usurped some power over the mind of every highlander who received the benefit of a lowland education – in fact who had any education at all.[12]

Anxious to avoid ridicule, the Highlander refused to speak of his beliefs to an outsider, unless 'in some instances, he affected to speak of them with contempt, to enforce his pretensions to literature or philosophy'.[13] Mrs Grant's observation is corroborated by Boswell's account of the Highlander who answered his questions on second sight with 'the fallacious arguments of Voltaire and Hume'[14], while in Macpherson's own work, a certain embarrassment about local traditions is abundantly evident.[15]

Despite this difficulty, a number of works survive which show a native understanding of the Highland people, uninhibited by any consciousness of patronising Lowland attitudes. Martin Martin, who was born in Skye, produced two important reports at the turn of the eighteenth century: *A Voyage to St Kilda*, 1698, and *A Description of the Western Islands of Scotland*, 1703. Both works have a strongly medical slant, but among the pages of dietary detail and strange remedies there are invaluable insights into the everyday life of the people of the islands. Although Martin's works appear to be objective reports, there is a tendency to idealise the Scottish people and St Kilda is presented almost as a Northern Arcadia:

> The Inhabitants of *St Kilda* are almost the only People in the World who feel the Sweetness of true Liberty; what the Condition of the People in the Golden Age is feigned to be, that theirs really is, I mean in Innocency and Simplicity, mutual Love and cordial Friendship.[16]

The tone of Martin's work is particularly relevant to Macpherson, who viewed the Highlands in a similarly idealised manner:

> The seats of the Highland chiefs were neither disagreeable nor inconvenient. Surrounded with mountains and hanging woods, they were covered from the inclemency of the weather. Near them generally ran a pretty large river, which, discharging itself, not far off, into an arm of the sea, or extensive lake, swarmed with variety of fish. The woods were stocked with wild-fowl; and the heaths and the mountains behind them were the natural seat of the red-deer and roe. If we make allowance for the backward state of agriculture, the valleys were not unfertile; affording, if not all the conveniences, at least the necessarys of life. Here the chief lived, the supreme judge and law-giver of his own people . . .
> In this rural kind of magnificence, the Highland chiefs lived,

for many ages. At a distance from the seat of government, and secured, by the inaccessibleness of their country, they were free and independent.

(*Temora*, xv-xvi)

Although Macpherson's eulogies have none of Martin's practical details or gossip about local beliefs, the same notion of the Highlands retaining qualities belonging to the Golden Age is apparent. In Macpherson's essays, traditional Highland society is presented romantically, as an ideal against which to judge a degenerate modern civilisation. But for a more accurate impression, the accounts of Macpherson and Martin must be balanced by the less sympathetic responses of the soldiers who were posted North.

Revealing comparisons can be made between the enthusiastic descriptions of Macpherson and Martin and the shrewd, but often uncomprehending, letters of Edward Burt. Instead of emphasising the snow and storms which Burt found so wearing, Macpherson reports that the Highlanders lived in places 'neither disagreeable nor inconvenient' and sheltered from the weather by the hills. For Burt, the mountain landscape was hostile and full of potential dangers, but in Macpherson's eyes it provided a secure retreat, protecting the natives from the influence of the degenerate Lowlands. Macpherson's vision of the healthy, outdoor life is very different from Burt's constant references to the 'fluxes, fevers, agues, coughs, rheumatisms, and other distempers',[17] which seemed part of Highland life. Similarly, where Macpherson perceived a plentiful supply of food, Burt stressed the sparseness of the Highland diet, which involved bleeding the cattle by the end of the winter to make cakes in order to avoid starvation.[18] Characteristics such as physical strength and hardiness, which contributed to the notorious Highland pride, provoked visitors' fear rather than admiration. Even the tartan plaid, which Martin described merely as an interesting local feature, was seen as a battle dress, fully camouflaged, allowing swift movement and attended by a huge armoury of weapons.[19]

The difference between the views of the Highlanders and those of outside observers is nowhere more apparent than in passages concerning the Clan system and the power of the Chief. To men such as Burt or General Wade, the Highland Clans were powerful military units, which represented a potential threat to the stability of Britain.[20] The soldiers, who came to the Highlands as part of the various attempts to reduce the chances of further Jacobite Risings, were quite unable to understand the workings of an army based on family ties. For Burt, the Chiefs were tyrants who forced their followers to live in appalling conditions in order to retain the blind obedience to the head of the Clan.[21] His inability to dissociate the idea of power from material wealth is evident in his remarks on the misplaced 'ostenta-

Macpherson's Childhood in the Scottish Highlands

tion' of the Chiefs, one of whom is described as living not in a castle, but in 'a house hardly fit for one of our farmers of fifty pounds a-year'.[22]

For writers who lived in the Highlands, however, references to the Clan system invariably glowed with enthusiasm. For Anne Grant, Highland society displayed the triumph of affection over adversity:

> Every one of the tribe or neighbourhood endeared by affinity or mutual good offices, was in a greater or lesser degree beloved. This genial climate of the heart, this perpetual spring of the affections softened every hardship and made privations tolerable, from which we should shrink affrighted.[23]

In Macpherson's portrait of the Chief, too, he describes his authority as being that of a 'father', rather than of a judge or general (*Temora*, xv). Even Burt eventually came to realise that loyalty to the Chief was the result of love rather than of fear or obligation.[24]

According to Anne Grant, the Clan system meant that 'no Highlander ever once thought of himself as an individual'[25] and it was in this kind of close-knit community that Macpherson grew up. It was normal for Highlanders to seek marriage partners from within the Clan and James Macpherson's parents were no exception: 'His father's name was Andrew Macpherson, son to Ewan Macpherson, brother to the then Macpherson of Cluny – His mother's name was Helen Macpherson, Daughter of a respectable tacksman of the Second Branch of the Clan.'[26] James' father was closely related to the Clan Chief, and appears to have been a first cousin of Ewan Macpherson of Cluny, who became famous during the '45 Rebellion.

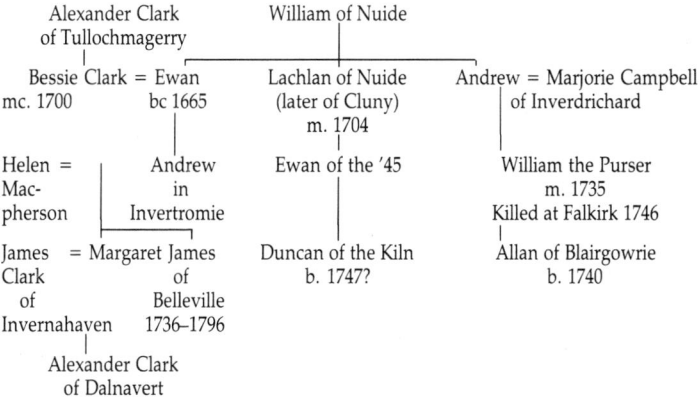

James' paternal grandfather was also called Ewan and, according to the research of Dr Alan G. Macpherson, he was the illegitimate elder brother of Cluny's father, Lachlan of Nuide.[27] J. N. M. Maclean, author of the only recent biographical study of Macpherson, seized on the notion of illegitimacy to suggest that Macpherson's father was a social outcast and probably destitute before marriage.[28] He then constructed an ingenious hypothesis suggesting that in returning to Badenoch as a wealthy man, James Macpherson's purpose was to humiliate the Cluny family, by forcing them to recognise his own illegitimate children as heirs to a large estate.[29] Given Macpherson's obvious affection for the Highlands and especially his own Clan, however, this argument seems ludicrous. The question of illegitimacy, which forms the crux of Maclean's argument is also completely misplaced. In the Highlands in the eighteenth century there was no social stigma attached to being a bastard. Although certain rights of inheritance might be forfeited, 'natural children' were very much part of the family:

> The love of kindred, so honourable to the Highland character, procures for *natural children* in that country a kindness and attention which they do not meet with elsewhere. A married lady in the Highlands would consider her children as disgraced if their *half-brothers* and *half-sisters* were not suitably provided for in the world; and, as they come out first, they not unfrequently fare the best[30]

Rather than being brought up with any sense of being an outcast by birth, then, James Macpherson seems to have come from close to the heart of his Clan. Far from being ashamed of his background, he is likely to have been proud of his relation to the Chief. Instead of being socially unacceptable, his family were from the upper class of Highland society and indeed, evidence exists to show that Allan Macpherson of Blairgowrie spent part of his childhood under the care of James' parents.[31]

The Highland emphasis on the family, or Clan, was in complete contrast to the urban civilisation that was developing in the rest of Britain. During the eighteenth century, a growing unease about the isolation of modern individuals can be discerned in the work of European writers. For Macpherson, the move to a modern city from Badenoch, where he knew everyone and was related to most, must have been particularly difficult. His childhood memories of a society based on family love rather than wealth or property undoubtedly contributed to the idealised vision of Highland life which he developed after moving South.

In a small community where everyone is interrelated, an interest in ancestry is inevitable. In the Scottish Highlands, genealogy was of great importance and many Clans could trace their forefathers back to

Macpherson's Childhood in the Scottish Highlands 13

one of the great Celtic heroes. Although the system of bardic patronage had largely died out by the eighteenth century, many Clan Chiefs were still attended by a bard who was responsible not only for the composition of poetry, but also for preserving the history of the Clan. Burt described the duties of the bard in his *Letters*:

> The *bard* is skilled in the genealogy of all the Highland families; sometimes preceptor to the young laird; celebrates, in Irish verse, the original of the tribe, the famous warlike actions of the successive heads, and sings his own lyrics as an opiate to the chief when indisposed for sleep.[32]

Knowledge of the past, of the deeds of one's ancestors, was a vital part of the Highland consciousness and was to emerge in 1762 as the theme of Macpherson's first Ossianic epic. Although Macpherson's motto, 'fortia facta patrum' (brave deeds of the forefathers) came from Virgil, it is not difficult to see the influence of traditional Highland values.

Although the position of bard to the Clan Chief was a specialised one, every village in the Highlands had its own poets and reciters. Music and poetry were an essential part of life, and songs accompanied everything from weddings and funerals to daily work in the fields, at sea, or at home. During the long winter evenings, which visitors such as Burt found intolerable, the local people would gather to listen to recitations of poems and stories. J. F. Campbell's collection, *Popular Tales of the West Highlands*, 1860–1862, includes a firsthand account of a traditional ceilidh by Hector Urquhart, the gamekeeper at Ardkinglas:

> In my native place, Pool-Ewe, Ross-shire, when I was a boy, it was the custom for the young to assemble together on the long winter nights to hear the old people recite the tales or sgeultachd, which they had learned from their fathers before them. In these days tailors and shoemakers went from house to house, making our clothes and shoes. When one of them came to the village we were greatly delighted, whilst getting new kilts at the same time. I knew an old tailor who used to tell a new tale every night during his stay in the village; and another, an old shoemaker, who, with his large stock of stories about ghosts and fairies, used to frighten us so much that we scarcely dared pass the neighbouring churchyard on our way home.[33]

The reciters of the stories were old men with a huge stock of tales which had been passed down from mouth to mouth, being embellished and recreated in each new recital. In a characteristic encomium, Mrs Grant described the old Highland sennachies as serving 'for song books, and circulating libraries, so faithfully do they preserve . . . "The tales of the times of old" and the songs of the bards, that now stroke the viewless harps on wandering clouds.'[34] Mrs Grant's quotation from *Ossian* shows that she saw distinct similarities between the old Highland storytellers and Macpherson's portrait of the Celtic bard. It is not unlikely that when Macpherson came to develop the character of Ossian, he was recalling the old men he had known since his childhood, such as Finlay Macpherson, who lived at Lynaberack, and spent his days and nights reciting Ossianic poetry to friends and neighbours.[35] For the Highlander who was no longer capable, physically, of continuing the traditional pursuits of hunting, fishing or driving cattle, contribution to the community seems to have consisted in entertainment.

The stories which Macpherson adapted for the **English**-reading public as *The Poems of Ossian* were traditional tales, well known throughout North West Scotland and Ireland. Macpherson's heroes, Fingal, Oscar, Ossian or Dermid, each had distinct characters, familiar to every Highlander from the earliest age, as can be seen in the following description of story-telling in Barra:

> During the recitation of these tales, the emotions of the reciters are occasionally very strongly excited, and so also are those of the listeners, almost shedding tears at one time, and giving way to loud laughter at another. A good many of them firmly believe in the extravagance of these stories.
>
> They speak of the Ossianic heroes with as much feeling, sympathy, and belief in their existence and reality as the readers of the newspapers do of the exploits of the British army in the Crimea or in India; and whatever be the extravagance of the legends they recite respecting them . . . the same character is always ascribed to the same hero in almost every story and by almost every reciter. Fingal, or rather Fionn, is never called the king of any country . . . but the king of the Finn, a body of men who were raised, according to the traditions current in the Long Island and other parts of the Highlands, in Ireland and in the Highlands, to defend both countries against foreign invaders, more especially the Scandinavians.[36]

The exploits of the Celtic heroes, handed down orally from generation to generation, had all the legendary appeal of the Arthurian myth, while retaining a vivid immediacy for the audience. The stories were primarily entertainment, but since the Highlanders claimed direct descent from the Celtic heroes, they also served to inspire the audience with memories of their heroic ancestors. One of James Macpherson's childhood friends described the use of Ossianic poetry in Badenoch as a moral guide:

> I heard my father tell that my Grandfather John Macpherson of

Benchar would different times cause my father to sit down by him to write some of them down from his mouth and strongly recommended their minds to adhere to some passages of them as a good rule for life.[37]

Thus the Highlanders were brought up to admire the ancient warriors of the Fiana, a military band consisting of the strongest and most able, whose purpose was to defend the Highlands against invasion.

The memory of the Fiana was not only perpetuated through popular stories, but through the very landscape of the Highlands. Any ancient monument whose origin was unknown, was attributed to the Celtic heroes.[38] Dunsgiath Castle in Skye was associated with Cuchullain, while in Badenoch, the huge Iron Age hill fort, Dun da Lamh, was generally regarded as the work of Fingal and his men as late as 1863.[39] Although Macpherson placed Ossian's river Conan in Glencoe, there were rivers, mountains and rocks bearing the names of the Fiana throughout the Highlands and Islands.[40]

The survival of ancient legends and monuments were part of the Highlanders' deep sense of the antiquity of their race, as can be seen in Hugh MacDonald's evidence of 1800:

> The Scandinavians who invaded the Isles and the Highlands, long after the time of the *Feinne*, were not able to change the language, or to destroy the monuments of our ancestors: for the descendants of those heroes maintained their independence on the main land, and retained the historical traditions and poetry of their fathers over every part of the country.[41]

The legends of the Fiana were symbols of the unconquerable spirit of the Highlanders, who saw themselves as a pure race, unsullied by foreign influences. Captain Burt observed the Highlanders' pride in their own unmixed blood and scorn of the hybrid English, remarking sardonically that he thought 'a little mixture in that sense would do themselves no manner of harm'.[42]

This particular form of Highland pride is clearly evident in Macpherson's descriptions: 'Their language is pure and original, and their manners are those of an ancient and unmixed race of men. Conscious of their own antiquity, they long despised others, as a new and mixed people' (*Temora*, ii). Macpherson's emphasis on language is highly significant because the Gaelic, as a Celtic language, was far older than English. Highlanders were fond of associating their tongue with the language of Adam and Eve, regarding English as an inferior hotchpotch of different languages.[43] In a revealing, if rambling, letter of 1806, Alexander Maclaurin asserted that Gaelic was 'the Mother of all the Languages in Europe, and . . . not derived from any other Language whatsoever'. After describing the movements of the Celts from Asia to Scotland, he concluded, 'neither the Romans, nor the Danes or Norwegians, the Saxons, nor the French were ever able to conquer the Gael . . . they kept their Country, their Language, and their Manners unto this day'.[44] To the Highlander, English was a debased, mongrel tongue belonging to a degenerate people who had no true heritage. Such an attitude, however, did little to endear the people of Northern Scotland to the rest of Britain.

Throughout the first half of the eighteenth century, the British Government was haunted by fears of Jacobite Rebellion. The warlike Highlanders, with their foreign language and culture, seemed ready to attack Britain from within at any moment, but after the Rising of 1715, the Government's vague anxiety became a serious political issue. The new policy was not to ignore the region, but to gain control, an objective which demanded a series of radical measures.

The survival of the Gaelic language was one of the principal factors dividing the Highlands from the rest of Britain. Not only did it increase the resistance to outside influences, but it also perpetuated the Highlanders' sense of their own special culture and society. As a consequence, after the Rising of 1715 the problem of the Gaelic was one of the first to come under attack. The decline of Gaelic has been documented in detail by Charles Withers in his excellent study, *Gaelic in Scotland, 1698–1981*, so it is only necessary to include a brief summary here. According to Withers, the spread of English and the simultaneous erosion of Gaelic in the Highlands went hand-in-hand with the establishment of Protestantism. Although the SSPCK were originally concerned primarily with stamping out 'Popish and even Heathenish Superstition',[45] after 1715 there was a new attitude towards the education of the Highlanders:

> Nothing can be more effectual for reducing these countries to order, and making them usefull to the Commonwealth than teaching them their duty to God, their King and Countrey and rooting out their Irish language, and this has been the case of the Society as far as they could, ffor all the Schollars are taught in English. (*sic*)[46]

The efforts of the SSPCK were evidently motivated as much by political as religious interests, and God was firmly aligned with a Protestant King and Country. The aim of the Government was to break down the division between the Highlands and the rest of Britain and in order to do this, the Gaelic language had to be 'rooted out'. Although areas on the borders of the Highland region such as south Perthshire had an increasing number of English speakers as a result of frequent contact with the Lowlands[47], the spread of English in the North and West required careful investment of resources. Moves had already been made in the seventeenth century to erode Gaelic through the establishment of parochial schools in the Highlands, but it was not until the eighteenth century that the teaching of English became widespread. In SSPCK schools, only English texts were permitted and by 1751, the use of Gaelic in schools was completely banned. Thus although Macpherson was born and bred in the Gaelic-speaking Central Highlands, remote from the rest of Britain, he would have been learning English as soon as he went to school.

The spread of Protestantism, which was an important part of the educational policy, was not left to the SSPCK alone. The dangerous link between Catholicism and the Jacobites meant that it was strategic to increase the power of the clergy. A glance at the minutes of the Kirk Sessions in Kingussie during the eighteenth century shows clearly the reforming zeal of the Ministers, who would impose penalties for such minor crimes as the gathering of nuts on a Sunday.[48] As the disciplinary powers of the Kirk grew, the traditional authority of the Clan Chief was gradually and very subtly diminished: no longer was the ordinary Highlander responsible to only one master.

The enforcement of law and order was not left entirely in the hands of the clergy, however. After 1715, the Government established four military barracks at strategic points in the Highlands, including one at Ruthven. From Macpherson's birthplace, the imposing stone fortress could be seen on its high mound in the Spey valley, commanding a view of the surrounding area. The garrison had a capacity for 120 soldiers and as a child, Macpherson would have been only too familiar with the intrusive presence of Government troops in his own village. He probably regarded the soldiers with suspicion, as an occupying force, but like the Kirk and the school, they were helping to open his mind to the possibilities of a very different life beyond Badenoch.

Although Ruthven barracks was an isolated fortress, it was part of the Government's overall plan to open up communications in the Highlands. The 1715 Rising demonstrated the need for an efficient road network, so that troops could move rapidly through the Highlands to subdue insurrections. Between 1726 and 1737, General Wade was commissioned to build 250 miles of roads and 40 bridges in Northern Scotland. Perhaps his most impressive achievement was the road running North West out of Badenoch through the Corrieyairack pass at 2519 feet. The 28-mile road required 18 bridges and the labour of 500 soldiers. Although the military roads could be seen as symbols of the Government's attempt to penetrate the Highlands, such feats of engineering could hardly fail to have impressed the young Macpherson. The road out of Ruthven could be seen as a dangerous link with the corrupt Lowlands, but at the same time, it provided a way out of rural Badenoch to the opportunities of the prosperous South.

If the Rebellion of 1715 gave the Government cause for alarm, the '45 was to intensify the fear. Although James Macpherson was too young to take up arms, the events of 1745–1746 and the aftermath of Culloden must have made a lasting impression on the nine-year-old boy. His own Chief and close relation, Ewan Macpherson of Cluny, joined forces with the Jacobite army and led the Clan in the campaign of Prince Charles Edward Stuart.[49] The young Macpherson saw his family leaving home to follow the Prince south, and undoubtedly witnessed the seige of Ruthven barracks by some 300 Highlanders. Although the first assault was unsuccessful, in February 1746 the Jacobite army seized the stronghold and set it on fire. The sight of the burning fort must have been visible for miles around, but rather than heralding a Jacobite victory, it was a forerunner of disaster for the Rebel army. The overthrow of the military barracks took place on the march to Culloden, so the moment of victory at Ruthven was rapidly extinguished by the devastating defeat that followed. If James Macpherson had watched the sack of Ruthven barracks, he would also have witnessed the return of some of the defeated rebels, who rallied there before dispersing for ever.

After Culloden, life in the Highlands changed. The activities of 'Butcher' Cumberland and his troops are notorious and although the Macpherson regiment had suffered less damage than most in the actual battle, the Clan did not escape the aftermath. A graphic account left by Captain John Macpherson of Strathmashie gives some indication of the survivors' experiences:

> Oh heavens! In what characters will what follows be writ! Murders, burnings, ravishings, plunderings! Ane army of fiends let loose from Hell, with Lucifer himself at their head! Barbarities unheard of – no distinction of sex or age – cruelties never as much named among any people who made profession of or pretended to Christianity, and all not only with impunity, but by command.[50]

As a child, James Macpherson witnessed not only the humiliation of his Chief and Clan, but scenes of appalling violence carried out by British soldiers.

Even after the Macphersons had surrendered their weapons, the Earl of Loudon sent 300 men with orders to burn down Cluny Castle. Strathmashie gave the following account:

> they not only burnt the house itself, with such office houses as were near it, but all the houses that they apprehended belonged to it at a good distance from it. It was a most pretty, regular, well-contrived house as any benorth the river of Tay; double built in the new way, only about two years before, pavilion roof'd, with two pretty pavilions joined to it by colonades.[51]

It is not unlikely that James joined his six-year-old cousin, Allan Macpherson of Blairgowrie, among whose earliest memories was hurling stones at the troops who were setting fire to the Chief's home.[52] Despite the protests of his young relations, however, Cluny himself was now an outlaw and was to spend the next nine years in hiding on his own lands.

Charles Edward Stuart did not escape Scotland immediately after Culloden and, in the late summer of 1746, he too was in hiding in Badenoch. Among Cluny's hideouts was a thatched shelter concealed in a wood on the inaccessible slopes of Ben Alder, overlooking Loch Ericht. The Prince spent a fortnight in 'The Cage', together with Cluny and the wounded Cameron of Lochiel, supported by members of the Clan. By late September, the Prince had received news of two French ships on the West coast and made his escape, leaving Cluny a fugitive in Badenoch until 1755.

During the years when Cluny was in hiding, the troops, making Ruthven their Headquarters, maintained a relentless search for the Clan Chief, offering a thousand guineas for his capture. After six years, the Government troops were no closer to running down their quarry, but according to Cluny's son, Duncan, instead of abandoning the hunt, they

> redoubled their Vigilance and placed a detachment of soldiers in almost every town of the parishes of Laggan and Kingussie – a measure so strongly resembling that adopted previous to the massacre of Glencoe as to induce some timid people to leave the country.[53]

The reference to Glencoe may, at first, seem melodramatic: the language of a son who wishes to glorify the memory of his father. When James Wolfe arrived in Ruthven in 1752, however, he was so incensed by the army's failure to capture Cluny that he ordered an intensified search. The 'Vigilance' referred to by Duncan Macpherson was the work of the man who was later to become famous as the hero of Quebec. Wolfe's letters demonstrate that the anxiety of the Macphersons was well-founded:

> I gave the sergeant orders (in case he should succeed) and was attacked by the clan with the view to rescue their Chief to kill him instantly, which I concluded would draw on the destruction of the Detachment, and furnish me with a sufficient pretext to march into their country 'on j'aurais fait main basse sans misericorde'[54]

Cluny, however, was on his own territory and had the support of the entire Clan. He had numerous hiding places, spending summers in caves in the high mountains and winters concealed under the floors of loyal clansmen. Although there are numerous stories of Cluny's narrow escapes from the red-coats, in nine years only one man ever tried to betray his Chief.[55]

Eventually Cluny escaped to France, but by this time, James Macpherson was eighteen. Throughout his late childhood and adolescence, his home and family had been under a constant threat of violence and repression. Not only was Badenoch affected by the strong military presence at Ruthven, but also by more far-reaching changes. The repercussions of the '45 Rebellion were felt throughout the Highlands, as the Government's displeasure gave rise to a series of Draconian Acts. After 1746, Highlanders were forbidden to carry arms, play the bagpipes or wear their distinctive dress. The estates of fourteen of the most prominent rebel Chiefs (including Cluny) were forfeited to the crown, while the ancient systems of wardholding and of heritable jurisdiction were abolished.[56] Such radical changes were designed to demoralise the rebellious Highlanders and, by destroying their traditional communities, force them into the 'civilised' society of the United Kingdom.

Such was the atmosphere in which James Macpherson spent his formative years. He left Badenoch for University in 1752, at a time when the search for Cluny was at its height, and it is perhaps not surprising that he was later to look back on the world of his childhood as a lost paradise. The local resentment towards the British Government cannot have eased the normal problems of leaving home for the first time and Macpherson must have set out for Aberdeen with mixed feelings. Despite his suspicions about the world beyond Badenoch, it was certain to offer greater prospects to a talented young man than were promised in the Highlands in the 1750s. Although he left home with the traditional distrust of the Lowlanders, his very background heightened the appeal of the wealthy south. When he returned to Ruthven after four years in Aberdeen and Edinburgh, Macpherson was no longer satisfied with life in a small Highland town. Although he always professed to defy the influence of English culture, Macpherson's own career demonstrates its inevitable domination. The Government's moves to 'improve' the Highlands gave Macpherson the opportunity to acquire an education and win a place at University. The sudden policy of severe repression after the '45 meant that once Macpherson finished at Aberdeen, his native country would hold little attraction. Like many a talented Highlander, James Macpherson was to find wealth and success in England, while remaining haunted by the memory of the Highlands. His interest in Ossian, the sole survivor of a heroic Celtic race, is already becoming more comprehensible.

NOTES
1. R.Carruthers, *The Highland Notebook*, (Edinburgh 1843), 311.
2. Macpherson to John Macpherson 14 December 1790, IO MS Macp 127.

Macpherson's Childhood in the Scottish Highlands

3. The Will of James Macpherson, PROB 11/1272 137.
4. Boswell's *London Journal, 1762–1763*, ed F. Pottle, (London 1950), 73 et passim.
5. *State of the Society in Scotland for Propagating Christian Knowledge, giving a brief Account of the Condition of the Highlands and Islands of Scotland, . . . Together with Some Account of this Society's Missionaries for converting the Native Indians of America*, (Edinburgh 1741).
6. A. Grant, *Essays on the Superstitions of the Highlands of Scotland*, 2 vols, (Edinburgh 1811), I, 138–139.
7. See P. Cruttwell, 'These are not Whigs', *EIC*, xv, 1965, 394–415; T. C. Smout, *A History of the Scottish People, 1560–1830*, 2nd edn, (Glasgow 1972); M. Chapman, *The Gaelic Vision in Scottish Culture*, (London 1978).
8. E. Burt, *Letters from a Gentleman in the North of Scotland to his Friend in London*, 1754, ed. R. Jamieson, 2 vols, (London 1818), I, 293. This edition has a large appendix of additional material by men such as Wade and Lord Lovat.
9. Ibid, I, 342.
10. A. Macpherson, *Glimpses of Church and Social Life in the Highlands in Olden Times*, (Edinburgh 1893), 21; I. F. Grant, *Everyday Life on an Old Highland Farm, 1769–1782*, (London 1924), 11–17.
11. A. Grant, *Essays*, I, 34.
12. Ibid.
13. Ibid, I, 35.
14. J. Boswell, *The Journal of a Tour to the Hebrides*, 1785, in Boswell's *Life of Johnson*, ed. G. Birkbeck Hill, rev. edn, L. F. Powell, 6 vols, (Oxford 1934–1950), V, 168.
15. Eg *Temora*, xxiii.
16. M. Martin, *A Voyage to St Kilda*, 1698, 4th edn (London 1753), 66.
17. Burt, *Letters*, I, 335–336; cf. J. Ray, *A Compleat History of the Rebellion*, (Manchester 1746), 387. The pages of remedies in Martin's works suggest that Burt's observation was not a Lowland prejudice.
18. Ibid, II, 28; but see also his description of salmon, trout, hare and game, I, 114.
19. M. Martin, *A Description of the Western Islands of Scotland*, 1703, 2nd edn, (London 1716), 206–09; cf Ray, 390; Burt, *Letters*, II, 120, 102–05n; J. Campbell, *A Full and Particular Description of the Highlands of Scotland*, (London 1752), 8–9.
20. See *An Authentic Narrative of Marshal Wade's Proceedings in the Highlands of Scotland*, 1725, Burt, *Letters*, Appendix, 268–316.
21. Burt, *Letters*, I, 52.
22. Ibid, I, 152; cf. I, 153, 321; II, 61–2.
23. A. Grant, *Essays*, I, 66.
24. Burt, *Letters*, II, 8.
25. A. Grant, op. cit., I, 51.
26. Notes from Rev. John Anderson, 25 October 1797, ADV MS 73.2.13 f26; see also A. Macpherson, *Glimpses of Church . . .*, 235–56. The best discussion of James Macpherson's ancestry is by Alan G. Macpherson, 'James "Ossian" Macpherson's Ancestry', *CD*, xvi, 1964, 20–26. Tacksmen had a high status in Highland society and were often closely related to the Chief. They leased land from the Chief and rented it out to tenant farmers.

27. Dr Macpherson discussed an alternative genealogy based on conflicting evidence from Douglas of Glenbervie's *Baronage of Scotland*, 1798, but concluded that Clark's evidence, supported by Aeneas Macpherson of Invereshie's genealogy, was the more reliable.
28. J. Maclean of Glensanda, 'The Early Political Careers of James 'Fingal' Macpherson (1736–1796) and Sir John Macpherson, Bart. (1744–1821)', (unpublished doctoral dissertation, University of Edinburgh, 1967), 15–26.
29. Ibid, 20–24; cf A. Macpherson, *Glimpses of Church* . . ., 260–61.
30. Jamieson's note, Burt, *Letters*, I, 149. The question of illegitimacy in the Highlands is examined in detail by Alan G. Macpherson, 'An Old Highland Parish Register: Survivals of Clanship and Social Change in Laggan, Inverness-shire, 1775–1854', *SS*, x, 1966, 1–43; xi, 1967, 149–192; xii, 1968, 81–111; see Part ii, 1967, 'illegitimacy in the Highlands until 1700 was not a result of casual immorality, but was the result of a socially acceptable practice entertained by many respectable tacksmen and leaders of the community', 107.
31. W. C. Macpherson, ed., *Soldiering in India 1764–1787*, (Edinburgh & London 1928), 'Extracts from the Journals and Letters left by Lt. Col. Allan Macpherson and Lt. Col John Macpherson of the East India Company's service',2.
32. Burt, *Letters*, II, 62. See also D. S. Thomson, *An Introduction to Gaelic Poetry*, (London 1974), 19–56; W. J. Watson, *Bardachd Ghaidhlig: Gaelic Poetry 1550–1900*, 3rd edn, (Inverness 1959); J. L. Campbell, ed, *A Collection of Highland Rites and Customs from the Manuscript of the Rev James Kirkwood (1650–1709)*, (London 1975), 40.
33. J. F. Campbell, ed, *Popular Tales of the West Highlands*, 1860–1862, 2nd edn, 1890, 4 vols, facsimile (London 1983), I, vi; cf. Macpherson, 'Their amusement consisted in hearing or repeating their songs and traditions, and these entirely turned on the antiquity of their nations, and the exploits of their forefathers', (*Temora*, ii).
34. A. Grant, *Letters from the Mountains*, (Edinburgh 1806) I, 60.
35. Evidence from Alexander Clark, Ruthven, ADV MS 73.2.12 f 55/2.
36. J. F. Campbell, op. cit., I, v.
37. Donald Macpherson, October 1797, ADV MS 73.2.13 f23; cf Lewis Grant to Robert Walker, 26 January 1764, 'People of old were wont to impress upon the minds of their Children the Songs of the Bards', ADV MS 73.2.13 f 8.
38. See Andrew Gallie to the Highland Society, 4 March, 1801, *Report*, 41–42.
39. A. Macpherson, *Glimpses of Church* . . ., 99–100.
40. For a discussion of the topography of the Fiana, see *The Poems of Ossian*, ed J. Sinclair, 3 vols, (London 1807), III, 498–542.
41. H. MacDonald, S. Uist, 12 August 1800, *Report* App 49.
42. Burt, *Letters*, I, 334.
43. See A. MacDonald, *Ais-Eiridh na Sean-Chanoin Albannaich*, (The Resurrection of the Ancient Scottish Language), (Edinburgh 1751).
44. A. Maclaurin, 18 July 1806, ADV MS 73.2.11 f 56.
45. See note 5 above.
46. C. Withers, *Gaelic in Scotland, 1698–1981*, (Edinburgh 1984), 122, quoting a statement of 7 June 1716, SRO GD 95 11, 294.
47. By 1755, places such as Crieff, Muthill or Dunblane were at least 87% English-speaking, Withers, 67.

48. A. Macpherson, op. cit., chapter 3.
49. A. Macpherson, op. cit., describes Cluny as a loyal Jacobite, 166, 449. More recent evidence shows that Cluny regarded the Rebellion as misguided, but was forced to lead the Clan in support of the Prince, CD, xvii, 1965, 14.
50. A. Macpherson, 'Incidents in the'45 and the wanderings of Prince Charlie in Badenoch after Culloden', TGSI, xxiv, 1899-1901, 293. See also D. Daiches, *Charles Edward Stuart*, (London 1973); A. J. Youngson, *After the Forty-Five*, (Edinburgh 1973).
51. A.Macpherson, ibid., 307–18; A. Macpherson, *Glimpses of Church* . . . 478–84; Daiches, op. cit., 254–58.
52. W. Macpherson, *Soldiering in India 1764–1787*, 2.
53. D. Macpherson, 'An Account of the Escapes of Cluny of the '45 After the Battle of Culloden as narrated in a letter by his son, Col. Duncan Macpherson of Cluny', 9 June 1817, CD, x, 1958, 5–8.
54. A. Macpherson Grant, 'Badenoch after the '45', *The Inverness Courier*, 7 June 1938, 3; cf Wolfe to Rickson, 1755, 'Mr Macpherson should have a couple of hundred men in the neighbourhood with orders to massacre the whole clan if they show the least symptom of Rebellion. They are a warlike tribe, and he's a cunning, resolute fellow himself', quoted by Alan G. Macpherson, *The Posterity of the Three Brethren, A Short History of the Clan Macpherson*, (Clan Macpherson Association 1966).
55. D. Macpherson, op. cit., 10. See also the Clan Macpherson Museum, Newtonmore.
56. A. Smith, *Jacobite Estates of the Forty-Five*, (Edinburgh 1982), 2; R. Mitchison, *A History of Scotland*, (London 1970), 342; Smout, *A History* . . ., 321–38; B. Lenman, *Integration, Enlightenment and Industrialisation: Scotland 1746–1832* (London 1981), 1–13.

Macpherson at the University of Aberdeen 1752–1755

> The education of Nature is most perfect in savages, who have no other tutor; and we see that, in the quickness of all their senses, in the agility of their motions, in the hardiness of their constitutions, and in the strengths of their minds to bear hunger, thirst, pain, and disappointment, they commonly far exceed the civilised. A most ingenious writer, on this account, seems to prefer the savage life to that of society. But the education of Nature could never of itself produce a Rousseau.
> Thomas Reid, *Inquiry into the Human Mind*, 1764[1]

Throughout his life, Macpherson was to draw on his Highland background for a symbol of ideal society, uncorrupted by civilisation. Yet his very praise of the Highlands, depended largely on having left them. The advantages of the physical 'education of Nature' became apparent only through his experience of urban life and, ironically, Macpherson's personal revolt against the advancing civilisation of the Lowlands owed more to his education at Aberdeen University than to his 'natural' education in Badenoch.

How did Macpherson come to see his declining home as an ideal society, infinitely superior to the prosperous cities of eighteenth-century Britain? Why did his family and friends, who were simply carrying on their normal daily lives, suddenly seem part of a living museum? And what was to make him want to record the popular songs and stories that people such as Finlay Macpherson would recite to anyone who came to visit? James Macpherson was only twenty-three when *Fragments of Ancient Poetry* was published, so it seems reasonable to look for answers to some of these questions at the University of Aberdeen. We know the subjects Macpherson would have studied and which tutors taught him, so it is possible to trace some of the ideas that influenced *Ossian* in the degree course.

The few surviving descriptions of Macpherson at University suggest that he was an able, but not particularly diligent, student. A fellow undergraduate remembered him as being 'more remarkable for quietness of parts and soundness of intellect than for application or proficiency in his studies'[2]. The biographical entry in the *Edinburgh Encyclopaedia* concurs: ' His talent for poetry displayed itself at this early age, and he employed himself more in the composition of humorous and doggerel rhymes than in the ordinary occupations of a student.'[3] Despite his later reputation as a 'good classical scholar'[4], Macpherson appears to have spent much of his time at university amusing himself with comic verse. A contemporary anecdote reveals both Macpherson's early facility for versemaking and the belligerent streak in his character, which was later to emerge in the dispute with Dr Johnson:

> When at the Greek class Macpherson took much pleasure in teasing a Hugh Machardy, a very poor, and withal a very ugly and awkward lad. In particular, he ridiculed him for things that were his misfortune rather than his fault. As he made use of Hudibrastic verse, Machardy, plucking up courage, retorted on Macpherson in mock heroics, which turned the laugh against him. The quarrel was coming to extremities when some body told Mr Broadfoot, the professor, of it, who ordered the culprits to produce their poems, which were read by him in the class with much gravity. After making severe remarks on the composition, he ordered both writers to keep peace, under pain of expulsion. Macpherson was exceedingly indignant.[5]

Although not too much should be made of a single school anecdote, the image of Macpherson that emerges is of an intelligent, high-spirited young man, with certain tendencies towards bullying. It is, perhaps, the character of a talented, but impoverished student, who is determined to prove his superiority to his colleagues. For Macpherson, the normal insecurities of the freshman would have been aggravated by the startling contrast between his home and the city of Aberdeen. The notorious 'Highland pride', invariably attributed to him in later years, seems to have developed during his days as a student.

James Macpherson arrived in Aberdeen in the autumn of 1752[6], when the city was enjoying a period of rapid economic expansion. The old woollen industry was flourishing, while new linen factories had just opened in 1749 and 1751.[7] At the same time, the city's first paper mill had been built, while the Aberdeen Infirmary, which had only opened in 1740, was already being extended. The booming economy was also reflected in ventures such as the establishment of the first independent Scottish bank outside Edinburgh. When Johnson visited Aberdeen in 1773, he was struck by the contrast between the Old Town and the New:

> Old Aberdeen is the ancient episcopal city, in which are still to be seen the remains of the cathedral. It has the appearance of a town in decay, having been situated in times when commerce was yet

unstudied, with very little attention to the commodities of the harbour.

New Aberdeen has all the bustle of prosperous trade, and all the shew of increasing opulence. It is built by the waterside. The houses are large and lofty, and the streets spacious and clean. They build almost wholly with the granite used in the new pavement of the streets of London, which is well known not to want hardness, yet they shape it very easily. It is beautiful and must be very lasting.[8]

The rapid changes in urban life, so typical of the eighteenth century, were particularly marked in the contrast between Old and New Aberdeen. For a young Highlander such as Macpherson, the city must have aroused somewhat mixed emotions. He spent the first two years of his degree at King's College, Old Aberdeen, before moving to Marischal College in the newer part of the city. Although the change was caused by financial difficulties, many people would see the move to the New Town as a great improvement. Alexander Gerard, for example, who taught at Marischal, described Old Aberdeen in 1753 as 'a village inhabited by the lowest people, and those of the most corrupt manners'.[9] For Macpherson, who had come straight from an impoverished Highland community, the sight of a wealthy, urban society was to provoke envy and ambition. Although the New Town was prosperous and exciting, however, the displacement of the old way of life was also a daily reminder of the changes taking place in the Highlands.

The changes taking place in Aberdeen in the 1750s were not confined to the town. The University was flourishing and could boast among the teaching staff many of the leading Scottish academics of the period, such as Thomas Blackwell, Thomas Reid, Alexander Gerard, James Beattie, John Gregory, and George Campbell. Many of the lecturers were also members of the vigorous Aberdeen Philosophical Society, and the close connection between the University and 'The Wise Club' contributed to the strong emphasis on philosophy in the degree course at Aberdeen.[10]

Macpherson's arrival at King's College in 1752 coincided with a major revision of the traditional Arts course.[11] Had he matriculated earlier, he would have undertaken a philosophical course based on Logic and Reasoning. Under the influence of the progressive young tutor, Alexander Gerard, the old system was rejected in favour of a new course based on empirical observation. The staff at Aberdeen were concerned that abstract philosophical studies turned students into 'subtle disputants', rather than educating them for the 'useful and important Offices of society'.[12] Just as Rousseau preferred Emile to be brought up among things rather than words, so Gerard argued that philosophy was no longer an image of 'human phantasies and conceits', but of 'the truth of things', based on an accurate and extensive history of nature'.[13] Thus the new course began with History, Geography, Mathematics and Natural Philosophy and moved on to Logic and Metaphysics only in the final year, as the conclusion rather than the foundation of the course.

In the pursuit of 'certain and general conclusions about the world'[14], Gerard advocated the observation of scientific or historical facts, an approach shared by Thomas Reid, who became Macpherson's Regent in the second year of his course: ' Human knowledge is like the steps of a ladder. The first step consists of particular truths, discovered by observation or experiment: the second collects these into more general truths: the third into still more general.'[15] Despite Reid's apparent confidence, however, his approach appears to be the result of a deep-seated horror of error and uncertainty. His letter continues with the following warning:

> But there are many such steps before we come to the top; that is, to the most general truths. Ambitious of knowledge, and unconscious of our own weakness, we would fain jump at once from the lowest step to the highest; but the consequence of this is, that we tumble down, and find that our labour must be begun anew.

The painstaking approach of the empirical philosopher is unlikely to have appealed strongly to the young Macpherson. The prevailing emphasis on fact and the utilitarian purpose of the course left little room for the imagination. In Thomas Reid's eyes, imagination 'adulterates philosophy, and fills it with error and false theory'.[16] The new curriculum's focus upon useful, factual subjects meant that literary criticism was completely left out until the third year, and even then it was only included 'as far as time would allow'.[17] Macpherson's creative talents were thus given no formal encouragement, while his reading of poets such as Milton, Pope, Dryden, Young, Gray and Blair, must have been a personal rather than academic choice.

Although the arts curriculum at Aberdeen was revised extensively, certain elements of the traditional degree were retained. Despite the strong philosophical emphasis, the philosophy course began only in the second year and the foundation year was still devoted to Latin and Greek. Macpherson would probably have studied Latin at school, in preparation for his degree, where classical studies continued for the first two years. In view of the new emphasis on fact and utility, the continued interest in Latin and Greek may seem surprising, but for the staff at Aberdeen there was nothing incongruous in the structure of the course. The classics were by no means seen as obscure, academic pursuits, but as an essential part of a proper education and invaluable to the future. The utilitarian attitude emerges clearly in Gerard's description of the task of a Greek master, which was not only to teach that elegant language in which the sciences were first delivered, and which, by returning to their original terms . . . must always be regarded as the foundation of knowledge, but to open the minds of youth, by explaining antiquity, by acquainting them with the lives and characters of the chief classical authors and by pointing out the uses of literature, or the various purposes it serves in life.[18]

Greek was, it appears, an eminently useful subject. Its advantages had nothing to do with the beauty or imaginative power of the literature, but related rather to the light it shed on the philosophy or history of the Ancient World.

Gerard's firm belief in the importance of the classical world was undoubtedly influenced by his own tutor, Thomas Blackwell. Blackwell was one of the foremost Greek scholars in Scotland and, during the 1750s and 1760s, his influence at Aberdeen was very extensive. As the Principal of Marischal College he was actively involved in the organisation of the University, as well as continuing to teach and give lectures, while many of his former students had remained at Aberdeen and obtained academic positions. In his first year, Macpherson studied Greek under Bradfut and Latin under Thomas Gordon. In the second year, he began the philosophy course with Thomas Reid as his Regent. After this he moved to Marisdal College and presumably entered the Tertian class under the tuition of William Duncan. All the men who taught him, with the possible exception of Bradfut, had originally been students of Blackwell and many of the Professor's ideas can be traced in their work. In Gerard's eyes, Blackwell's ability to 'inspire young minds with the love of learning' was superior to anyone's and his own admiration for his old tutor glows through the description.[19] Although Macpherson was introduced to Greek at King's, he can hardly have avoided Blackwell's influence, even if he failed to attend any lectures, he would certainly have read the influential *Enquiry into the Life and Writings of Homer*, (London 1735), which sold out so quickly that it went into a second edition in 1736. Blackwell's books are among the most interesting and popular works to come out of the University of Aberdeen in the mid eighteenth century. They are certainly the most relevant to the study of *Ossian*.

Blackwell's popularity among his students rose partly from his own determination to make education attractive. Convinced that the 'unnatural Separation of *Learning* from *Life*, had done infinite harm to both'[20], he made a conscious effort to prevent his work from seeming dry and lifeless. Thus for his work on mythology, he adopted a chatty, epistolary form, while in the *Enquiry into Homer* he avoided all 'those Divisions, Subdivisions and Repetitions which afford artificial Helps to the Memory, but stiffen a Treatise like an old Sermon'.[21]

Blackwell's anxiety about the division between academic pursuits and real life emerged strongly in the work he published while Macpherson was a student at Aberdeen, *Memoirs of the Court of Augustus*, 1753–1763. Here, he addressed himself to the problem of 'Whether the Gentlemen in the learned Professions, *by confining* themselves to their Books and Routine of Business, acquire not a *narrow monkish* Cast, which disqualifies them for the *active* Scenes of Life?'[22] The ensuing discussion included the following advice to the youth of Britain:

> along with their Studies at home, to look much abroad: not to plunge into the Gayety and Foppery of the *idle* . . . but to view a variety of Objects – *Towns, Fields, Forts, Harbours, Magazines*, and especially to converse with *Men of all Characters, Professions and Trades*; . . . nor would it be much amiss, if the . . . Student have Address and Agility of Body, that he made trial of it, and essayed to wield the Weapons or handle the tools of the several Callings he is inspecting. Why for instance, should Letters disqualify a Man to take up a Foile, mount in the great Saddle, or rein in the hunting Horse?[23]

Such enthusiasm for physical action must have seemed strange to a Highland student such as James Macpherson. Having been raised in a society where the normal methods of subsistence were hunting, fishing or farming, and where climbing mountains or swimming rivers was part of everyday life, the Greek Professor's enthusiasm for such activities must have seemed very odd. Instead of emphasising the importance of libraries, Blackwell was advocating wide experience, just at a time when Macpherson was turning his back on the very lifestyle most admired. Such views must surely have begun to open Macpherson's eyes to the value of his home community and fostered his native contempt for city dwellers.

The man whom Blackwell upheld as an ideal was the Irish philosopher, Bishop Berkeley (1685–1753). Not only was he well-read, and an original thinker, but he was also a man of action. After an enthusiastic description of Berkeley's first-hand researches into the causes of volcanos during an expedition to Sicily, Blackwell observed, 'I enter not into his Peculiarities, either religious or personal; but admire the extensive Genius of the Man.'[24] Although Blackwell showed more interest in physical action than most of the staff, his emphasis on the capacity of human beings was shared by all. Despite certain differences in approach, the degree course at Aberdeen was unified by the same goal: the study of man in society. As William Duncan, who probably taught Macpherson in the third year at Marischal, observed: 'Of all human Sciences, that concerning Man, is certainly the most worthy of Man, and the most necessary Part of Knowledge.'[25]

Thomas Reid, too, attacked the materialism of the French philosophers, exclaiming angrily, 'I detest all systems that depreciate human nature.'[26] At Aberdeen, the study of man was a noble pursuit and the desire to find an ideal society of superhuman beings was eventually to find expression in *The Poems of Ossian*.

Blackwell's fascination with human potential was an important part of his interest in Homer. If Berkeley possessed an 'extensive Genius', in Blackwell's eyes Homer was the greatest genius who had ever lived. His *Enquiry* was not a work of literary criticism, but an attempt to investigate the causes which had resulted in Homer's extraordinary ability. It was a study of Homer the man, rather than of the *Iliad* and the *Odyssey*.

Although Blackwell acknowledged Homer's 'exalted Genius, and comprehensive Mind'[27], he thought that the ability to compose an epic depended largely on the poet's environment. The *Enquiry* examined general factors such as the climate of Ancient Greece, as well as looking at Homer's own particular circumstances. Blackwell saw Homer as an impoverished bard, but regarded this poverty as a vital part of the poet's development. Since he was forced to travel to support himself, Homer enlarged his experience and, therefore, his genius. Blackwell's theory of poetry was essentially empirical: great descriptions resulted from the ability to report first hand experience accurately. Homer could present the battles of the Trojan War convincingly because his own country was still so unsettled:

> the Struggle was fresh in *Homer's* Days: Arms were in Repute, and *Force* decided *Possession*. He saw Towns taken and plundered, the Men put to the Sword, and the Women made Slaves: He beheld their despairing Faces, and suppliant Postures; heard their Moanings o'er their murdered Husbands, and Prayers for their Infants to the Victor. On the other hand, he might view Cities blessed with peace, spirited by Liberty, flourishing in Trade, and increasing in Wealth.[28]

Blackwell showed no interest in Homer's imagination; for him, the ideal poet, like the ideal philosopher, was a man of action.[29] He saw a direct connection between epic poetry and periods of violence:

> It was when *Greece* was ill-settled, when Violence prevailed in many Places . . . that Homer produced his immortal Poem: And it was when *Italy* was torn in Pieces . . . that *Dante* withdrew from his Country, and made the strongest Draught of Men and their Passions, that stands in the Records of modern Poetry . . . And . . . it was when unhappy *Britain* was plunged in all the Calamities of *Civil Rage*, that our high-spirited Poem took its Birth.[30]

According to Blackwell it was in such periods of unrest that the human spirit expanded most fully: 'Every Man finds himself on such

Occasions his own Master, and that he *may be* whatever he can *make* himself: He knows not how high he may rise, and is unawed by Laws, which are then of no force.'[31] If war affected ordinary people so dramatically, then those who had outstanding natural ability would suddenly produce works of supreme genius.

It is not difficult to imagine the young Macpherson, who had witnessed the events of the '45 Rebellion, being strongly attracted to Blackwell's theories on the association between warfare and genius. Fancying himself as a budding poet, the idea of violence both stimulating poetic ability and furnishing it with materials would have obvious appeal. It is not surprising that the first long poem published by Macpherson after leaving Aberdeen was an epic entitled *The Highlander*. Blackwell's survey of the connection between poetry and genius also emphasised the importance of the epic as the highest form of poetry, and often connected with nationalism.[32] It was therefore, the only genre suitable for the great Scottish poem Macpherson hoped to write when he left University.

Despite Blackwell's obvious attraction to the wild society of Ancient Greece, he was also fully aware of the less desirable aspects of uncivilised states. He believed firmly in the power of the arts to improve mankind, ridding societies of 'inhuman customs' such as cannibalism.[33] The *Enquiry* contains not only images of the violence of early societies, but also approving portraits of 'a Colony led out, a City founded, the Foundations of Order and Policy laid, with the Provisions for the Security of the People'.[34]

This optimistic view of the arts as contributing to the stability of society and softening of manners was difficult to reconcile with Blackwell's views on great poetry. If the finest creations resulted from a turbulent state, then the development of a peaceful community must gradually destroy the impulse to produce work of epic quality. Blackwell appears to have been aware of the dilemma:

> The Things that give the greatest Lustre in a regular Government; the greatest Honours and highest Trusts, will scarcely bear Poetry: The *Muse* refuses to bestow her Embellishments on a *Duke's* Patent, or a *General's* Commission. They can neither raise our Wonder, nor gain our Heart: For Peace, Harmony and good Order, which make the happiness of a People, are the *Bane* of a Poem that subsists by Wonder and Surprize.[35]

Art seemed to be, ultimately, self-defeating. As poetry contributed to the civilisation of savage society, it helped to destroy the conditions most suitable for its creation.

Similar difficulties emerge in the discussion of language. Again, Blackwell was fully aware of the advantages of a sophisticated language and regarded English as superior to any modern tongue.[36]

At the same time, however, he was deeply concerned about the restrictive tendency of refined language:

> what we call *Polishing* diminishes a Language; it makes many Words obsolete; it coops a Man up in a Corner, allows him but one Set of Phrases, and deprives him of many significant Terms, and strong beautiful Expressions.[37]

The history of the Greek language offered little comfort; Blackwell noted that as the national genius gradually turned from poetry to philosophy, the language became more refined and abstract. Although he recognised that the speech of the early Greeks was 'broken, unequal and boisterous', his criticism was balanced by his obvious admiration for its poetic qualities.[38] Paradoxically, the 'simplicity' of ancient man did not produce a plain style of diction, but a language naturally suited to poetry, being 'full of Metaphor; and that Metaphor of the boldest, daring and most natural kind'.[39] The ancient language may not have been suitable for communicating science or philosophy, but as a medium for poetry, it was infinitely superior to any sophisticated language.

Blackwell's anxiety about abstract language appears to have been passed on to his students. Gerard's lengthy criticism of Logic in the new *Plan of Education* shows a similar distrust of sophisticated argument, while Thomas Reid made the following observations:

> Is it not pity that the refinements of a civilized life, instead of supplying the defects of natural language, should root it out and plan in its stead dull and lifeless articulations of unmeaning sounds, or the scrawling of insignificant characters? The perfection of human language is commonly thought to be, to express human thoughts and sentiments distinctly by these dull signs; but if this is the perfection of artificial language, it is surely the corruption of the natural.
>
> Artificial signs signify, but they do not express; they speak to the understanding, as algebraical characters may do, but the passions, the affections, and the will, hear them not.[40]

Reid's emphasis on the emotions is closely related to Blackwell's association between great art and strong passions. He associated 'natural language' with children and savages, who communicated their emotions freely, while the 'artificial language' of more sophisticated thinkers could only address the understanding.[41] Reid went on to suggest that man was creative by nature, but was prevented from fulfilling his potential by the development of language: a view which seems to owe much to Blackwell.

Again, we can imagine Macpherson absorbing his tutors' ideas and applying them to his own experience. As a Gaelic speaker, he had been taught to reject his 'natural' language and adopt the sophisticated language of the South. The parallels between Blackwell's survey of the history of Greek and the contemporary changes in the Gaelic are not difficult to discern: English might be the more suitable medium for philosophy, but Gaelic had all the energy of a primitive tongue. Thus Macpherson's eyes were suddenly being opened to the importance of Gaelic, despite the efforts of his old school in Badenoch, where he would have been forced to learn English.

Blackwell's concern about the 'unnatural Separation of *Learning* from *Life*' echoes in the background of the various discussions about language. Although it would be misleading to label the men of Aberdeen University as 'primitivists'[42], given their interest in improvement and academic advance, they seem to have shared a burden of anxiety about the progress of civilisation. The confidence that is apparent in the planning of a new curriculum, for example, was constantly being undermined by doubt: indeed, Gerard's emphasis on 'certain and general conclusions' suggests a degree of uncertainty. In Reid's work, too, the bold advocation of 'observation and experiment' was checked by the knowledge that David Hume's adoption of a similar approach in the *Treatise of Human Nature* (1736) had led to conclusions that were far from reassuring.[43] Although Blackwell himself made frequent references to the intellectual freedom of modern society, resulting from an enlightened education, he nevertheless regretted the route which had to be taken to reach this liberty:

> We live within Doors, cover'd, as it were, from Nature's Face; and passing our Days supinely ignorant of her Beauties, we are apt to think Similies taken from her *low*, and the ancient Manners *mean*, or absurd.[44]

The alienation of modern man made the Ancient World doubly attractive, but the rediscovery of Homeric Greece required many hours of labour in a library, surrounded by heavy tomes. For Blackwell, the very life of the academic rendered him incapable of appreciating the literature he was eventually able to read.

Although Blackwell's criticisms were aimed primarily at those pursuing academic goals, many of his statements suggest a general dissatisfaction with the contemporary world. In the passage just quoted he goes on to observe that 'the Moderns admire nothing but Pomp, and can think nothing Great or Beautiful, but what is the Produce of Wealth.' This association between civilisation and corruption was to become a commonplace of the late eighteenth century, finding its most famous expression in Edward Gibbon's *Decline and Fall of the Roman Empire* (1776–88). For Macpherson, the notion fitted well with his traditional Highland prejudices, and emerged strongly in *The Poems of Ossian*.

The anxiety about the effects of luxury on modern civilisation fuelled the enthusiasm for the Ancient World. Blackwell's works were symptomatic of the prevailing interest in the past, which developed with the growing dissatisfaction with the present. History was part of the introduction to philosophy in the new course at Aberdeen, because it helped to explain the development of society and to evaluate the modern world.[45] Modern man could learn salutary lessons from the most ancient historians, seeing his own society in the perspective of world history.[46] According to Blackwell, a mere catalogue of dates and battles was of little use compared with a proper, philosophical analysis of the progress of society:

> A *moral* or *philosophical* History of the World well writ wou'd be a very useful work; to observe . . . in what Simplicity Men began at first, and by what degrees they came out of that Way by Luxury, Ambition, Improvement or Changes in Nature in them . . . This wou'd be a View of Things more instructive, and more satisfactory, than to know what King reigned in such an Age, and what Battles were fought, which common History teacheth and teacheth little more.[47]

Again, the utilitarian emphasis is obvious.

A good example of the contemporary use of classical history can be found in William Duncan's translation of *Caesar's Commentaries*, a huge folio volume which was published in London in 1753. The translation was prefaced by an essay on 'The Roman Art of War', a historical piece which was nevertheless designed to make contemporary readers examine their own society. In the Dedication, Julius Caesar was presented as a model for the young Prince of Wales to emulate. Duncan praised Caesar not only for wisdom and physical courage, but also for patriotism, comparing him with Henry V as an ideal king, who 'reigned not for himself, but for his People'. The classical past was being used partly as an inspiration to young readers, but also to expose the deficiencies of contemporary society. Thus, the vigour of the Roman Army was exalted in comparison with the soldiers of eighteenth-century Europe, and an account of the Roman troops concluded with the comment, 'we daily see Armies, without once engaging, perish and melt away'.[48]

Although Duncan appears to have admired some aspects of the Roman Empire, there is also evidence of a certain ambivalence in his attitude:

> their very Conquests proved their Ruin, and they sunk under the weight of their own Greatness. For the Countries they had brought under Subjection, not considering themselves as Parts of the State, but rather as Tributaries and Slaves, were glad of an Opportunity of shaking off the Yoke.[49]

Duncan recognised the power of the Roman Army at its height, but he was also strongly aware of the decline of Rome. He shared Blackwell's suspicions about the effects of luxury, commenting:

> It is well known that the *Spartans*, so long as they adhered to their primitive Institutions and Poverty, were the most powerful people of all Greece, and never proved unsuccessful in their Wars, till they became possessed of great Riches and Reserves.[50]

With the growing uneasiness about Rome came a tendency to celebrate peoples such as the Spartans, as symbols of austerity, strength and courage. The Germans and Gauls provided a similar alternative to the potentially corrupt ideal of Rome, so Duncan's translation of Caesar's *Gallic Wars* can be read as an appraisal of the virtues of primitive versus civilised society.

Macpherson would have found much of interest in Duncan's *Caesar*, especially in the descriptions of the Germans and Gauls. Caesar's account of the Germans, with their warlike spirit, physical strength, ability to endure poverty and their unmaterialistic values had much in common with eighteenth-century descriptions of the Highlanders. The German reverence for ancestry and division of land among groups of kinsmen would also seem familiar to the Highland student. Even the institution of bards and the tradition of oral poetry were normal parts of Macpherson's native community. Duncan's cool appraisal of the Roman attempt to subdue rebellious nations by absorbing them into the Empire also had clear parallels with the Government policy on the Highlands, so it is not difficult to imagine Macpherson's growing sympathy for the Germans.

Works such as Duncan's *Caesar* or Blackwell's *Enquiry into Homer* were certainly opening Macpherson's eyes to the values of primitive societies. For Duncan, the Germans, Spartans and early Romans represented strength and austerity, uncorrupted by wealth or selfish ambition. For Blackwell, the Homeric world offered the energy and adventure needed for the creation of great poetry, as well as an unsophisticated language lively enough to capture that energy. Through the influence of his tutors, Macpherson began to regard aspects of his own society, which he had always taken for granted, as special and worthy of preservation. His pride in the antiquity of the Highlanders, in the purity of the Gaelic language and in the importance of his native culture was now being nurtured after the battering it had received after the '45. At the same time, he began to recognise the irreversible changes that now threatened to destroy this ancient society by absorbing it into the corrupt civilisation of modern Britain.

But while the recognition of parallels between the Highlands and the Ancient World made Macpherson value his native society, it also gave rise to less reassuring feelings. For Blackwell, primitive society was attractive because it was remote, but Macpherson had actually been brought up in such a world. Did he wish to be regarded as a savage? Or should he try and compensate for his background by a display of education?

Not everyone at Aberdeen shared Blackwell's enthusiasm for primitive people and Gerard, for example, observed: 'As savages can be touched with nothing but what excites the utmost extravagance of passion, so a gross and barbarous taste can relish nothing that is not either palpable or overdone.'[51] The 'grossness both of taste and passion' which Gerard associated with savage races was not mere squeamishness, but a moral objection. In Gerard's eyes, taste was an important ingredient of sympathy:

> Refinement of taste makes a man susceptible of delicate feelings on every occasion; and these increase the acuteness of the moral sense . . . On this account, a man of nice taste will have a stronger abhorrence of vice, and a keener relish for virtue.[52]

Rather than exalting the Noble Savage, Gerard regarded uncivilised man as a coarse, amoral creature incapable of true sympathy. He even denied the association between early man and poetry, seeing the latter not as the spontaneous expression of emotion, but as an art requiring careful cultivation. Unlike Blackwell's theory of the genius who merely reported his experiences accurately, Gerard's ideal poet was a conscious artist, who moulded his observations to his vision:

> as Zeuxis produced an Helen, by selecting, from many beautiful virgins, the parts that were in each more beautiful; we form in our minds the model of perfection . . . A man of genius, possessed of so sublime a standard, endued with such exquisite refinement of taste . . . will represent his objects, not merely as they are, but like Sophocles, as they ought to be.[53]

Although Gerard was also referring to Ancient Greece, it represented to him not a wild, uncultivated world, but the height of civilisation.

Macpherson's pride in being an uncorrupted Highlander was thus being undercut by the contradictory emphasis on refinement. While he learned to value the 'primitive' virtues on one hand, he was also being taught that a refined taste was essential to both art and morality. How could Gerard's views be reconciled with Blackwell's notion that the greatest poetry rose spontaneously from periods of violence? Or that the metaphors of early languages were more suitable for expressing the high passions that constituted the stuff of the epic?

The conflicting emphases on spontaneity and refinement, on emotional expression and utilitarianism, were characteristic of Aberdeen in the mid eighteenth century. Despite the confident tone of the academics, the underlying confusion emerges as they veer between praising the effects of modern education on one hand and attacking the progress of contemporary civilisation on the other. This confusion extended to the aesthetic theories: Blackwell's emphasis on the spontaneous record of personal experience was completely at odds with Gerard's vision of the artist selecting and rearranging his material according to his specially refined taste. Indeed, any attempt to *account for* great art seemed doomed to failure. Whether the poet was seen as a passive mirror of his society, or whether his successes were attributed to the mechanical faculty of taste, there was something lacking. In the empirical approach to literature and in the efforts to prove its usefulness to society, any recognition of imaginative power was lost. The idea of Original Genius both obsessed and eluded the academics at Aberdeen in the mid-eighteenth century and when Macpherson came to tackle the ancient poetry of the Celts, the conflicting influences of his education were to come pouring out.

NOTES
1. *The Works of Thomas Reid*, ed. W. Hamilton, (Edinburgh 1846), 200–01.
2. Quoted by J. Ramsay, *Scotland and Scotsmen in the Eighteenth Century*, ed. A. Allardyce, 2 vols, (Edinburgh 1888), I, 545; cf G. Gleig, 'James Macpherson', *Encyclopaedia Britannica*, 3rd edn., (Edinburgh 1801), Supplement, vol ii, 109: 'he displayed more genius than learning entertaining the society of which he was a member, and even diverting the younger part of it from their studies, by his humorous and doggerel rhymes'.
3. *Edinburgh Encyclopaedia*, ed. D. Brewster, 18 vols, (Edinburgh 1830), xiii, 222.
4. The words are John Home's, who met Macpherson in 1759, *Report*, App., 68.
5. Ramsay, op. cit., I, 545–46. cf. Carruthers, *The Highland Notebook*, 309: 'The acrimonious controversy with Johnson irritated him extremely; and there are many coarse epigrams, lampoons, and parodies, among his unpublished papers, in which the great moralist is treated very unceremoniously'.
6. Macpherson's name appears on the Matriculation List, P. J. Anderson, *Roll of Alumni of the University and King's College, Aberdeen, 1596–1860*, (Aberdeen 1900), 78.
7. A. Keith, *A Thousand Years of Aberdeen*, (Aberdeen 1972), 300–30.
8. Johnson, *A Journey to the Western Islands*, 10.
9. J. M. Bulloch, *A History of the University of Aberdeen 1495–1895*, (London 1895), 148. Gerard was elected Regent at Marischal in 1750 at the age of 22.
10. P. J. Anderson, *Studies in the History of the University*, (Aberdeen 1906), 73–96; D. D. McElroy, 'The Literary Clubs and Societies of Eighteenth Century Scotland', (unpublished Ph.D dissertation, University of Edinburgh 1952), 127–37.
11. The new curriculum was adopted in December 1752, according to the *Scots Magazine*, xiv, 1752, 606. Full details were later published,

A. Gerard, *A Plan of Education in the Marischal College and University of Aberdeen*, (Aberdeen 1755).
12. J. Chalmers, *Abstract of Some Statutes and Orders of King's College in Old Aberdeen*, (Aberdeen 1753), 13.
13. Gerard, op. cit., 5.
14. Ibid 9–10; cf William Duncan, *Elements of Logick*, (London 1748), 337: 'In this way of putting together our Thoughts, it is evident at first sight, that however far we carry our researches, *Science* and *Certainty* will still attend it . . . we hereby see Knowledge arising out of its first Elements, and discern distinctly how these Elements are combined and interwoven, in order to erect a goodly Structure of Truth.'
15. Reid, *Works*, 53.
16. Ibid, 99.
17. Gerard, op. cit., 32.
18. Gerard, op. cit., 27–8.
19. A. F. Tytler, Lord Woodhouselee, *Memoirs of the Life and Writings of the Honourable Henry Home of Kames*, 2 vols, (Edinburgh 1807), II, 73–4.
20. Blackwell, *Letters Concerning Mythology*, (London 1748), Preface.
21. Ibid 38–9. The *Letters* contain invaluable insights into the *Enquiry*.
22. Blackwell, *Memoirs of the Court of Augustus*, 3 vols, (Edinburgh 1753, 1754, 1763), II, 276–77.
23. Ibid, II, 277–78.
24. Ibid, II, 278.
25. Duncan, *Elements of Logick*, 1.
26. Reid, *Works*, 95.
27. Blackwell, *An Enquiry* . . ., 10.
28. Ibid, 23.
29. See 304–05, 'The *making* or *feigning* Faculty, be it ever so rich and inventive, after an Effort or two, recoils upon itself.'
30. Ibid, 65–6.
31. Ibid, 64–5.
32. For contemporary theories of the epic see H. T. Swedenberg, *The Theory of the Epic in England 1650–1800*, (Berkeley 1944); K. Simonsuuri, *Homer's Original Genius, Eighteenth-Century Notions of the Early Greek Epic, 1688–1798*, (Cambridge 1979).
33. Blackwell, *An Enquiry* . . ., 254.
34. Ibid, 23.
35. Ibid, 27; cf. Rousseau, *A Discourse on the Arts and Science*, 1750, tr. G. D. H. Cole, ed. J. H. Brumfitt & J. C. Hall, (London 1973), 4–5: 'So long as government and law provide for the security and well-being of men in their common life, the arts, literature, and the sciences, less despotic though perhaps more powerful, fling garlands of flowers over the chains which weigh them down. They stifle in men's breasts that sense of original liberty, for which they seem to have been born; cause them to love their own slavery, and so make of them what is called a civilised people.'
36. Blackwell, op. cit., 61.
37. Ibid, 58–9; cf. 125: 'the *Scholastick* Turn, *Technical* Terms, imaginary Relations, and wire-drawn Sciences, spoil the natural Faculties, and marr the Expression.'
38. Ibid, 43–7.

39. Ibid, 41; cf. 43.
40. Reid, *Works*, 118.
41. Ibid. Cf. Rousseau, *A Discourse* . . ., 6: 'Before art had moulded our behaviour, and taught our passions to speak an artificial language, our morals were rude but natural; and the different ways in which we behaved proclaimed at first glance the difference of our dispositions'.
42. See e.g. L. Whitney on the 'Aberdeen Primitivists' in 'English Primitivistic Theories of Epic Origins', *Modern Philology*, xxi, 1924, 337–78.
43. Reid, *Works*, 97. Reid was appalled by the consequences of Hume's scepticism, and his own *Inquiry into the Human Mind* was the direct response of a Christian philosopher.
44. Blackwell, *An Enquiry* . . ., 25.
45. See R. Rawlinson, *A New Method of Studying History*, (London 1728); D. B. Horn, 'Some Scottish Writers of History in the Eighteenth Century', *SHR*, xl, 1961, 1–18.
46. See Adam Smith's *Lectures on Rhetoric and Belles Lettres*, ed. J. M. Lothian, (London 1963), 85–112.
47. Blackwell, *Letters Concerning Mythology*, 113.
48. *The Commentaries of Caesar*, xl.
49. Ibid, xxix.
50. Ibid, xlii.
51. A. Gerard, *An Essay on Taste*, (Edinburgh 1759), 127. The Essay was written in 1756 for a competition set by the Edinburgh Society, in which it won first prize.
52. Ibid, 205; cf. the review of Dodsley's *Collection* which appeared in the *Edinburgh Review*, i, 1755, 58–61, where taste is seen as an indication of moral standards. The review, however, was less optimistic than Gerard about the progress of taste: 'no sooner does taste arrive at to this degree of perfection than the symptoms of decay are ready to appear. Refinement becomes excessive . . . That amiable simplicity, which is the chief ornament of composition, is despised and lost. By these steps did the Roman taste go to ruin. And the age of Nero followed soon after the age of Augustus.'
53. Gerard, *An Essay on Taste*, 125.

Macpherson's Early Poetry

> Thus every good his native wilds impart
> Imprints the patriot passion on his heart,
> And even those ills, that round his mansion rise,
> Enhance the bliss his scanty fund supplies . . .
> So the loud torrent and the whirlwind's roar
> But bind him to his native mountains more.
>   Such are the charms to barren states assigned;
> Their wants but few, their wishes all confined.
> Yet let them only share the praises due:
> If few their wants, their pleasures are but few.
> Goldsmith, The Traveller, 1755–1764

In 1756, Macpherson returned to his native town of Ruthven. He had spent three years at Aberdeen and a further few months in Edinburgh, but now his days as a student were over and he had to begin to earn a living. According to Bailey Saunders, Macpherson was hoping to enter the Church, but given his temperament and general character, this seems a little unlikely.[1] What is certain is that he took up a post as a teacher in the school where he had been a pupil a few years before. Despite his deep affection for Badenoch, the move back home does not appear to have been a happy one.

Macpherson's experience of city life made settling down in the Highlands again very difficult. Whatever the theoretical drawbacks of urban life, in practical terms it offered entertainment and intellectual stimulation, as well as opportunities for acquiring wealth and status. Life in Badenoch was very different. By 1756 the repressive policies which had followed the '45 were beginning to tell, while much of the old Clan spirit had departed with Cluny, who had finally escaped to France in 1755. The literary notion that the country was the happiest environment for the poet was to prove something of a fallacy when Macpherson put it into practice. Donald Macpherson, one of James' childhood friends, was later to draw a vivid picture of the moody young schoolmaster:

> When he taught the Grammar School of Ruthven, near his father's and my father's Dwellings, I know he composed several

ludicrous poems and catches upon Countrie emergencies, and even one upon myself, was the author of several such. He published in newspapers or magazines of these times. I married in 1759, and I mind perfectly well that a year or two before then, upon a Sunday, one publick service began at Kingussie. I met Mr Macpherson off the road near the Church, walking alone. Upon joining, I found him more morose, silent and pensive than usual. With a serious feeling, I asked the reason. He said, in the same humour, that he was quite wearied of teaching a school, was at a loss how to acquire genteel bread. I told him that he was blessed with several talents, singular good memory, particularly poetry. Did he hit right, he had no reason to perish (?) so soon. He said there was little room there for him.[2]

Just as Macpherson had entertained fellow students at Aberdeen with comic verses, so his friends in Ruthven were familiar with his compositions. Donald Macpherson seems to have been quite proud of being the subject of one of James' humorous poems, especially since the author was also publishing work in magazines. Despite his local reputation, however, Macpherson seems to have felt pessimistic about his prospects and frustrated by his circumstances. Unfortunately, none of Macpherson's light verse has survived. Any assessment of his early ability is thus based on an incomplete range, apparently consisting of the few pieces Macpherson deemed worthy of preservation.[3] These early compositions nevertheless shed important light on the author's personal preoccupations, and as the only surviving examples of Macpherson's own poetry, they are of great importance to the study of *Ossian*.

Getting into print is a perennial problem for the unknown poet but for James Macpherson, who had neither money nor literary connections, the idea of having work published for the first time must have seemed remote indeed. All Scottish writers of the mid eighteenth century were burdened to some extent by a sense of inferiority about their native tongue. The belief that English was the only correct medium for literature caused even the leading authors to devote themselves to developing a refined style, uncontaminated by the dreaded 'Scotticisms'.[4] For Macpherson, already labouring under the sense of coming from a 'primitive' society, the pressure to develop an elegant, English style must have been particularly heavy. Furthermore, once Macpherson had left University, he had no tutor to guide his development. Although Ruthven was a reasonable size for a Highland town, it could not offer the educational resources of Aberdeen or Edinburgh. Macpherson's only access to contemporary literature would have been through the periodical press which, according to Tytler, had a considerable following among young Scots of the eighteenth century:

> A taste for polite literature, had . . . begun gradually to diffuse itself in Scotland, even from the time of the publication of the *Tatlers, Spectators* and *Guardians*; and, as in England, the effect of these writings, and more particularly of the papers of *Addison*, was conspicuous in substituting an ease and elegance of composition as a more engaging vehicle for subjects of taste, in room of the dry scholastic style in which they had hitherto been treated; so, in Scotland, the attention of our youth, fresh from their academicall studies . . . was insensibly attracted to the more pleasing topics of criticism and belles lettres. The cultivation of style became an object of study . . .[5]

After the strongly classical and philosophical bias of his degree, it is not difficult to imagine Macpherson turning with relish to the contemporary periodicals, to improve his taste in literature and his own style of writing. Scottish periodicals included extracts from the English journals,thus bringing tantalising glimpses of an exciting outside world to rural Inverness-shire. In the pages of the *Scots Magazine*, Macpherson could read of the latest international events and scientific discoveries as well as new book reviews and poems. To the frustrated schoolmaster, it provided both an escape and a constant reminder of the limitations of his circumstances. At the same time, the literary section offered Macpherson a challenge: the opportunity to gain fame even when living in the remote mountains of Badenoch.

Although the *Scots Magazine* was modelled on the *Gentleman's Magazine* and contained a great deal of English material, the editors nevertheless shared the nationalistic ambitions prevalent in Scotland in the eighteenth century. The rivalry between England and Scotland gave rise to a host of schemes for the improvement of Scottish arts and sciences, which were given regular publicity in the *Scots Magazine*. The editors also maintained their own policy of encouraging new writing in Scotland, anxious that 'the Caledonian muse might not be restrain'd by want of a publick Echo to her Song'.[6] This enlightened attitude meant that the *Scots Magazine* was the first to publish work by writers who were later to be famous: writers such as James Beattie, James Boswell and James Macpherson.

The question of Macpherson's contributions to the *Scots Magazine* is somewhat problematic. D. S. Imrie in *The Scots Magazine 1739–1826*, refers only to the poems published in May, 1755, ('To a Friend, mourning the Death of Miss . . .'), and October 1758 ('On the Death of Marshal Keith').[7] When the indefatigable Malcolm Laing edited *Ossian* in 1805, he also collected Macpherson's own poetry and included a further three poems which had been published in the *Scots Magazine* between 1758 and 1760.[8] These had appeared in the journal with the initials 'J. McP' or 'JM' and had then been republished with James Mapherson's name in *A Collection of Original Poems, by the Rev.*

Mr Blacklock and Other Scotch Gentlemen, 1760. The poems made useful ammunition for Laing in his attempt to prove that Macpherson was the author of *The Poems of Ossian*, but the authorship of the three pieces is uncertain owing to the following note on Blacklock's *Collection*, which appeared in the *Scots Magazine* in 1762:

> The public are desired to take notice of three erratas, being three pieces inserted in pages 134, 170 and 176. These, by mistake, are said to be written by James Macpherson, whom some have supposed to be the same person who translated Fingal. We are now certainly informed that they are not composed by him. These pieces were taken from the Scotch Magazine (xxi, 527, 255 and xxii, 459) and have the initials J. M. annexed to them, which corresponding to Mr Macpherson's name, occasioned this mistake.[9]

Considering Macpherson's poetic ambitions, it seems highly improbable that he would have denied the authorship of poems selected to appear beside the foremost Scottish poets of the day had they been his own work. As Alexander Carlyle remarked when Macpherson was suspected of being the author of Colonel Dow's *Tragedy of Zingis*, 'Could Macpherson have Claim'd it, he was not the Man to Relinquish Either the Credits or Profits which might arise from it.'[10] The following discussion of the early poetry, therefore, will focus only on those poems which were definitely written by Macpherson.

Macpherson's first published poem appeared in the *Scots Magazine* in May 1755, when he was only nineteen and this early success must have fired his literary aspirations. 'To a Friend mourning the Death of Miss . . .' was a formal elegy based on Horace's Ode, 'Quis desiderio?' (Book I, Ode 24).

> To a FRIEND, mourning the death of Miss ---
> Hor. Lib 1 ode 24 imitated
>
> What measure can there be to grief?
>   What joy can give the soul relief,
>   Since MIRA is no more?
> Come, mournful muse of hapless love,
> Whose voice and lyre proceed from Jove,
>   With me her fate deplore.
>
> Does then eternal sleep infold
>   Those sparkling eyes? does pallid cold
>   Congeal that balmy breath?
> Lo! that sweet bloom that once did move,
> And kindle all the soul of love,
>   Lies blasted in grim Death.

Where now can will and virtue find
  So sprightly and so pure a mind,
    Adorn'd with every grace?
Such innocence, such early truth,
Such beauty, parts, and blooming youth,
    Her all divine confess.

By all bemoan'd the virgin fell.
  On ev'ry tongue her praises dwell;
    Each throbbing bosom sighs;
But most, my friend, bemoan'd by thee,
Whose muse still mourns her destiny
    In woful elegies.

In vain you importune the shade,
  Whose blast makes youthful beauty fade,
    Relentless to your pain:
Though sweeter than the Thracian bard,
Thy muse by list'ning woods was heard,
    To him your lays are vain.

No more that lamp extinct will burn,
  To warm that corse; no more return
    That breath which heav'd before
Her breast; no more that stream will dye
The ruby cheek; nor shall that eye
    E'er softly languish more.

'Tis hard. But patience, constant fair,
  Thy woes, thy mournful woes will bear,
    And ease the loaden soul;
Till slow-pac'd Memory shall fail,
  And kind Oblivion draw the vail,
    And all thy griefs controul.

Published in the *Scots Magazine*, xvii, 1755, 249.

The use of a classical model was not surprising, given that the poem was written at the end of Macpherson's course at Aberdeen. The overt classicism indicates not only Macpherson's desire to show off his education but also his diffidence about publishing original work. Although the poem is based on Horace, Macpherson described it as an 'imitation' rather than a translation, and it is characteristic of the period that he should not only copy but also try to 'improve' upon a classical source. The treatment of the Latin Ode sheds interesting light on Macpherson's subsequent use of his Gaelic sources in the *Ossian* 'translations'.

Although Macpherson's poem borrowed the ideas, structure and even some complete lines from Horace, it is by no means a literal translation. The Latin poem was inspired by the death of Quintilius and by Virgil's grief for the deceased, but in Macpherson's version the death of a young woman is lamented by her lover. The theme is typical of Macpherson and stories of lovers whose happiness has been interrupted by death were to recur frequently in *The Poems of Ossian*.

Just as the subject of the Ode was altered to suit Macpherson's preoccupations, so the taut language of the original was embellished freely, as Horace's tragic 'Melpomene' became the 'Mournful Muse of hapless love'. While Macpherson's conclusion remained close to the Latin in meaning, it was couched in elaborate, eighteenth-century diction, and 'durum: sed levius fit patientia/ quidquid corrigere est nefas' ('It is hard, but patience alleviates whatever wrongs must be healed') was rendered:

> Tis hard. But patience, constant fair,
>   Thy woes, thy mournful woes will bear,
>   And ease the loaden soul;
> Till slow-pac'd Memory shall fail,
>   And kind Oblivion draw the vail,
>   And all thy griefs controul.   (37–42)

In some cases, the embellishments were obviously added for the sake of the metre or rhyme scheme, but there are instances where Macpherson's variations on the original reveal characteristic preoccupations. In stanza 2, for example, a single line of Latin, 'ergo Quintilium perpetuus sopor urget ?' ('Then does perpetual sleep overwhelm Quintilius?') was expanded to:

> Does then eternal sleep infold
>   Those sparkling eyes ? does pallid cold
>   Congeal that balmy breath ?
> Lo! that sweet bloom that once did move,
> And kindle all the soul of love,
>   Lies blasted in grim Death.   (7–12)

The contrast between a happy past and a miserable present is a persistent theme in Macpherson's work and was to find its fullest expression in *Ossian*'s 'tales of the times of old'. The celebrated 'joy of grief' that was to accompany Ossian's nostalgic songs also seems to be anticipated in the emotional extravagance of the elegy. Indeed, Macpherson seems to have relished demonstrations of grief, adapting Horace's 'multis ille bonis flebilis occidit' ('He fell, mourned by many a good man') to

> By all bemoan'd the virgin fell;
>   On ev'ry tongue her praises dwell;
>   Each throbbing bosom sighs;   (19–21)

The 'throbbing bosom' of the bereaved is then echoed, two verses later, by the recollection of 'that breath which heav'd before /Her breast'. In Macpherson's poetry, sexual love is frequently associated with death. Laments tend to be expressed in erotic terms, while love scenes are generally confined to tragic deaths or separations. *The Poems of Ossian* are littered with the corpses of dead lovers while the pervading atmosphere is one of gloom: a gloom so unrelenting that it appears to have been a strange source of pleasure for the poet.

Despite Macpherson's early success with the imitation of Horace, he had to wait three years before having the satisfaction of seeing his name in the *Scots Magazine* again. 'On the Death of Marshal Keith', published in October 1758, was also an elegy, but a far more successful one than 'To a Friend'.[11] Again, Macpherson was exploring a romantic theme, the death of a Jacobite hero. James Keith had been forced to leave Scotland after the failure of the Jacobite Rising of 1715, but spent the rest of his life gaining fame through courageous acts in battles on the Continent. His death gave Macpherson the opportunity to blend the panegyric for an individual hero with his larger concern for the Highlands and her exiled sons.

Marshal Keith could be seen as a symbol of the Jacobite leaders, powerful in battle but doomed to exile and death in a foreign land. It is not difficult to read some of Macpherson's grief for his own banished Chief in the poem, for example in lines 39–40: 'Sad from his native home the chief withdrew;/But kindled Scotia's glory as he flew'. In the same way, a passage that appears to be a typical mid-eighteenth-century description of ruins has special significance when seen as the work of a Highland poet:

> See! the proud halls they once possessed, decayed,
> The spiral tow'rs depend the lofty head;
> Wild ivy creeps along the mould'ring walls,
> And with each gust of wind a fragment falls;
> While birds obscene at noon of night deplore,
> Where mighty heroes kept the watch before.   (53–58)

Although the description owes much to contemporary poetry, it can also be related to Macpherson's personal experience of castles ruined in the Jacobite rebellion, especially with the reference to 'mighty heroes'.

The contrast between the past and the present which Macpherson stressed in the imitation of Horace, has an equally prominent place in 'Marshal Keith'. Here the use of the heroic couplet emphasises the suddenness of the change:

> With silent eyes they run the hero o'er,
> And mourn the chief they shall obey no more; (15–16)

> Sadly she sits, and mourns her glory gone;
> He's fallen, her bravest, and her greatest son!
> While at her side her children all deplore
> The godlike hero they exiled before. (35–38)

Although Macpherson is glorifying the memory of the Jacobite hero, it is essentially a 'glory gone'. Just as Ossian was to be called the 'last of a race of heroes', so the Keiths are among the last survivors of a heroic people:

> But chief, as relics of a dying race,
> The Keiths command, in woe, the foremost place;
> A name for ages through the world revered,
> By Scotia loved, by all her en'mies feared;
> Now falling, dying, lost to all but fame,
> And only living in the hero's name. (47–52)

Although Keith had been part of the 1715 Rising, the image of the Jacobite hero as a 'relic of a dying race' had equal relevance to those who had fled abroad after the '45. For Macpherson they represented the glory of Scotland, and the death of Keith is presented partly as a reminder to 'Scotia' that the sons who had been driven from home were, in fact, her greatest strength. The elegaic tone, however, suggests that the glory of both Keith and the Highland people had now become part of history. Despite the echoes of 'Lycidas', Macpherson's poem includes no reference to any Christian resurrection and the only solace offered is that of Fame:

> On Mem'ry's tablet mankind soon decay,
> On Time's swift stream their glory slides away;
> But, present in the voice of deathless Fame,
> Keith lives, eternal, in his glorious name:
> While ages far remote his actions show;
> And mark with them the way their chiefs should go;
> While sires unto their wond'ring offspring tell,
> Keith lived in glory, and in glory fell. (59–66)

In Highland society, however, fame was a matter of great importance, since stories of the forefathers' bold deeds served both as entertainment and inspiration to their descendants. By writing the poem on Keith, Macpherson was following the Highland tradition: immortalising the memory of the dead and thus, inspiring the living.

Macpherson's preoccupations with death and the Highlands also emerged as the themes of two longer poems which were written during the time he spent as a schoolmaster in Ruthven. The poems were never finished and have only survived as a result of Malcolm Laing's attack on *The Poems of Ossian*. When the Reverend John Anderson was sorting out the papers at Belleville, after Macpherson's death in 1796, he came across a small notebook containing the poet's 'first Essays in English Verse'[12]. After some hesitation Anderson sent the book to Laing, who was delighted to include the contents along with the other poems he attributed to Macpherson, in the attempt to prove him a poet capable of creating *Ossian*.[13]

Of the two long poems in the notebook, the earlier is less ambitious and rather less interesting. Entitled 'Death', it follows the graveyard tradition of Young's *Night Thoughts* and Blair's *The Grave*, a choice suggesting that both 'To a Friend' and 'On the Death of Marshal Keith' were symptoms of a morbid preoccupation with death. The formalised grief of the published elegies, however, pales beside the overwhelming gloom of the longer poem, where the vague emotions shamble formlessly, unrelieved for some five hundred lines.

Macpherson's preoccupation with death and despair was bound up with his sense of frustration. In the central passage of reflection, the idea of death is closely related to a sense of guilt about being ambitious:

>O man! what is thy boast ? A beauteous face?
>That soon is blasted. Strength itself decays.
>Strong is the foe, and all his allies strong.
>Ev'n Nature's self and elements combine
>With death, with force confederate. Hapless man!
>How fallen, fallen from that high estate
>Of innocence and love, thy prior boon:
>When Pleasure stretched the untainted wing
>O'er fields of bliss; where fair Content and Joy,
>With Meditation and Serenity,
>Led the eternal choir, and Virtue smil'd
>To see her children sport; when, far removed,
>Death pin'd in hell's deep bounds: But, oh the pow'r
>Of vile ambition, virtue-hated fiend!
>Heaven's changed to hell, and death to life preferr'd;
>Hatred to love, and vice to innocence;
>Content, and virtue, and serenity,
>Are chang'd to folly, woe, and gloomy thought.   (188–205)

Rather than concentrating on the death of an individual, Macpherson was contemplating the nature of fallen man. His own sense of Original Sin can be seen in line 205, where the symptoms of melancholy are seen as the direct result of 'vile ambition'. The sense of guilt was, perhaps, derived from the discontent Macpherson experienced on returning to the home of his childhood, where he could not recapture the 'innocence and love...Content and Joy'. As long as Macpherson's ambitions remained unfulfilled, Badenoch was not a paradise, but a prison. Macpherson's account of the power of ambition suggests that it was an obsession which affected every aspect of life: 'Heaven's changed to hell, and death to life preferr'd;/Hatred to love, and vice to innocence' (202-203). The man corrupted by ambition is seen to reject life, love and innocence in favour of death, hatred and vice; and this notion emerges throughout the poem, which contemplates not only death, but also the destruction of innocent love.

After opening the poem with a gloomy parade of abstractions ('Sorrow . . . Death . . . grisly Terror, shivering Dismay, and cloud-envelop'd Horror'), Macpherson piled on the misery with two brief tales of tragic love, in the style of Thomson.[14] The first is particularly interesting, as it shows his tendency to associate love with death, mixing violence with romantic descriptions. The reader is plunged into a chaotic scene, where the hero, Doricles, is seen searching a ruined city for his lost love, Daphne:

> He starts, he views, he flies; no dangers fright
> But those of Daphne: her he shivering found,
> Rock'd in the tottering hall; her azure eyes,
> Like two fair fountains, watered the plain
> Of roses on her cheek.   (63–67)

Already, the style of Ossian is anticipated, as a moment of high drama is frozen by a beautiful, but strangely unreal, image. The lyricism of the lovers' reunion, however, is shortlived for just as they are reaching safety, disaster strikes:

> The field appears, and joy begins to dawn;
> When from a tottering roof a fragment falls,
> And crush'd the lovely Daphne in his arms!   (70–72)

The untimely death gives Macpherson the opportunity for a typical contemplation:

> How did Doricles stand aghast! How beat,
> With broken sighs, his sorrow-wounded breast!
> Still, still he grasps the dying innocent;
> Yet sweet in death, and lovely in decay.   (73–76)

While this unhealthy delight in corpses is reminiscent of the imitation of Horace, it is also a foretaste of *The Poems of Ossian*.

The sad tale of Doricles and Daphne is not only interesting stylistically, but also because of Macpherson's choice of disaster. Since there is no mention of flames or explosions, the cause of devastation appears to be an earthquake, which links the passage to the meditation on fallen man, quoted above. After the discourse on the effects of 'vile ambition', Macpherson continues with the lines:

> Escap'd from hell once, Discord gnashed her teeth,
> And roll'd her glaring eyes: the nations quake,
> Affrighted peace the sinful earth foregoes,
> And truth is gone: Death recognised the sign,
> Smiles grimly and begins to whet his shafts;
> Then o'er Hiberian floods, with mighty noise,
> Self-balanced, through midheaven wings his way,
> Eager for war. The affrighted waves subside,
> And with retreating hosts invade the earth:
> Earth dreads, and shivers from her inmost womb;
> Her mountains tremble, and her rough rocks fall
> Thundering along the ground; while through the chink
> Flames subterraneous flash, smoke wraps the sky,
> Domes throw their stately towers to earth; men groan,
> Torn in the jaws of death; half-stiffl'd cries
> Of suffocated infants, from the embrace
> Of cold maternal arms, invade the ear.   (206–222)

There is a direct parallel between the consequences of ambition, turning love to hatred, life to death, and the natural disaster. The earth is described as 'sinful' (208), which implies that the earthquake is some sort of punishment, thus making the story of Doricles and Daphne part of the general guilt that pervades the poem. The notion that natural disasters were punishments sent from God to chastise the wicked world was not peculiar to Macpherson. On 1 November 1755, Lisbon had been devastated by an earthquake, which provoked an enormous response throughout Europe. Although Voltaire's sceptical treatment of the incident in *Candide* is probably the most famous, many of the articles about the disaster were full of religious fervour. Earthquakes were seen as agents of God and according to one, fairly typical writer they were

> judgments, and may be foretold, not by signs in the heavens, but signs of the times; that these signs are infidelity and corruption of manners, which, he says, are the characteristics of these times in Great Britain, and leaves the inference to his readers.[16]

Macpherson's personal feelings of guilt were part of a much larger anxiety, shared by many of his contemporaries. The misgivings about the progress of modern civilisation were by no means confined to the University of Aberdeen, but appear to have been pervasive. The reference to 'infidelity' in the passage above indicates the common anxiety about the consequence of scientific advance and new philosophical ideas. The mere suggestion that the world could function without God roused complicated feelings of guilt, anger and fear.

Such feelings emerged forcibly in the articles which seized on the Lisbon earthquake as proof of God's power.

Apart from the earthquake, the poem includes many lines on sickness, which suggests a similar fascination with forces beyond man's control:

> Behind her comes Consumption – meagre ghost!
> With slow, weak, languid pace, and self-devour'd:
> Born drooping on a tedious flux of time,
> With pain deep loaden, sluggish, flowing down:
> Then ulcers, swellings, apoplectic fits,
> Convulsive trances, fever scorching hot,
> The sage Physician – all a gloomy train!
> Their general parent follow; while grim Death,
> Wide-wasting Terror! shuts the dismal scene (41–49)

In a society where disease was rife, Macpherson's interest is, perhaps, understandable, but there is a curious sense of satisfaction in the parade of symptoms and the eventual defeat of the 'sage Physician'[17]. Although part of Macpherson's relish stems from the idea that Consumption follows prosperity (the 'her' of line 41), thus humbling the envied rich, there is also a dim sense of relief that modern medicine is not omnipotent.

A similar mixture of despair and satisfaction can be felt in the section of the poem that deals with war. Rather than allowing his imagination to run over battlefields or naval encounters, Macpherson opened his discussion with the image of an old soldier: 'How feeble is that arm /Robust, that often foil'd his country's foe!' (179–180). The image of the impotent old soldier recalls the Aberdonian anxieties about modern society and its loss of strength, while the fact that the soldier is also mad seems to make a mockery of the idea that man's intellect can somehow guide and redeem society.

After this gloomy portrait, Macpherson's discussion turned upon the victims of war, which he describes as the 'woe of mothers and new-married maids' (370). The most striking passage is the graphic description of a sailor who manages to escape the destruction of his ship in a naval battle, by floating on a broken mast, only to be drowned within sight of the shore, where his unfortunate mother is waiting to pull him to safety. The melodrama is typical of the poem but again the morbid story can be related to wider issues. The theme of the parent outliving the child, which was to be an important feature of *Ossian*, has much in common with the image of the active man losing his strength, or indeed, with the death of young lovers. All these images, so characteristic of Macpherson's work, suggest the same profound pessimism about the future.

Despite the morbid nature of 'Death' and the two elegies, not all Macpherson's early work was the product of adolescent depression.

We know from Donald Macpherson's account and the anecdotes from Aberdeen that Macpherson actually had a reputation as a comic writer. Some indication of the lighter side of his talent can be seen in the other poem from the notebook. Again, the autobiographical elements are pronounced, but the whole tone is lighter and the poem concludes with the comic motif of marriage. 'The Hunter' is the earliest example of an attempt by Macpherson to fuse his native Highland culture with the influences of an academic education. Although superficially an English poem in rhyming couplets, the basic framework of 'The Hunter' is a fairytale, set in the Highlands and incorporating elements of the traditional culture. This blend of Highland culture and English style is thus an important forerunner of the Ossianic poems.

The storyline of 'The Hunter' has much in common with Macpherson's own experience. When the young Highlander, Donald, is out hunting, he accidentally kills a faun belonging to a fairy princess. To avenge the death, the fairy plants the seeds of ambition in Donald's hitherto untroubled mind and, as a result, Donald is plunged into internal conflict. His discontent drives him away from the Highlands, south to Edinburgh, which just happens to be under attack from an invading English army. Without a moment's hesitation, the vigorous Highlander leaps to the defence of his country and leads the Lowland army to victory. Donald's daring deeds gain him high favour with the Scottish King Fergus and, once in Court, he falls in love with the beautiful Egidia. Although Egidia is also secretly in love with Donald, he is so embarrassed by his lack of social graces, that he fails to make any approach at all. Eventually the situation is resolved when it transpires that Donald is the lost son of the King. As a prince, any diffidence about his social position is completely inappropriate, so Donald can propose and the poem ends happily.

Despite its light, romantic tone, 'The Hunter' dramatises a problem close to Macpherson's heart: the conflict between the attractions of the city and a native attachment to the Highlands. In 'Death', ambition is condemned as an influence entirely evil, but in 'The Hunter', things are less straightforward. Instead of the fundamental opposition between ambition and love which was asserted in the earlier poem, we find ambition leading not only to material success, but also to a family reunion and a happy marriage. In spite of the guilt and unhappiness surrounding Donald's desertion of his Highland home, such feelings have completely vanished by the conclusion. The poem is essentially optimistic and suggests Macpherson's own romantic hopes about the possibilities beyond Badenoch.

'The Hunter' opens with an idealised portrait of Donald in his mountain home, which is very different from the melancholy exclamations of 'Death':

Macpherson's Early Poetry

> Once on a time, when Liberty was seen
> To sport and revel on the northern plain,
> Immortal fair! and was supremely kind
> On Scotia's hills to snuff the northern wind;
> There lived a youth, and DONALD was his name.
> To chace the flying stag his highest aim;
> A gun, a plaid, a dog, his humble store;
> In these thrice happy, as he wants no more.
> The flesh of deer his food; the heath his bed;
> He slept contented in his tartan plaid.
> Sprightly as morn he rose with dawning light,
> And strode o'er hills until the approach of night;
> Then bounding homeward, joyful burden bears
> Of heath-hens, woodcocks, or of fearful deers.
> Then Bessy gets upon the homely board
> What Donald's gun and oaten field afford.
> Blest in the chace, blest in his barren soil,
> And more than happy in his temperate toil,
> Our Donald lived; but, oh! how soon the light
> Of happiness is sunk in blackest night!   (1–20)

The description of the Highlander is carefully handled and it is clear that Macpherson's purpose was not merely the creation of a fairytale atmosphere. When the poem was written, in 1756, the Highlanders were forbidden by law to wear tartan or carry weapons, so Macpherson's idealisation of young Donald had a strongly political aspect. Donald's physical prowess, his gun and his plaid were the distinctive features of the Highlander most feared by the British Government. And yet Macpherson did not present his hero as a man of violence, but as a man of peace. The description can be read as a nostalgic plea for the traditional Highland way of life, at a time when it was being destroyed. Already, in the opening line, where 'Liberty' is associated with a romantic past, Macpherson's view of the Highlands as a personal Golden Age is evident.

Although the passage is based on Macpherson's own affection for the Highlands, it is coloured by his education. In order to create an idealised atmosphere, Macpherson incorporated echoes of Virgil's *Georgics* and the Horatian *Beatus ille*, which had become the common currency of the eighteenth-century pastoral. The neo-classical ideal was nevertheless being adapted to produce a more active hero than the traditional shepherd or farmer. According to Boswell, Macpherson had a vigorous contempt for agriculturalists:

> We were talking of Gray's fine Elegy in a Churchyard. 'Hoot!' cried Fingal (James Macpherson) 'to write panegyrics upon a parcel of damned rascals that did nething but plough the land

and saw corn'. He considered that fighters only should be celebrated.[18]

A similar prejudice appeared in Macpherson's essay on *Temora*, where the development of arable farming was associated with the decline of the heroic society.[19] It is not surprising then to find that although Donald has an 'oaten field', the emphasis is entirely upon his abilities as a hunter. Donald is a man of action, and here we can see the fusion of Macpherson's Highland background with Blackwell's vision of Homeric Greece. Both seemed ideal worlds, characterised by liberty and simplicity, and filled with men of outstanding physical ability. Both were inspired by an anxiety about the effects of moving away from a natural way of life to an urban civilisation.

The sense of harmony between Donald and his surroundings is achieved partly through the use of natural imagery, as in the description of the Hunter swimming the Tay:

> Refresh'd he rose, then plunged into the tide;
> The waves arose, and, bubbling, wash his sides;
> He gains the farther shore; then, with a bound,
> The Hunter rises: Showers descend around.
> Thus water-fowl their downy bodies lave
> In the bright bubbles of the silver wave;
> Then seek the shore, and clap the ruffled wing;
> Then through the air on well fledged pinions sing.
>
> (II, 179–186)

Although Macpherson was following Blackwell's ideal of drawing on personal experience, however, much of the freshness was marred by the attempt to produce 'refined' descriptions, according to the demands of contemporary taste. In his account of 'Grampus', for example, Macpherson shows his knowledge of the Scottish mountains, but also forces the landscape into elaborate, ornamental diction:

> A hill there is, which forms a sable wall
> Through all the north, and men it Grampus call.
> Here lean-cheek'd Barrenness terrific strides;
> A tattered robe waves round her iron sides;
> Two baleful eyes roll in her iron face;
> Her meagre hand supports a pile of grass;
> Her bare white skull no decent covering shows;
> Eternal tempests rattle on her brows;
> Lank-sided Want, and pale-eyed Poverty,
> And sharp-tooth'd Famine, still around her fly;
> Health-gotten Hunger, want-descended Pain,
> Vein-numbing Cold – are all her gloomy train. (II, 55–66)

It is almost as if by using the abstractions and compound epithets of contemporary English verse, Macpherson was somehow compensating for the Scottish subject matter.

A similar blend of cultures can be seen in Macpherson's use of the supernatural, which forms an important part of the poem. Although the fairies were given the lofty, classical names of Xanthe and Euchenor, they were deeply rooted in traditional Highland culture. The motifs of the enchanted faun and the revenge of the fairies both occur in old Gaelic poetry, but Macpherson would have been familiar with many such stories simply through being a native of Badenoch.[20] Anne Grant's *Essays on the Superstitions of the Highlands* give ample evidence of the local belief in fairies, including descriptions of the 'fairy glades' at Corrieyairaick, or of the ghosts that haunted the Spey valley.[21] One of the well-known Clan legends was that the Black Chanter of Clan Chattan had been given to a Macpherson piper by a fairy woman.[22] Fairies were not pretty little elves but supernatural beings, and stories of marriages between fairies and human beings were common.

Whatever Macpherson's own view of such beliefs, he certainly recognised their imaginative potential. The Highland legends could provide a supernatural dimension to his poetry without seeming artificial or merely ornamental. The traditional association between fairies and fallen angels, for example, gave Macpherson the opportunity to draw on both the Highland beliefs and English literature.[23] Thus, the assembly of the Fairy 'Senate', which meets to discuss Donald's punishment for the death of the faun, is strongly reminiscent of Satan's Council in *Paradise Lost*, II. Although Macpherson handles the allusions lightly, with a tone almost mock heroic, the parallels are obvious. While Milton's Devils decide to send evil to corrupt the innocent earth, Macpherson's fairies agree to ruin Donald with ambition:

> Content upon the green the peasant lives,
> While damn'd in the courts of state the courtier grieves
> For power, for grandeur, pours the eternal pray'r,
> Wakes sleepless nights, and yawns whole days of care.
> Should some foe-fairy glide through fields of light,
> And to the regal seat direct his flight,
> Take the black humour, boiling round the brain,
> Then, soft-transported, seek the northern plain;
> Around the hunter the black humour shed,
> And fill, with vile ambition, all his head;
> Then, damn'd to care, the deer-destroying man
> Shall rue the slaughter of the bounding fawn.   (I, 109–120)

Thus, Macpherson elevates the Gaelic motif of the fairies' revenge through allusions to both Milton and the pastoral tradition. By drawing parallels between the Fairies' Court and Milton's Hell, the Highlands become a kind of Paradise, which must then be lost.

Although Macpherson exploits the imaginative power of the supernatural, there is also a psychological realism in the poem. Donald's ambition may be attributed to the fairies, but his emotions would not be unnatural for any penniless young man who had glimpsed the lifestyle of the wealthy:

> In Donald's eye now fade the blissful scenes:
> The rough brow'd rocks, the sloping hills and plains,
> Delight no more; no chace, no winged fowl,
> No goat, no cattle, cheer the troubled soul;
> The hut is hateful, and the fields of corn
> Contract their bounds, and promise no return.
> All is one blank – O envy'd envy'd state,
> The hunter cries, of all the happy great!
> While press'd in poverty's hard iron hand,
> I force poor sustenance from barren land,
> Remote from life, and curs'd by fate unkind,
> To struggle on the hill with northern wind,
> Secure, in stately halls, the feast they ply
> And swim through life in deluges of joy.
> The hut, the heathy wild, the barren fold,
> The rattling hail, the north-descended cold,
> Is all my portion. (II, 1–17)

The parallels between Donald's state of mind and that of the author require little comment.

The haziness of the boundary between the supernatural and the psychological are examined in the poem itself. After Donald has been driven from home by ambition, he spends a night on the mountain and is visited by an apparition:

> When, lo! before the sleeping hunter's eyes
> His father Malcolm's phantom seem'd to rise.
> Thin are the snowy honours of his head;
> An half-worn shroud waves round the long since dead.
> (II, 87–90)

The vision rebukes Donald for deserting the Highlands, and warns him of the 'Care', 'Corruption' and 'Ambition' which he will find in Court. Although the sleepy Hunter is initially terrified by the apparition, he begins to debate the existence of ghosts and ultimately rejects his experience, turning his back on the Highlands and its culture. Since he subsequently learns that his real father is not Malcolm but King Fergus, the decision seems justified and the episode suggests that Macpherson wished to emphasise the imaginary nature of Highland beliefs. The influence of the fairies, which was an acceptable notion in the Highland setting, now seems a metaphor for the development of ambition in a young man who wishes to fulfil his natural potential.

Macpherson's Early Poetry

Although Donald rejects the phantom as imaginary, however, the feelings of guilt from which it rose were real enough. Even when Donald has been reunited with his real father, he cannot forget his Highland guardian, whose spirit was broken by the young man's departure. The problem of the two fathers symbolises the conflicting loyalties which face Donald: while the Highland guardian sinks into despair and death, the Lowland father welcomes his son into the prosperous society of Edinburgh.

Macpherson's first description of the Scottish capital was hardly complimentary:

> On rocks a city stands, high-tower'd, unwall'd,
> And from its scite the hill of Edin call'd,
> Once the proud seat of royalty and state,
> Of kings, of heroes and of all that's great;
> But these are flown, and Edin's only stores,
> Are fops, and scriveners, and English'd whores. (I, 137–142)

His disgust at the decline of Scottish glory in the face of the degenerate English is plain. However, it is the very failings of the South that provide Donald with the opportunity to display his talents. The situation is carefully arranged to demonstrate the inferiority of the Lowland army, so that the Highland hero can burst in and rally the troops to victory:

> Ah! glory gone!
> Ah! ancient virtue now for ever flown!
> What blessed corner does the godhead rest?
> No more you swell the generous Scottish breast,
> When thus, O Scotland! Saxons dare deride
> Thy steel-clad warriors, ranged side by side –
> I can no more – my panting vitals swell;
> I'll give thee glory, or thy soul to hell! (IV, 49–56)

The Lowlands were attractive not only in material terms, but also for providing a background against which the Highlander could shine.

The situation in 'The Hunter' allowed Macpherson to indulge similarly romantic ideas about the relationship between Scotland and England. The unspecific historical setting gave him the opportunity not only to express his feelings about the 'English thunder' (III, 6) that was threatening Scotland, but also to do something about it. As Donald slays the English leader in the battle, he is freeing Scotland from 'Hateful slavery and the aspiring Rose' (III, 12). By celebrating a Scottish victory over the English, led by a Highlander in full tartan dress, Macpherson was attempting to reverse the double disgrace of the 1707 Union and the '45 Rebellion.

Ironically, however, the victory is presented in English verse, while the poem itself contains hints of the real situation. As the English leader breathes his last, he gasps out an ominous prophecy:

> The hill-descended shall retain the prize,
> Until a race, deep-versed in policies,
> Shall sprout from Saxon trunk, and schemes unfold
> To change their steely points to fusil gold;
> Then shackled on his heath, the hill-born swain
> Shall crawl along, and move his hard-bound limbs with pain.
> Fair Liberty to them shall lose her charms,
> And Scots shall tremble at the sight of arms. (IV, 181–89)

The 'prophecy' obviously reflects Macpherson's own opinion of the contemporary situation in Scotland.

The very idealisation of Donald, 'Who saves his country, nor is basely sold /To sordid interest and the love of gold' (V, 97–8), has a somewhat ironic edge. His reasons for being in Edinburgh at the crucial moment had nothing to do with any noble desire to save Scotland, but resulted from his own ambitions, which led eventually to fame and fortune. Thus Macpherson's poem embodies the conflict between non-materialistic ideals and the natural desire for success. The Highlander is deeply attached to his home and aware of the perils of life in the city, nevertheless he chooses to leave the Highlands to take advantages of the opportunities elsewhere.

In Macpherson's poem, the decision is presented as an inevitability. Hunting was a normal part of Highland life, so Donald is driven from home as a result of exercising his natural abilities. In much the same way, Macpherson's talents had taken him away from Badenoch to be educated, but in doing so, made him unable to settle there again. Macpherson was fully aware of the inevitable domination of English culture, and in the dissertation on *Fingal*, he was to emphasise the fact. Rather than dwelling upon Culloden, he discussed the effects of communications, trade, industry and education:

> Many have now learned to leave their mountains, and seek their fortunes in a milder climate; and though a certain *amor patriae* may sometimes bring them back, they have, during their absence, imbibed enough of foreign manners to despise the customs of their ancestors. (*Fingal*, xv)

The changes in the Highlands became irreversible, once the inhabitants *wanted* to be part of the United Kingdom.

NOTES
1. B. Saunders, *The Life and Letters of James Macpherson*, (London 1894), 42. The theory appears to be based on the supposition that because Macpherson's name does not appear on the matriculation list at the

Macpherson's Early Poetry

University of Edinburgh, he must have enrolled as a student of divinity.
2. D. Macpherson to Rev. J. Anderson, Laggan, October 1797, ADV MS 73.2.13 f23. Punctuation has been modernised.
3. After reading some of Macpherson's lampoons and epigrams at Belleville, Carruthers noted, 'Macpherson's genius was, at all times, an overmatch for his taste, and his principles were likely to be overpowered by the impulse of the moment. His returning good sense, or right feeling, however, prevented the publication of such effusions, which appear to have been thrown aside when the fit was off.' *The Highland Notebook*, 309.
4. See James Beattie to Glenbervie, 5 January 1778: 'We who live in Scotland are obliged to study English from books, like a dead language. Accordingly, when we write, we write it like a dead language, which we understand but cannot speak; avoiding, perhaps, all ungrammatical expressions, and even the barbarisms of our country, but at the same time, without communicating that neatness, ease and softness of phrase, which appears so conspicuously in Addison, Lord Lyttelton, and other elegant English authors.' W. Forbes, *An Account of the Life and Writings of James Beattie*, 2 vols, (Edinburgh 1806), II, 17–18. See also D. Craig, *Scottish Literature and the Scottish People 1630–1830*, (London 1961), 40.
5. Tytler, *Memoirs of . . . Kames*, I, 164. See also M. E. Craig, *The Scottish Periodical Press 1750–1789*, (Edinburgh & London 1931); R. C. Elliott, 'The Early Scots Magazine', *MLQ*, xi, 1950, 189–96; G. A. Sinclair, 'Periodical Literature of the Eighteenth Century', *SHR*, ii, 1905, 36–49.
6. *Scots Magazine*, i, 1739, Preface.
7. D. S. Imrie, *The Scots Magazine 1739–1826*, (Edinburgh 1939), 55.
8. Laing ed., 1805, II, 587–600. The additional poems are 'On the Death of a Young Lady', *Scots Magazine*, xxi, 1759, 255; 'To the Memory of an Officer killed before Quebec', ibid, 527; 'The Earl Marischal's Welcome to his Native Country,' ibid, xxii, 1760, 459.
9. *Scots Magazine*, xxiv, 1762, 204.
10. A. Carlyle, *Anecdotes and Characters of the Times*, ed. J. Kinsley, (Oxford 1973), 258.
11. The text is Laing's, 1805, II, 588.
12. Anderson to Chalmers, 1 November 1797, ADV MS 73.2.13 f28. The book contained no Gaelic poetry but included a 'Variety of draughts which he never finished for public Inspections'.
13. Laing ed., 1805, II, 445. Laing noted that the manuscript 'contains memorandums concerning his school and housekeeping at Ruthven, in Badenoch, with a few dates, from which the Hunter appears to have been written towards the end of the year 1756. The poem upon Death is an earlier and worse composition'.
14. Cf. *The Seasons*, 'Summer', 1171–370, in the *Poetical Works*, ed. J. Logie Robertson, (London 1908).
15. Ibid, 1214–16.
16. *Scots Magazine*, xviii, 1756, 54–5; cf. J. Wesley, *Serious Thoughts Occasioned by the late Earthquake at Lisbon*, (Bristol 1755).
17. Each month a list of burials appeared in the *Scots Magazine*: in January 1756 there were 111 burials in Edinburgh, 21 of children

under the age of two. Causes of death were: Aged, 6; Apoplexy, 2; Asthma, 1; Childbed, 2; Chincough, 5; Colic, 1; Consumption, 20; Dropsy, 2; Epilepsy, 1; Fever, 33; Gravel, 1; Measles, 8; Smallpox, 10; Stillborn, 2; Suddenly, 9; Teething, 8. See also J. McManners, *Death and the Enlightenment*, (Oxford 1981).
18. 29 December 1762, *Boswell's London Journal 1762–1763*, 110.
19. *Temora*, xii–xiii; see Chapter Nine below.
20. A. Bruford, *Gaelic Folk-Tales and Mediaeval Romances*, (Dublin 1969); A. Polson, *Our Highland Folklore Heritage*, (Dingwall & Inverness 1926); F. Thompson, *The Supernatural Highlands*, (London 1976).
21. Grant, *Essays*, I, 267ff.
22. A. Carmichael, *Carmina Gadelica*, 6 vols, 2nd edn, (Edinburgh & London 1928–1971), II, 354.
23. Ibid, II, 353: 'The Proud Angel fomented a rebellion among the angels of Heaven, where he had been a leading light. He declared that he would go and found a kingdom of his own . . . Many angels followed him so many that at last the Son called out 'Father! Father! the city is being emptied!' Whereupon the Father ordered that the gates should be close. This was instantly done; and those who were in were in, and those who were out were out; while the hosts who had left heaven and had not reached hell, flew into the holes of the earth . . . These are the fairy folks – ever since doomed to live under the ground.'

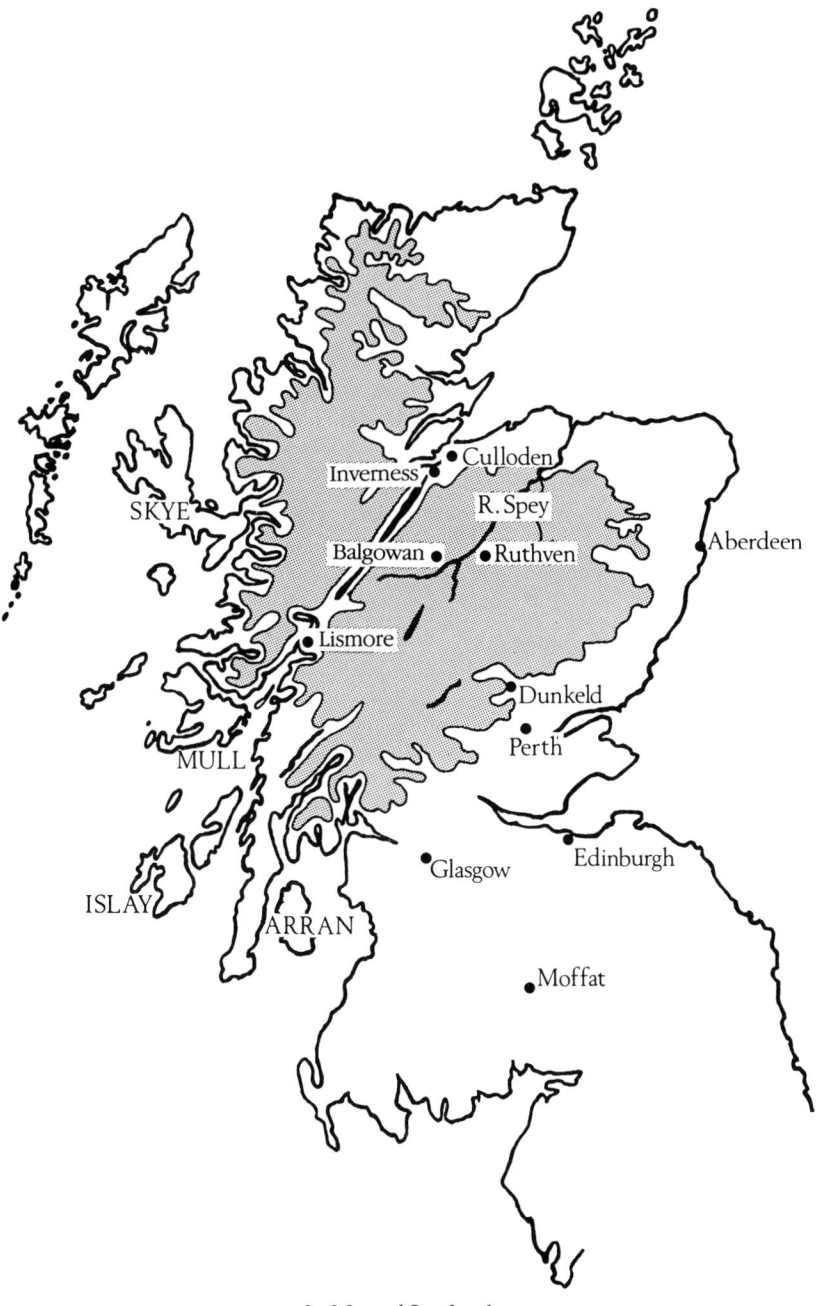

2. Map of Scotland

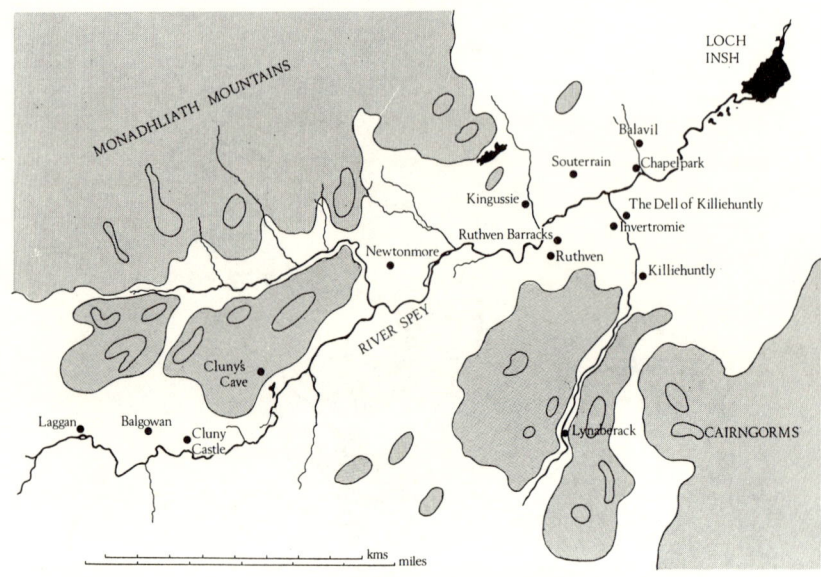

3. Map of Badenoch area

4. Map of the North-West Highlands and Islands showing places visited by Macpherson

5. Weird Scene, Moonlight, 1803 (by Cotman)

FINGAL,

AN

ANCIENT EPIC POEM,

In SIX BOOKS:

Together with several other POEMS, composed by

OSSIAN the Son of FINGAL.

Translated from the GALIC LANGUAGE,

By JAMES MACPHERSON.

Fortia facta patrum.   VIRGIL.

THE SECOND EDITION.

LONDON;
Printed for T. BECKET and P. A. DE HONDT, in the Strand.
M DCC LXII.

6. Title page of Fingal

THE HIGHLANDER

> There Shakespeare's self, with every garland crowned,
> In musing hour his Wayward Sisters found,
> And with their terrors dressed the magic scene . . .
>
> Proceed, nor quit the tales which, simply told,
>   Could once so well my answering bosom pierce;
> Proceed, in forceful sounds and colours bold
>   The native legends of thy lands rehearse;
> To such adapt thy lyre and suit thy powerful verse.
>
> Collins, 'Ode on the Superstitions of the Highlands of Scotland,'
> 1749–50

Although Macpherson felt frustrated by the limitations of Ruthven after his experience of city life, his affection for Badenoch remained unabated. During the years he spent there, immediately after University, his interest in the local area developed rapidly. While working as a teacher in Ruthven he began to collect old Gaelic poetry, while his interest in the Highlands was reflected in his own compositions. 'The Hunter' was never finished for publication, but in 1758 Macpherson published a work which owed much to the earlier piece, his first 'epic': *The Highlander*.

Given the Government attitude towards Northern Scotland in the mid eighteenth century, Macpherson's publication of a long poem celebrating the deeds of a heroic Highlander may seem highly subversive. By 1758, however, the threat of any further Jacobite Rebellion had virtually been removed so the old prejudices were slowly changing. As fears dwindled, the romantic image of the Highlands began to grow and by 1773 Boswell could write

> The very Highland names, or the sound of a bagpipe, will stir my blood, and fill me with a mixture of melancholy and respect for courage; with pity for an unfortunate and superstitious regard for antiquity, and thoughtless inclination for war; in short, with a crowd of sensations with which sober rationality has nothing to do.[1]

The Highlands were now safe for tourists and sentimentality. Although Macpherson's work drew on his own knowledge of the Highlands, it also owed much to this general shift in attitude. Johnson and Boswell set off for the North in the hope of finding 'simplicity and wildness' and 'a system of life almost totally different from what they (we) had been accustomed to see'.[2] A similar idea can be seen in Smollett's *Humphry Clinker*, where the Bramble household greets the Highlands as a 'Scottish Paradise' after weeks in the corrupt spa towns of England, searching for health.[3] Suddenly, the Highlands were no longer regarded as a hostile country full of barbarians, but as a simple, pastoral world, refreshingly different from the cities of eighteenth century Britain.

The appeal of an alternative society can be seen in Collins' praise of the 'sincere and plain' lifestyle of St Kilda in his 'Ode on the Popular Superstitions of the Highlands of Scotland',

> Thus blest in primal innocence they live,
> Sufficed and happy with the frugal fare
> Which tasteful toil and hourly danger give   (167–169)

For Collins, however, the Highlands offered something far more exciting than the traditional virtues of the simple life: they offered freedom to the imagination. His Ode is full of references to 'gliding ghosts', 'fairy people' and 'Runic bards', subjects which had no place in the poetry of post-Lockean England.[4]

It was not only South of the Border that attitudes towards the Highlands were changing. Natives of Northern Scotland were beginning to recognise the value of their own culture, as they became aware that its survival was threatened. In 1751, Alexander MacDonald published a collection of Gaelic verse, underlining the importance of the ancient language:

> We cannot . . . but testify our surprise, that, in an age in which the study of antiquity is so much in fashion, and so successfully applied to so many valuable purposes . . . this language alone, which is the depository of manners, customs and notions of the earliest inhabitants of this island, and consequently seems to promise . . . the most authentic accounts of things useful for us to know, should remain in a state, not only of total abandon, but, which is more astonishing . . . this people and this language should be alone persecuted and intolerated.[5]

In an age when philosophical enquiries into the origin of society were giving ancient languages a new status, it seemed absurd that Britain's oldest language should be repressed. Gaelic had a pedigree as distinguished as Greek or Hebrew, and yet it was being replaced by English. MacDonald saw his native tongue as a precious relic from an ancient civilisation and in his preface, he proposed that a collection of traditional Gaelic poetry should be made, 'to discover the progress of genius through all its different degrees of improvement'.[6]

Although MacDonald was the first to make public his concern about the erosion of Gaelic in the eighteenth century, his desire to preserve the ancient language in the form of poetry was by no means unique. The most important collection of old Gaelic verse, which included a substantial number of Ossianic pieces, had been made two centuries before by James MacGregor, the Dean of Lismore.[7] By the middle of the eighteenth century, a few more people were beginning to recognise the importance of the local oral poetry and started to write it down. The *Report on Ossian* includes a letter from Alexander Pope, the Minister of Rea in Caithness, describing a collection of Gaelic poetry he had made in 1739. Pope's collection was eventually recovered by J. F. Campbell and published with the collections of Donald MacNicol (*c.* 1755), Jerome Stone (*c.* 1755) and Archibald Fletcher (*c.* 1750), in *Leabhar na Féinne*, 1872.[9]

Although some Gaelic poetry was being preserved, the collections were chiefly made for the satisfaction of the individual collector. The literature remained completely inaccessible to non-Gaelic speakers, who were largely unaware of its existence. In January 1756, however, the first translation of a Gaelic ballad was published in the *Scots Magazine*.[10] The translator, Jerome Stone, was not a Highlander by birth, but had learned Gaelic during the five years he had spent as the Minister at Dunkeld in Perthshire. When he died prematurely in 1756, Stone was working on a study of Celtic and had already made a considerable collection of Gaelic poetry.[11] The letter published with the translation shows both his disgust at the general neglect of the Gaelic language and his excitement about the traditional poetry:

> Those who have any tolerable acquaintance with the Irish language must know, that there are a great number of poetical compositions in it, and some of them of very great antiquity, whose merit entitles them to an exemption from the unfortunate neglect, or rather abhorrence, to which ignorance has subjected that emphatic language in which they were composed. Several of these performances are to be met with, which, for sublimity of sentiment, nervousness of expression, and high spirited metaphor, are hardly to be equalled among the chief productions of the most cultivated nations. Others of them breathe such tenderness and simplicity, as must be affecting to every mind that is in the least tinctured with the softer passions of pity and humanity. of this kind is the poem of which I here send you a translation. Your learned readers will easily discover the conformity there is betwixt the tale on which it is built, and the story of Bellerophon, as related by Homer[12]

Stone's evaluation of the Gaelic poetry is strongly reminiscent of

Blackwell's response to the literature of Ancient Greece. The 'energy', 'sublimity' and 'high-spirited metaphor' of the early poetry were seen as vital features which were rarely found in the 'productions of the most cultivated nations'. Stone himself drew attention to the Homeric parallel by commenting on the similarity between the Gaelic story of Fraoch and the Greek Bellerophon.

Despite his enthusiasm, there is a certain defensive quality in Stone's criticism, as he praised not only the energy of the verse, but also its 'tenderness and simplicity'. Even the reference to Homer suggests an attempt to justify his interest in the Gaelic verse, while the letter concluded with an apology for the very metaphors he had been admiring:

> It is hoped the uncommon turn of several expressions, and the seeming extravagance there is in some of the comparisons I have preserved in the translation, will give no offence to such persons as can form a just notion of these compositions, which are the productions of simple and unassisted genius, in which energy is more sought after than neatness, and the strictness of connexion less adverted to than the design of moving the passions and affecting the heart.[13]

Although Jerome Stone valued the popular poetry of the Highlands so greatly, he was obviously aware that a Lowland audience might need some convincing. Despite his praise of the 'simplicity' of the Gaelic poetry, his own translation of 'Bas Fhraoch' ('The Death of Fraoch') was a florid composition using the sentimental diction of eighteenth-century English verse. The Gaelic original was expanded and embellished to fit an eighteenth-century stanza, while even the hero's name was changed from Fraoch to Albin. In the *Report on Ossian*, Stone's version of 'Albin and the Daughter of Mey' was reprinted together with the original Gaelic poem and a literal translation. The differences between them give some indication of the contemporary attitude to translation:

> Thogamar anois an cluin Fhraoich,
> Corp an Laoich an Caiseal Chro.
> On Bhas ud a fhuair am fear,
> Mairg is mairion na dhaigh beo.
>
> Gu mhi sud an tuabhar Mna,
> Is mo chonnairceas air mo dha Roisg,
> Fraoch a chur a bhuain a Chrainn,
> An deis an Caoran a bhi bhos.
>
> Air a chluain thugte an t ainm,
> Loch meidhe raite ris an Loch,

Am biodh a Bheist anns gach uair,
Is a Craos a suas ris an Dos.

(We bore to the grave of Fraoch,
The body of the hero to its circular pale;
After the worthy has died,
To be alive is our regret.

Cruelest of women was she,
That ever were seen by eyes,
Who sent Fraoch to tear the branch,
After the fruit had been born away.

The grove bears his name,
Loch Meyv is the name of the lake,
Where the monster kept watch,
And its open jaw to the tree.)[14]

Stone's rendering of these last three verses was as follows:

But now he's gone! and nought remains but woe
For wretched me; with him my joys are fled,
Around his tomb my tears shall ever flow,
The rock my dwelling, and the clay my bed!
Ye maids, and matrons, from your hills descend,
To join my moan, and answer tear for tear;
With me the hero to his grave attend,
And sing the songs of mourning round his bier,
Through his own grove his praise we will proclaim,
And bid the place forever bear his name.[15]

Whatever the quality of Stone's translation, the fact that it appeared at all was of great importance to the development of public interest in the Highlands. For the first time, Lowland readers were discovering that the Highlanders not only had a great store of poetry, but that this poetry could be seen on a level with Homer. 'Chevy Chase' had already attracted the attention of the great English arbiter of literary taste, Joseph Addison, in his discussions of popular ballads as works of art in the *Spectator*.[16] Suddenly, the ballads of the Highlands also seemed to merit the consideration of an educated man : a man such as James Macpherson.

Although no solid evidence exists to prove that Macpherson read Stone's translation, it seems likely that he would have been an avid reader of the *Scots Magazine* in 1756, since his own 'To a Friend' had been published there the year before. Stone's publication would certainly have attracted his attention, with its strong Highland interest and the Blackwellian praise of the poetry. It was gradually dawning on Macpherson that the poems he had known since his childhood might have some importance for antiquarian and literary reasons.

When Macpherson published his own translations of the Gaelic poetry, he said that he had 'admired the poems, in the original, very early, and gathered part of them from tradition for his own amusement' (*Fingal*, xiv). More detail was given by Ramsay of Ochtertyre, who suggested that Macpherson began his collection when he returned to Badenoch, in order to stave off the boredom of life as a country schoolmaster:

> After finishing the academical course, he found it necessary, for want of something better, to accept of the charity school at Ruthven of Badenoch . . . There, it is believed, he began to collect Gaelic poetry, without any other view at the time but to amuse himself in that solitude. That was no difficult task in the then state of Badenoch, when a number of old men were still alive who had a great mass of poetry stored up in their memory, which they used to recite to their countrymen when assembled beside a cheerful fire in the long winter nights.[17]

One of Macpherson's pupils, John Clark, remembered his teacher 'going round that neighbourhood, to take down in writing such Gaelic Poems, and Songs, as he judged of most merit'.[18] Apparently, Clark accompanied Macpherson on several occasions to attend dramatic presentations of the heroic poems, 'when it was customary for one person to represent Ossian an other Oscar &c and each to repeat their respective parts just as ever players do on a stage'.[19]

Although John Clark's evidence is subject to a degree of doubt, it nevertheless confirms that Macpherson began collecting Ossianic poetry in Badenoch, long before the literati of Edinburgh gave him their patronage. There is even some suggestion that Macpherson was collecting old manuscripts as well as jotting down the poems from the lips of the reciters:

> Mr Macpherson's sister was married to my kinsman Mr Clark of Ruthven at whose house I was often. I saw many of the Manuscripts in the Gaelic language, but recollect nothing more of them than they were written in a most beautiful hand.[21]

Clark's memory may have been a little hazy and the manuscripts he recalled could well have been those collected by Macpherson under the sponsorship of Hugh Blair and his colleagues, in 1760–1761. However the Graham family, who employed Macpherson as a tutor after he left the school in Ruthven, also remembered Macpherson's collection of Gaelic poetry, which must have antedated the publication of the *Fragments of Ancient Poetry*, 1760. When Thomas Graham was asked about Ossian he replied that 'he had never had any doubts on the subject, he having seen in Mr Macpherson's possession several manuscripts in the Gaelic language, and heard his speak of them repeatedly'.[22] It seems that Macpherson's collection was started during his time as a schoolmaster and continued to be enlarged while he was working as a private tutor. There is no evidence to suggest that he was collecting the poems with any intention of publishing translations, so his collection must have grown from a personal interest and a desire to save the poetry from disappearing.[23]

Although Macpherson's Gaelic collection seems to have sprung from impulses rather different from those which inspired his own compositions, by 1758 the two pursuits were beginning to merge. Macpherson's preoccupation with the Highlands was already obvious in 'The Hunter', but in *The Highlander*, there are elements to suggest the influence of traditional Gaelic heroic verse. The letter written by Donald Macpherson which described James's frustrated literary ambitions is of particular interest here:

> I told him he was blessed with several talents, singular good memory, particularly poetry. Did he hit right he had no reason to perish (?) so soon. He said there was little room there for him. I answered that there was a theme and meaning out, for which I was very sorry untouched hitherto, which in the general greatly pleased whoever heard it . . . admired by me: to witt, Ossian's poems . . .
>
> For instance, I heard my father tell that my Grand father, John Macpherson of Benchar, would (at) different times cause my father to sit down by him to write some of them from his mouth, and strongly recommended them to adhere to some passages of them as a good rule for life...which my father might still inlarge upon, did he ask him.
>
> Mr Macpherson heard me without a word from him, in the same humour. I proceeded to enforce the thought by showing Greek, Latin, English and French Poets brought themselves forward to esteem by such means; that if he did not take up some or others at that new period, it would sleep for ever.
>
> In my memory, the generality and people of taste valued themselves upon hearing these poems, with full applaus from the auditors of all degrees. And so (I) went on, he being mostly muit all the time. I followed this, strong as I could, till the Bell rang when we went in to preaching.
>
> Some time thereafter, he was at Edinburgh Collidge, & I in Town. We lodged in one house, but different rooms. He was still late up and rose very early, much upon this topick. Then it was that he published *The Highlander*, of which he sent me a copy, when he travelled through the highlands to collect the remains of these poems.
>
> I saw him amongst the first in the country. From my house he

went to my father's and got what could be given on that head: for in my early years, I mind to have heard several of those poems, not yet published and probably never will. But times are altered since. Perpetual labour leaves little room for unprofitable amusement for the lower classes.[24]

Donald's reference to *The Highlander* comes in the middle of his account of the Ossianic poetry, which shows that the two were closely connected in his mind. The description of Macpherson's long hours of labour on 'this topick' could refer to either and suggests that for Donald Macpherson, *The Highlander* was part of Macpherson's work on the traditional poetry.

A brief glance at *The Highlander* might suggest that the poem published in April 1758 was merely a reworking of 'The Hunter'.[25] In both poems, the central character is a young Highlander who saves Scotland from invasion by his heroic deeds in battle and then discovers he is the lost son of a King. The motif is slightly more elaborate in *The Highlander*, since young Duffus (who has had to abandon his old name, Alpin) is faced with the problem of succeeding to the throne when it has been occupied for years by an amiable usurper, King Indulph. The dilemma is nevertheless resolved peacefully by the marriage of Duffus and Indulph's daughter Culena, so that when the old king dies, the young hero can ascend the throne and the poem ends happily.

In both *The Highlander* and *The Hunter*, Macpherson examines the idea of the prince raised in obscurity, proving his worth through deeds rather than merely inheriting his power. In both, the military interest of Scotland being close to defeat but emerging victoriously is mingled with a romantic tale of love and marriage. While 'The Hunter' appears to have sprung straight from Macpherson's imagination, however, The Highlander owes something to historical and literary sources.

One of the chief differences between the two poems is the nature of the invading force. In 'The Hunter', the threat to Scotland was undisguised, as 'Hateful slavery and th'aspiring Rose' (III, 12) were coupled in angry indignation. In the later poem, the enemy does not come from South of the Border but from Scandinavia. This choice of setting suggests that Macpherson was already drawing on traditional Highland tales to inspire his own poetry, because many of the heroic ballads current in the eighteenth century dealt with the raids of the 'Lochlinners' or Vikings.[26] One of the principle sources for Macpherson's Ossianic epic, *Fingal*, was the Magnus ballad which was popular throughout the Highlands.[27] It described the arrival of Magnus with his Danish fleet and the great battle which followed, where Fingal managed to defend Scotland and defeat the Vikings. Not only is the situation similar in *The Highlander*, but the name of the invading

Danish hero is Magnus. It seems plausible that the ballad which inspired *Fingal* in 1761 may also have provided Macpherson with material in 1758.[28]

In addition to the general situation, there are certain details in *The Highlander* that have parallels in the Gaelic tradition. Macpherson's tale of the unknown nobleman discovering his true birth and atoning for the death of his father has much in common with the legend of Finn MacCumhail or Fingal.[29] Finn's father was traditionally slain by Goll Mac Morna in the battle of Cnuch, so that the orphaned boy had to be brought up in obscurity. Eventually, the son discovers his true identity and reclaims his father's position as head of the militia, reconciling the two warring factions of Clan Baoisgne and Clan Morna.

There are also parallels between the legendary militia, commanded by Finn, and Alpin's Highland army. The heroes of Gaelic legend, the Fiana, were a band of warrior-huntsmen, ready to defend their country against foreign invasion. In *The Highlander*, Macpherson emphasised that the skill required for hunting provided an excellent military training:

> The mountain-chiefs, in burning arms incased,
> And carrying all their country in their breast,
> Undaunted rear their useful arms on high,
> Now fought for food, now for liberty,
> Now met the sport of hills, now of the main,
> Here pierced a stag, and there transfixed a Dane.
> Though nature's walls their homely huts inclose;
> To guard their homely huts, though mountains rose;
> Yet feeling Albion in their breasts, they dare
> From rocks to rush, and meet the distant war.   (II, 31–40)

The idea of the Highlanders being ready for battle whenever Scotland should come under fire has obvious similarities with the role of the Fiana, while even some of the details of the battle may be derived from a traditional source. The description of the standards, for example, is very similar to a passage in *Fingal*:

> Each clan their standards from the beam unbind;
> They float along, and clap upon the wind:
> The heiroglyphic honours of the brave
> Acquire a double horror as they wave.
> (*The Highlander*, II, 12–15)

We reared the sun-beam of battle; the standard of the king. Each hero's soul exulted with joy, as, waving, it flew on the wind. It was studded with gold above, as the blue wide shell of the nightly sky. Each hero had his standard too; and each his gloomy men. (*Fingal*, 57)

This is one of the passages in Ossian for which Derick Thomson has traced a recognisable Gaelic source: the Magnus Ballad in Jerome Stone's collection.[30] The same ballad continues with an account of Finn fighting Magnus in single combat, which may also be in the background of the fight between Alpin and Magnus, which turns the course of the battle in Macpherson's poem.[31]

Although various elements in *The Highlander* suggest the influence of the heroic ballads of the Highlands, Macpherson appears to have bolstered up the popular legends by referring to Scottish history. In Buchanan's catalogue of the early kings of Scotland in *Rerum Scoticarum Historia*, 1582 (translated as *The History of Scotland*), Malcolm, Indulphus and Duffus are named as the 76th, 77th and 78th monarchs, who ruled Scotland in the tenth century.[32] After the murder of Malcolm, Indulphus ascended the throne and enjoyed seven years of peace before being attacked by Viking raiders. Although the Danes were defeated, Indulphus was killed, giving Malcolm's son, Duffus, the opportunity to regain the throne.[33]

Buchanan's history clearly provided much of the plot of *The Highlander*, though as so often with Macpherson, the differences between his work and his source are more revealing than the similarities. In *Rerum Scoticarum Historia*, for example, the Danish leaders are Hago and Helvicus, and although Macpherson uses Haco for one of the Viking heroes, the main leader is Magnus, who does not feature in Buchanan. More interesting is the transformation of King Indulphus' son, Culenus, into the beautiful princess Culena. Buchanan states that Duffus made Culenus the Governor of Cumberland, but in Macpherson's poem the conclusion is a union between the true heir and the usurper's daughter.

This romantic quality is typical of Macpherson, who was later to embellish his translations of the heroic Gaelic ballads with tales of amorous maidens and thwarted love. His vision of the Celtic past was not an accurate, historical delineation of Scotland in the Dark Ages, but a romantic ideal along the lines of Arthurian England. Throughout the poem, the ancient Caledonians adhere to eighteenth-century ideals of morality. For example, when Alpin has defeated Haco in a hand-to hand combat, he refrains from killing him and receives warm gratitude from his enemy: 'Accept, brave man, the friendship of a Dane,/Who hates the Scot, but yet can love the man' (I, 245–46).[34] The curious scene concludes with an exaggerated demonstration of affection: 'His brawny arms he round the hero flung;/As they embrace the clashing corslets rung' (I, 253–54). It is hard to imagine such an embrace between Achilles and Hector: Macpherson constantly imbued his 'primitive' heroes with the virtues of the civilised.

In order to show the moral superiority of the Celts to the heroes of classical literature, Macpherson frequently evoked passages from

The Highlander 71

Virgil or Homer. The best example is the romantic encounter between Alpin/Duffus and Culena, which is modelled closely on that of Dido and Aeneas, who were forced to seek refuge in a cave from the rain that interrupted their hunting party.[35] The scene is lightly handled, as Macpherson builds up the tension, relying on the reader's classical education to fuel the anticipation:

> Amazed, astonished, fixed in dumb surprise,
> The lovers stood, but spoke with silent eyes:
> At length the distant colloquy they rear,
> Run o'er the chace, the mountain, and the deer.
> Far from the soul th'evasive tongue departs,
> Their eyes are only faithful to their hearts.
> The winding volumes of discourse return
> To hostile fields by gallant Duffus shorn.
> Th'imperial maid must hear it o'er again,
> How fell Dovalus was by Duffus slain,
> How by the son the father's murderer fell.
> The kindling virgin flames along the tale.   (VI, 87–98)

At this point the passion is deflated by the unexpected entrance of Culena's father and a hermit. Unlike the classical prototype, Dido, Culena emerges from the cave as a 'virgin whole' (VI, 125) and the encounter with Duffus is a 'harmless secret in her soul' (VI, 126). She may be part of a primitive age, but her behaviour would not shame a heroine of mid-eighteenth-century sentimental literature.

Macpherson's attempt to reconcile the virtues of the civilised with his obvious relish for swashbuckling adventures was often unsuccessful. The incongruities are particularly obvious in the hunting scene, where the energetic account of the agile hunters and eager hounds seems strange after the sympathetic use of the deer imagery, describing a Highland maid earlier in the poem:

> Thus, on the heathy wild the hunted deer
> Start at each blast, together crowd through fear,
> Tremble and look about, before, behind,
> Then stretch along, and leave the mountain-wind. (IV, 77–80)

Culena herself is guilty of a similar confusion as she joins eagerly in the hunt, only to sink into depression once she has shot her prey. Despite the inconsistencies, Macpherson's purpose is plain: he was creating a new heroic ideal for his Scottish epic. The characters of *The Highlander* were meant to possess all the vigour of the classical heroes, but not give offence to the refined sensibilities of an eighteenth-century audience.

Although he was drawing on Highland legend, the deeds of the

Scottish warriors could be seen only through a thick neoclassical veneer. Macpherson intended his poem to be regarded as an epic, and his purpose is plain from the opening lines:

> The youth I sing, who, to himself unknown,
> Lost to the world and CALEDONIA'S throne,
> Sprung o'er his mountains to the arms of Fame,
> And, winged by Fate, his sire's avenger, came;
> That knowledge learn'd so long deny'd by Fate,
> And found that blood, as merit, made him great.   (I, 1–6)

Unlike the pastoral tone of 'The Hunter', the introduction to *The Highlander* alludes directly to the *Iliad*, the *Aeneid* and *Paradise Lost*.

The debts continued throughout the poem, with the latinate diction reflecting Macpherson's reading (the curious use of 'forky' (V, 264) to describe lightning for example, is a standard epithet in Dryden's *Aeneid*). The battle scenes, in particular, owed much to Pope's translation of Homer:

> Onward they rush, and in a shout engage.
> The swords through air their gleaming journeys fly,
> Crash on the helm, and tremble in the sky,
> Groan follows groan, and wound succeeds on wound,
> While dying bodies quiver on the ground.
> Thus, when devouring hatchet-men invade,
> With sounding steel, the forest's leavy head,
> The mountains ring with their repeated strokes
> 　　　　　　　　　(*The Highlander* II, 104–111)

Macpherson's description of the battle between the Scots and the Danes is very similar to Pope's account of the Trojan War:

> Now Shield with Shield, with Helmet Helmet clos'd,
> To Armour Armour, Lance to Lance oppos'd,
> Host against Host with shadowy Squadrons drew,
> The sounding Darts in Iron Tempest slew,
> Victors and Vanquish'd join promiscuous Cries,
> And shrilling Shouts and dying Groans arise;
> With streaming Blood the slipp'ry Fields are dy'd,
> And slaughter'd Heroes swell the dreadful Tide.
> As Torrents roll, increas'd by numerous Rills,
> With Rage impetuous, down their ecchoing Hills,
> Rush to the Vales and pour'd along the Plain,
> Now thro' a thousand Chanels to the Main.
> 　　　　　　　　　(*The Iliad*, IV, 508–19)

Although the borrowings are heavy, Macpherson always adapted them to suit his own purpose and the ubiquitous epic similes invariably drew on features peculiar to the Highland landscape.

When Macpherson alluded to specific classical scenes or images he usually altered them slightly, to make some point, as in the encounter between Duffus and Culena in the cave. In the traditional epic scene of the War Council, Macpherson adapted the epic image of the Balance:

> Around great Indulph, in the senate, sat
> The noble chiefs of Caledonia's state.
> In mental scales they either forces weigh,
> And act, before, the labours of the day. (I, 26–30)

When the image of the scales are used by Homer, Virgil or Milton, they are always a divine instrument, exerting power over the lesser beings.[36] In Macpherson's poem, however, they are 'mental scales', suggesting that the course of events is man's responsibility rather than the result of Fate or God's will. This idea is typical of the poem, where there is no divine machinery, but the heroes themselves are described as 'godlike' and inspiration comes from the example of their forefathers:

> The youthful warrior thus reviews, with joy,
> The godlike series of his ancestry.
> The godlike forms the drooping hero cheer,
> And keen ambition half believes the seer. (I, 57–60)[37]

Macpherson may have been keen to demonstrate that his Celts were morally superior to the Homeric heroes, but he was by no means following Milton in creating a new Christian ideal. In *The Highlander*, Macpherson was glorifying man and the allusions to great epic poems were part of this purpose.

There was also a strongly nationalistic intention in his poem. The epic model placed Scottish history on a level with that of classical Greece or Rome and the poem was evidently designed to stir up feelings of national pride. While Donald, the hero of 'The Hunter' had been motivated by personal ambition and saved his country almost by accident, Alpin is driven from the beginning by a noble patriotism:

> Midst rocks afar,
> I heard of Denmark, and of Sueno's war.
> My country's safety in my bosom rose:
> For Caledonia's son should meet her foes. (I, 79–82)

The patriotism is not confined to Scotland but extends to the whole of Britain:

> See Scot and Saxon, coalesced in one,

Support the glory of the common crown.
Britain no more shall shake with native storms,
But o'er the trembling nations lift her arms.

(V, 177–180)

Such a sentiment seems surprising after the Anglophobia of 'The Hunter', but Macpherson's sudden change of heart becomes easier to understand once contemporary events are taken into account.

In 1758, Scotland was under threat of invasion from the sea. The Seven Years War had broken out in 1756, severing the traditional links with France and making Scotland dependent on England for survival. Macpherson's native dislike of the Sassenachs, therefore, had to be swallowed, as the two countries united in the face of a common enemy.

Although the perennial rivalries between North and South Britain were being repressed, the Government remained suspicious of the Scots. Memories of the Jacobite Rebellions, together with a lack of confidence in the Scottish economy, made the Government reluctant to extend the English militia system to Scotland.[38] North Britain, with its long coastlines and lack of communications was thus in a very vulnerable position: a situation particularly galling to those who had remained loyal to the Government throughout the '45. The fears of a French invasion turned out to be well founded in October 1759, when Admiral Thurot landed in Islay before proceeding to Carrickfergus and eventual destruction in a naval battle in the Irish Sea.

Even before Thurot's bold voyage, the atmosphere in Scotland was tense. Throughout the War, the *Scots Magazine* published monthly reports of bloody battles in Europe and North America, as well as lists of the ships that had been captured. In the same year that *The Highlander* was published, James Beattie's 'Ode to Peace' appeared, expressing the mood of the time:[39] The poem lamented the departure of Peace from Albion, its 'once beloved retreat' (121) and voiced the contemporary longing for the return of a Golden Age:

Oh, whither art thou fled, Saturnian age?
Roll round again, majestic years!
To break the sceptre of tyrannic rage,
From Woe's wan cheek to wipe the bitter tears,
Ye years, again roll round! (13–17)

The contemporary poem, *The Highlander*, can be seen as Macpherson's own attempt to roll back a 'Saturnian age'. Although in some ways the poem was a traditional Highland *Brosnachadh Catha*, (battle incitement) designed to stir up Scottish spirits at a time of national danger, it was also an expression of the desire to escape contemporary events. Conscious of Scotland's vulnerability, Macpherson

The Highlander 75

turned to traditional legends to find the ideal warriors who would embody her essential greatness. His Celtic heroes moved in a remote world, untroubled by realistic details, where invading navies could be repelled easily and battles were merely part of the picturesque romance. Macpherson's Golden Age was a romantic vision of the Highlands, filled with invincible warriors of impeccable character. The step from here to *The Poems of Ossian* was not very large.

NOTES
1. *Boswell's Life of Johnson*, V, 140.
2. Ibid, 1–2. See also, E. Hanson, 'Johnson's Quest for the Fictions of Romantic Chivalry in Scotland', *Prose Studies*, vii (2), 1984, 97–128.
3. T. Smollett, *The Expedition of Humphry Clinker*, 1771, ed. L. M. Knapp, (London 1966), 240.
4. Cf. Thomson, 'The Castle of Indolence', I, xxx; W. Forbes, *James Beattie*, I, 220–21.
5. A. MacDonald, *Ais-Eiridh* . . ., vii–viii.
6. Ibid, v. See also F. Wise on Celtic as the 'Universal language of the post-diluvian world', *Some Enquiries concerning the First Inhabitants, Language, Religion, Learning and Letters of Europe*, (Oxford 1758), 30–31.
7. See N. Ross (ed), *Heroic Poetry from the Book of the Dean of Lismore*, (Edinburgh 1939); W. J. Watson (ed), *Scottish Verse from the Book of the Dean of Lismore*, (Edinburgh 1937); T. McLauchlan (ed), *The Dean of Lismore's Book*, (Edinburgh 1862); D. S. Thomson, *Gaelic Sources*.
8. *Report*, App. 52.
9. J. F. Campbell, *Leabhar na Féinne*. See also D. S. Thomson, 'A Catalogue and Indexes of the Ossianic Ballads in the Maclagan Manuscripts', *SGS*, viii, 1958, 177–224.
10. *Scots Magazine*, xviii, 1756, 15–17.
11. D. Mackinnon, 'A Collection of Ossianic Ballads by Jerome Stone', *TGSI*, xiv, 1887–1888, 314–69; Saunders, *James Macpherson*, 53–6.
12. *Scots Magazine*, xviii, 1756, 15–16.
13. Ibid.
14. *Report*, App. 104–05; 116–17.
15. Ibid, 111.
16. 'Spectator, No 70', *The Spectator*, ed. D. F. Bond, 5 vols, (Oxford 1965), I, 297.
17. J. Ramsay, *Scotland and Scotsmen* . . ., I, 545–46.
18. Clark to the Highland Society, 1803, ADV MS 73.2.15 f11 (b).
19. Ibid, 27 July 1806, ADV MS 73.2.76 f43.
20. Clark was a zealous supporter of Macpherson's *Ossian* and presented the spurious poem 'Mordubh' as a translation from ancient Gaelic in *The Works of the Caledonian Bards*, (London 1778). See D. S. Thomson, 'Bogus Gaelic Literature, c. 1750–1820', *TGSG*, v, 1958, 172–88.
21. See note 19.

22. Quoted by J. F. Campbell, *Popular Tales of the West Highlands*, I, xxx. See also A. M. Delavoye, *The Life of Lord Lynedoch*, (London 1880), 3: 'These Poems, so much the object of inquiry, were many of them collected and translated at the time Mr Macpherson resided as private tutor in the house . . . at Balgowan'.
23. See *Fingal*, xiv–xv.
24. D. Macpherson to Rev J. Anderson, October 1797, ADV MS 73.2.13 f23. See Chapter Three, above.
25. As suggested by the *Edinburgh Encyclopaedia*, 1830, 222. *The Highlander* was published in Edinburgh in 1758. References, incorporated in the text, are to the text included in Laing's edition of *Ossian*.
26. See R. T. Christiansen, *The Vikings and the Viking Wars in Irish and Gaelic Tradition*, (Oslo 1931).
27. Thomson, *The Gaelic Sources*, 23–6; J. F. Campbell, *Leabhar na Féinne*, vi. The poem survives in the collections of Pope, Turner, Stone, MacNicol, Fletcher, Maclagan and Kennedy. See also J. F. Campbell, *Popular Tales*, III, 363–95.
28. On the similarities between *Fingal* and *The Highlander*, see A. MacBain, 'Macpherson's Ossian', *Celtic Magazine*, xii, 1887, 145–54, 193–201, 240–54; Anon (J. F. Campbell?), 'Ossian Redivivus', *The Times*, 14 October 1869.
29. For details of the legends, see G. Murphy, *The Ossianic Lore and Romantic Tales of Mediaeval Ireland*, (Dublin 1955); E. Knott & G. Murphy, *Early Irish Literature*, (London 1966); A. Nutt, *Ossian and the Ossianic Literature*, (London 1899); M. Dillon, *Early Irish Literature*, (Chicago 1948).
30. Thomson, *The Gaelic Sources*, 23. See also *Report*, App. 30 on Fingal's standard.
31. Ibid, 23–6, on Fingal, 62–3; cf. Macleod to Blair, March, 1764, 'The poem in book the 4th is handed down pretty entire in this country, in which each of Fingal's chiefs singles out the chief among the enemy he was to fight, leaving to Fingal the honour of engaging the king of Lochlin', *Report*, App. 30.
32. G. Buchanan, *The History of Scotland*, 4th edn, 2 vols, (Edinburgh 1751), 8.
33. Ibid, 221.
34. Cf. 'An Essay on Charity', *Scots Magazine*, xxii, 1760, 577, on prisoners of war, arguing that 'no man be longer deemed an enemy than while his sword is drawn against us'.
35. *The Highlander*, VI, 1–118; cf. *Aeneid*, IV, 120–80; Dryden's *Aeneid*, IV, 231–50.
36. *Iliad*, VIII, 68–77; XXII, 208–13; *Aeneid*, XII, 725–27; *Paradise Lost*, IV, 996–1004.
37. Cf. Dryden's *Aeneid*, VII, 241–42.
38. See J. Robertson, *The Scottish Enlightenment and the Militia Issue*, (Edinburgh 1985); J. R. Western, *The English Militia in the Eighteenth Century*, (London & Toronto 1965); R. Sher, *Church and University in the Scottish Enlightenment*, (Edinburgh 1985).
39. The poem was published in the *Scots Magazine*, xx, 1758, 482.

The Death of Oscur

> I Believe both Macpherson & Chatterton, that what
> they say is Ancient Is so.
>
> Blake, 'Annotations to Wordsworth', 1826

In the autumn of 1759, the Scottish playwright, John Home, was making his annual visit to the fashionable Spa town of Moffat in Dumfriesshire. This year his trip was to prove particularly memorable, not only for Home, but also for James Macpherson. For some years, Home had been developing an interest in the culture of the Scottish Highlands. Though not a Highlander by birth, Home's interest in Highland beliefs went back at least as far as 1749, when his conversations with William Collins had resulted in the composition of Collins' 'An Ode on the Popular Superstitions of the Highlands of Scotland, Considered as the Subject of Poetry'.[1] Further stimulation came from his friend Adam Ferguson, the philosopher, who had given Home enthusiastic descriptions of the ancient poetry of the Highlands.[2] Ferguson's accounts may well have been prompted by the publication of Jerome Stone's translation in the *Scots Magazine*, which would also have fuelled John Home's growing interest.

James Macpherson, who had finally escaped Ruthven School and was now working as a private tutor to Graham of Balgowan, was staying with his pupil at Lord Hopetoun's house in Moffat. There is evidence to suggest that Macpherson had already met Adam Ferguson, when he visited Ferguson's father in Perthshire with his young charge.[3] The meeting with John Home, which took place on the Bowling Green at Moffat, was therefore well prepared.

Home was thrilled to have come across someone who could give him an idea of what the Gaelic verse was really like. Macpherson, however, appears to have been rather puzzled by Home's request to see some of the poetry in his collection, since the Lowland gentleman could speak no Gaelic. John Home's own account of the conversation is well worth reading:

> When Mr Home desired to see them, Mr Macpherson asked if he understood the Gaelic? 'Not one word,'
> 'Then, how can I show you them ?'

'Very easily,' said Mr Home; 'translate one of the pieces which you think a good one, and I imagine that I shall be able to form some opinion of the genius and character of the Gaelic poetry.'

Mr Macpherson declined the task, saying, that his translation would give a very imperfect idea of the original. Mr Home, with some difficulty, persuaded him to try, and in a day or two he brought him the poem on the death of Oscar; with which Mr Home was so pleased, that in a few days, two or three more were brought him.[4]

The poetry Macpherson produced was even better than Home had hoped. As soon as he had read the pieces, he rushed to show them to George Laurie and Alexander Carlyle, who happened to be spending the day in Moffat. Carlyle was as excited as Home: 'I was perfectly astonished by the poetical genius displayed in them. We agreed that it was a precious discovery, and that as soon as possible, it should be published to the world.'[5]

Within days John Home was in Edinburgh, showing off Macpherson's translations to his influential friends, who were equally impressed. The man who took the greatest interest was Hugh Blair, who was soon to become the Professor of Rhetoric and Belles Lettres at the University: 'I being as much struck as Mr Home with the high spirit of poetry which breathed in them, promptly made enquiry where Mr Macpherson was to be found.'[6] Blair was so impressed by the translations that he sent for Macpherson at once, eager to see further examples of the Highland poetry and to publish them, if possible.

But Macpherson was less than delighted with the invitation. Just as he had been reluctant to translate any poetry for Home, he now refused to produce more for Hugh Blair. As at Moffat, Macpherson seemed convinced that 'no translation of his would do justice to that spirit and fire of the original' and he was also worried that the crude Highland verse would not please the public.[7] Blair, however, was even more determined than Home had been and refused to be fobbed off with the excuses of a twenty-two-year-old. Eventually, 'after much and repeated importunities' (the most effective seems to have been the appeal to Macpherson's Highland loyalties), Blair managed to persuade him to translate more of the poems, with a view to publication. Even after he had promised to co-operate, Macpherson continued to write letters to Blair, asking to be released from the agreement. But by then, the eyes of the Edinburgh literati were on the project and copies of Macpherson's work had already been despatched to Gray, Walpole, Shenstone and other Englishmen of letters.[8] The matter was now beyond Macpherson's control, and the young Highlander was heading for fame, willy-nilly.

The story of Macpherson's sudden rise from obscurity is interesting for a number of reasons, not the least for his own reactions to the various events. The popular image of Macpherson as a skilful swindler, setting out to make a fortune from a literary hoax, is hard to reconcile with the descriptions of what actually happened. In each account Macpherson's reluctance to produce translations is stressed, while it is obvious that the publication of the Ossianic poetry was due entirely to the pressure exerted by Blair and his colleagues. Although Macpherson had made some collection of Gaelic verse, he had had no intention of publishing the poetry in English until he gained the attention of the literati. Accusations of fraud and forgery should therefore be withheld until some explanation has been found for Macpherson's initial reluctance to produce an English text.

This unwillingness could be attributed to a fear of detection. It is easy to assume that Macpherson, aware of Home's ignorance of the Gaelic, simply concocted a poem but then became alarmed at the prospect of his work being read by men familiar with the genuine Fenian legends. This theory, however, falls down for a number of reasons. In the first place, Macpherson knew that Home had discussed the poetry with Adam Ferguson, who could speak some Gaelic and was familiar with the genuine verse. The poem he produced for Home was likely to find its way to Ferguson, so a fraudulent piece would quickly be found out and Macpherson's reputation would be destroyed before it had begun. Secondly, there is no reason why Macpherson should have wanted to concoct a poem, since he already knew several pieces of ancient poetry by heart. If he was going to co-operate at all, why not just translate part of his Gaelic collection? Alexander Carlyle's description of the young Highlander at Moffat is revealing: 'He was Good looking, of a Large Size, with very thick Legs, to Hide which he Generally wore Boots, tho' not then the Fashion. He appeared to me Proud and Reserv'd and Shun'd Dining with us on Some Pretence.'[9] James Macpherson, a red-headed Highlander of six foot three, must have felt somewhat conspicuous in the smart Lowland Spa. Carlyle's jibe about his 'thick Legs' suggests that Macpherson's appearance of being 'Proud and Reserv'd' masked an acute self-consciousness. The refusal of an invitation to dinner probably rose not from any anti-social streak, but from nervousness over the unexpected attention of one of the best known writers in Scotland.

Home and Carlyle were not only famous, they were also Lowlanders. Macpherson was, after all, trying to establish a reputation as a poet in the neo-classical tradition of Pope and Dryden. He wanted to impress Home as a 'good classical scholar'[10], so any connection with the quaint society portrayed in Collins 'Ode' was potentially embarrassing. According to George Laurie, Macpherson's real reason for refusing to produce English versions of Gaelic poetry was 'that his

Highland pride was alarmed at appearing to the world only as a translator'.[11] Macpherson himself was later to observe that

> Those who alone are capable of transferring ancient poetry into a modern language, might be better employed in giving originals of their own, were it not for that wretched envy and meanness which affects to despise contemporary genius.[12]

Macpherson's epic, *The Highlander*, had been published in April 1758, but it had failed dismally to attract critical attention. How could the original work of a young poet be less interesting to men such as Home and Blair than the popular songs of uneducated Highlanders? At a time when originality was the new criterion for judging art, Macpherson was being forced into the position of a mere translator.

Apart from his personal pride, Macpherson had his native loyalties to consider. Macpherson's collection had stemmed from his concern about the erosion of Highland culture in the face of the advancing Lowland civilisation, so the idea of translating Gaelic verse into the language that threatened its destruction was something of a breach of trust. Highland poetry was handed down orally, forming a living link from generation to generation, so any written translation might turn it into inanimate, public property. Should the heroic traditions of the Highlanders be made accessible to outsiders? If Macpherson had any plans to publish his collection, it was to be in Gaelic, 'for the use of natives who held these poems in very high estimation'.[13] There was no guarantee that the Lowlanders would respond to the ancient poems with the appropriate respect: Blair noted that Macpherson thought 'they would be very ill relished by the public as so very different from the strain of modern ideas, and of modern connected, and polished poetry.'[14] The Gaelic tradition was totally different from the English, so Macpherson was doubtful whether the simple ballads would impress readers used to the elaborate literature of English and classical authors. It was no good translating the poems of the Highlanders if they were to be scorned by English speakers.

The great differences between the Gaelic and English traditions gave rise to objections of a practical nature. Even if Macpherson had been anxious to co-operate, Home's request for a translation could not be satisfied easily. The 'text' from which he had to translate consisted of poems he knew from memory or those he had jotted down from Highland speakers in Badenoch (any manuscripts he may have had at this stage would probably have been left at home). Any English version he might produce would inevitably fall short of the original, but unless he could show Home something of a high standard, it would be better to leave the poetry in the safe custody of the Gaelic. John Clark's account of Macpherson's conversation with Home is illuminating on this point:

Mr Macpherson repeated that he could not gratify Mr Home's curiosity in that respect because the Genius of the Gaelic language was so different from the English that a Translation of the former into the latter, would prove merely a simple inanimated tale, when stript of that energetic gracefulness, and harmonious phrasiology which so strongly mark the originals.[15]

The unfortunate transformation from 'energetic gracefulness' to a 'simple inanimated tale' was not merely the problem faced by any translator of poetry from one language to another. The difficulties confronting Macpherson were increased by the very nature of Gaelic poetry. The verse of the Highlands was essentially oral, and was never intended to be read from the page, especially in a foreign language. Twentieth-century studies of Gaelic story-telling have found that the tales drew 'the breath of life from the lips of men and from the applause of the appreciative fireside audience', an idea confirmed by J. F. Campbell's descriptions of traditional ceilidhs.[16] Even old manuscripts of Gaelic verse were only shadows of the real poetry, as the Irish scholar, Gerald Murphy concluded:

> When . . . we form a picture of the orally narrated Irish tale as something immeasurably superior to the suggestion of it a monastic scribe has recorded, we are not creating a figment of the imagination, we are merely restoring to the corpse buried in the manuscript the soul that once animated it.[17]

Writing down Gaelic poetry at all was like producing song lyrics without the music: the beauty of the performance was lost and all that was left was the 'simple inanimated tale'. If this was then transferred to another language, the resulting version could bear little resemblance to the original recital.

The issue was further complicated by prevailing attitudes towards the spoken word. Johnson, for example, saw his duty as a lexicographer as lying in the correction of spoken English, which seemed a chaos of 'improprieties and absurdities':

> As language was at its beginning merely oral, all words of necessary or common use were spoken before they were written: and while they were unfixed by any visible signs, must have been spoken with great diversity, as we now observe those who cannot read to catch sound imperfectly, and utter them negligently. When this wild and barbarous jargon was first reduced to an alphabet, every penman endeavoured to express, as he could, the sounds which he was accustomed to pronounce or to receive, and vitiated in writing such words as were already vitiated in speech.[18]

Johnson's desire to clarify language and establish rules for meaning and pronunciation had much in common with the Aberdonian emphasis on ascertaining a firm foundation for knowledge. The new empirical attitude demanded facts and documentation, while traditional truths suddenly seemed to be old wives' tales. Locke's *Essay concerning Human Understanding* had dealt with traditional truths as Chinese Whispers, becoming more unreliable as they passed from speaker to speaker:

> *in traditional Truths, each remove weakens the force of the proof*: And the more hands the Tradition has successfully passed through, the less strength and evidence does it receive from them. This I thought necessary to be taken notice of: Because I find amongst some men quite the contrary is commonly practised, who look on Opinions to gain force by growing older.[19]

As a Highlander, educated at a University in the eighteenth century, Macpherson was confronted with apparently irreconcilable attitudes towards oral verse. The Highland veneration of ancient tradition and respect for oral recitation was the complete antithesis of Locke's sceptical approach. Indeed, many of the doubts that were to be raised about the authenticity of Ossian rested upon the improbability of poems surviving over several centuries without being committed to the safety of paper.

Macpherson was influenced by both his Highland roots and his education. The Ossianic poems and the essays published with them are full of admiration for the Highland bards and the oral tradition, but there are also passages which suggest the voice of the empiricist. The essay on *Temora* opens with remarks on the unreliable nature of traditional history: 'Probability is all that can be established on the basis of tradition, ever dubious and uncertain' (*Temora*, xi), while even the Gaelic ballads are treated with scepticism:

> They are entirely writ in that romantic taste, which prevailed two ages ago. – Giants, enchanted castles, dwarfs, palfreys, witches and magicians form the whole circle of the poet's invention. The celebrated Fion could scarcely move from one hillock to another, without encountering a giant, or being entangled in the circles of a magician. (*Temora*, xxiii)

Macpherson's dismissal of the ballads has often been interpreted as a skilful concealment of his sources, but it seems that he did, in fact, regard the poems current in the Highlands as the corrupt remnants of an ancient tradition. The poetry Macpherson heard being recited in

The Death of Oscur 83

Badenoch, though admirable in its way, did not entirely accord with his preconceptions about the nature of ancient poetry. Although the leading characters were the traditional, third-century heroes, their adventures were very different from those of the truly ancient, Homeric epic. The exploits of Fingal and his warriors appeared to have been altered on their way down through the generations, with different reciters making fresh contributions to the poems at each new performance. Andrew Gallie, who worked with Macpherson on the Gaelic poems for *Fingal*, expressed the following belief:

> It was, and I believe still is well known, that the broken poems of Ossian, handed down from one generation to another, got corrupted. In the state of the Highlands, and its language, this evil, I apprehend, could not be avoided; and I think great credit is due, in such a case, to him who restores a work of merit to its original purity.[20]

Anne Grant's assessment of Macpherson's translation suggests a similar view:

> Something no doubt has been added, and much subtracted; and this latter it was necessary to do, in justice to the old Bard, to whom his successors had appended many extravagant and grotesque ornaments.[21]

Macpherson seems to have shared a belief common in the Highlands: that Ossian's poems had been distorted by the succession of bards who had recited or recreated his poetry. In the eyes of both Andrew Gallie and Anne Grant, the task of the translator was to restore the corrupt relics of ancient poetry to a state of 'original purity'.

This idea of a pure original from which there has been a decline is crucial to the understanding of Macpherson's practice. His contempt for the existing poetry of the Highlands was the corollary of his idealised vision of Celtic Scotland, which was to emerge clearly in his 'historical' essays on *Ossian*. Macpherson's Celtic world was one of noble warriors, not a quaint fairyland of giants and magicians, so the witches and monsters which feature in the popular Highland ballads had to be condemned as interpolations and stripped away. (Ironically, the stories of the Viking invasions, which were obviously a later addition to the third-century Fenian cycle, were perfectly acceptable, since they suited Macpherson's vision of Fingal as a national hero, defending the honour of Scotland). While certain elements had to be removed, the task of elevating the Gaelic poems also involved numerous embellishments: Ossian's successors might have added too much, but they had also lost much of the original beauty. Although Macpherson was to draw on the genuine ballads, then, his Ossianic poems were by no means accurate translations of the poetry which was still being recited in the Highlands. He was making an attempt to restore these 'broken' poems to their 'original purity', but this ideal of restoration was to prove highly creative.

Standards of translation have changed considerably from the eighteenth century, when attempts to be true to the 'spirit' of the author resulted in works that seem only loosely connected with the original. Dryden had asserted that 'the way to please the best judges is not to translate a poet literally' but according to the taste of the translator.[22] Omissions and additions were therefore permissible, providing the translator's contributions to the original author did not appear to be 'stuck into him, but growing out of him'.[23] The method depended on an intuitive sympathy between the translator and the translated, as the Earl of Roscommon had suggested:

> Examine how your Humour is inclin'd,
> And which the Ruling Passion of your Mind;
> Then seek a Poet who your way do's bend,
> And chuse an Author as you chuse a Friend:
> United by this sympathetick Bond;
> You grow Familiar, Intimate and Fond;
> Your thoughts, your Words, your Stiles, your Souls agree,
> No longer his Interpreter, but He.[24]

The identification between the translator and the original author reached an extraordinary degree in Macpherson's 'ancient poetry'. By dismissing his principal sources as corrupt, Macpherson felt free to 'restore' the Gaelic poems to what he thought they ought to have been. The traditional figure of Ossian, familiar throughout the Highlands as the last survivor of the Fiana, was thus to be presented to the English-speaking world with the ideas and preoccupations of James Macpherson. Macpherson had failed to find an original voice in the poetic language of his own age, producing only derivative poems which interested no one. Now, by speaking through the mouthpiece of the old Highland bard, he was to produce poetry that seemed more original than his own compositions.

The plot of 'The Death of Oscur', the first poem Macpherson produced for John Home, bears little resemblance to any surviving Gaelic ballad.[25] The central characters, Oscur and Dermid, were well known throughout the Highlands, but the traditional stories of their deaths were nothing like the tale produced by Macpherson. In Gaelic legend Oscur was killed by Cairbre at the battle of Gabhra, while Dermid was slain by a poisonous bristle after the boar hunt on Ben Gulben. The fragment Macpherson showed Home is a romantic story, in which the two heroes are drawn into an emotional triangle and killed as a result of their passion. Since Macpherson was supposedly translating from a poem he knew by heart, it is possible that he had heard such a story in the Highlands. The dialogue framework suggests the influence of traditional Gaelic verse, as do various elements of the style. The story itself, however, has more in common with the tragic vignettes in Macpherson's own poem, 'Death', than with any of the genuine ballads that have survived in the eighteenth-century Gaelic collections. It seems that from the beginning, Macpherson adopted the imaginative approach that he was later to advocate for historical writing: 'He looks upon antiquity through the medium of the ancients and thinks he sees it in its genuine state.'[26] Macpherson was looking through the eyes of an early bard and felt free to create his own stories, even though he used traditional names and developed a suitably 'ancient' style. If the existing poems were too corrupt to show off the genius of the Highlands to the outside world, Macpherson would use only the parts he considered fit and 'restore' the rest, according to his own ideas on ancient literature. Of his first collection of fifteen 'Fragments of Ancient Poetry' only two of the poems are based closely on recognisable Gaelic ballads: Fragment VI 'The Maid of Craca', and Fragment XIII (XIV in the 2nd edition), which was based on the Garbh MacStairn ballads. The rest appear to have been a blend of Highland tradition and Macpherson's imagination.

Although Macpherson seems to have indulged his romantic imagination in the plots of his poems, the style suggests that he made considerable efforts to develop the voice of the ancient Celtic bard. Macpherson had no model for the translation of Gaelic poetry except the poem published by Jerome Stone under the title 'Albin and the Daughter of Mey'. As we saw in Chapter Four, Stone had obviously been equally concerned that the poem would not suit contemporary taste, as he had altered the names of the characters, embellished the Gaelic poem with various additions, and presented his 'translation' in elaborate eighteenth-century diction. But the presentation of the poem is unlikely to have pleased Macpherson. When he translated *The Iliad* in 1773, he used a style similar to that which he developed for his Gaelic translations:

> The fetters, which the prevailing taste of modern Europe, has imposed on poetry, may well be admitted, as an excuse, for a man of the best genius, for not succeeding in the characteristical simplicity of Homer. The same taste may likewise be permitted to seduce him into those modernised terms of language, which, however pleasing they may be in themselves, are utterly inconsistent with the solemn gravity of an ancient epic poem. The best translators have not, in short, occupied the whole ground. The simplicity, the gravity, the characteristical diction, and, perhaps, a great part of the dignity of Homer, are left untouched. They have rendered the father of poetry, in a great measure, their own: And, in stripping him of his ancient weeds, they have made him too much of a modern beau.
> (*The Iliad*, Preface, xv–xvi)

Although Macpherson followed Dryden in the attempt to adopt the 'spirit' of an original author, he was strongly opposed to Dryden's idea of making Virgil 'speak such English as he would himself have spoken, if he had been born in England, and in this present age'.[27] For Macpherson, ancient poetry was painfully separate from contemporary literature, and should be brought into the modern world with a suitably dignified style. Stone's florid rendering of the Gaelic ballad tamed the original by putting it in the language of contemporary periodical poets. Macpherson, though anxious not to offend eighteenth-century readers, was nevertheless determined to 'do justice to that spirit and fire of the original'.

Macpherson's remarks on modern translations of Homer show that he had strong views both on ancient literature and on contemporary poetic diction: the two things were simply not compatible. Here was another important reason for his reluctance to translate his own collection of Gaelic verse. The language of contemporary English poetry was quite alien to the Gaelic tradition, but a literal translation of a corrupt Gaelic ballad could not do justice to the great Ossian. What style should Macpherson adopt for presenting the ancient poems, restored to their 'original purity'?

After three years at Aberdeen, Macpherson's notions on the nature of ancient poetry were well developed. They were, indeed, largely responsible for his view that the existing poems of the Highlands were corrupt remains of a great original. He had learned from Blackwell's work that the epic was a natural form for the early bard, so it seemed reasonable to assume that Ossian, too, was an epic poet. The heroes of the existing Highland poems would not be out of place in an epic, but Ossian's great original work must have become scattered through the centuries into shorter poems or 'Fragments'.

Macpherson's own work is easier to understand in the light of contemporary theories on ancient poetry, which provoked numerous aesthetic discussions in the 1750s and 1760s. In 1753, Robert Lowth had published his influential *Lectures on the Sacred Poetry of the Hebrews*, while the poetry of the early Scandinavians had been introduced to the British public in 1755–1756, by Mallet's *Introduction à l'Histoire de Dannemarc* (later published as *Northern Antiquities*). Ancient poetry also dominated the new investigations into 'Original Genius', and provided evidence for Burke's revolutionary *Enquiry into the Sublime and the Beautiful*, 1757.

For writers of the mid-eighteenth century, ancient poetry represented an expression of strong emotion. Lowth asserted that the origin of poetry could be 'traced into the vehement affections of the mind'[28] and the association between early poetry and overwhelming emotion, or 'sublimity', was a commonplace of the period. In his *Lectures on Rhetoric and Belles Lettres*, Adam Smith discussed the work of the ancient Greek poets:

The Death of Oscur

> All passions, especially admiration, express themselves in a very loose and broken manner, catching at whatever seems connected with the subject of the passion . . . The higher the rapture, the more broken the expression.[29]

Smith's observations are very similar to Lowth's discussion of Hebrew 'enthusiasm', which issued forth in

> sudden exclamations, frequent interrogations, apostrophes even to inanimate objects: for to those, who are violently agitated themselves the universal nature of things seems under a necessity of being affected with similar emotions.[30]

The parallels between the early poetry of different nations led to assumptions about the general nature of ancient poems. The style reflected the feelings of the early bard, so Gray's savage youth, for example, must speak in 'loose numbers wildly sweet'.[31] Both the Pindaric Ode and the metres of the Bible seemed to offer the passionate bard the necessary freedom of expression. Macpherson must, therefore, find a form suitable for the strong emotions of the Celtic bard, which could not be conveyed in the 'fetters' of modern poetry.

The powerful emotions of the early bard were not only seen to affect the form of his poetry. Blackwell had associated the rich metaphors of the Greeks with their strong feelings, while Lowth described the Hebrew practice of using familiar objects to give their ideas concrete form, rather than relying on cold abstractions. The great appeal of primitive, figurative language comes across strongly in Mallet's account of Scandinavian poetry:

> The stile of these ancient poems is very enigmatical and figurative, very remote from the common language, and for that reason, grand, but tumid; sublime, but obscure. If it be the character of poetry to have nothing in common with prose, if the language of the gods ought to be quite different from that of men, if every thing should be expressed by imagery, figures, hyperbole, and allegories, the Scandinavians may rank in the highest class of poets[32]

Mallet was aware that the claims he was making might seem extravagant, so the passage continues with a defence that turns out to be an extraordinary condemnation of contemporary poetry:

> The soaring flights of fancy may possibly more peculiarly belong

to a rude and uncultivated, than to a civilised people. The great objects of nature strike more forcibly on rude imaginations. Their passions are not impaired by the constraint of laws and education. The paucity of ideas and the barrenness of their language oblige them to borrow from all nature, images fit to cloath their conceptions in. How should abstract terms and reflex ideas, which so much enervate our poetry, be found in theirs? They could seldom have been met with in their most familiar conversations. The moment the soul, reflecting on its own operations recurs inwards, and detaches itself from exterior objects, the imagination loses its energy, the passions their activity, the mind becomes severe, and requires ideas rather than sensations; language then becomes precise and cautious, and poetry, being no longer the child of pure passion, is able to affect but feebly. If it be asked, what is become of that magic power which the ancients attributed to this art? It may well be said to exist no more. The poetry of the modern languages is nothing more than reasoning in rhime, addressed to the understanding, but very little to the heart. No longer essentially connected with religion, politics, or morality, it is at present, if I may so say, a mere private art, an amusement that attains its end when it has gained the approbation of a few select judges.[33]

Contemporary poetry was nothing but a 'mere private art', produced to please an élite group of critics. It had no real feeling and no function in society, having abandoned all the issues of any value. Ideally, poetry should have a 'magic power': it was the 'language of the gods' and 'essentially connected with religion, politics, or morality'. The early poet had special gifts; he was often associated with prophecy and divine inspiration and fulfilled a crucial role in society. These were the ideal qualities which Macpherson must attempt to recapture in his translations of ancient Gaelic verse. The idea of restoring poetry to a state of 'original purity' had implications far more profound than either Andrew Gallie or Mrs Grant of Laggan could ever have guessed.

The excitement that greeted 'The Death of Oscur' shows that Macpherson had succeeded in creating an 'ancient' poem which could satisfy the demands of contemporary readers. Certainly, it was a very different production from his earlier poems, even though there were a number of familiar elements. The story of tragic love is reminiscent of the tales of Doricles and Daphne, Damon and Delia, while the noble characters of Oscur and Dermid are very similar to the ideal warriors of *The Highlander*. The style of the new 'translation' was, however, completely different. Macpherson's early poetry had been presented in the elevated language of eighteenth-century blank verse, complete with latinate vocabulary, personifications and rhetorical flourishes. In 'The Death of Oscur', however, Macpherson employed simple language and a strongly rhythmical prose style:

> Dermid and Oscur were one: They reaped the battle together. Their friendship was strong as their steel; and death walked between them to the field. They came on the foe like two rocks falling from the brows of Ardven. Their swords were stained with the blood of the valiant: warriors fainted at their names. Who was a match for Oscur, but Dermid? and who for Dermid, but Oscur! (32)

The convoluted sentences, lasting for several lines of verse, were now replaced by short phrases, often consisting largely of monosyllables: 'She went. He stood behind the shield. Her arrow flew and pierced his breast' (35). The blank verse and heroic couplets, too, were abandoned in favour of prose paragraphs of varied lengths and rhythms, to suggest the 'irregularity' of the passionate early poet. The entire poem reads as the spontaneous utterance of an ancient bard, whose grief is too strong to be controlled. Critical writers such as Lowth had seen 'sudden exclamations' as evidence of powerful emotions, and so the poem opens with these anguished cries:

> Why openest thou afresh the spring of my grief, O son of Alpin, inquiring how Oscur fell? My eyes are blind with tears, but memory beams on my heart. How can I relate the mournful death of the head of the people! Prince of the warriors, Oscur, my son I shall see thee no more! (31)

The influences of both Macpherson's native roots and his education can be seen in the very first Fragment he produced, which is a curious blend of the Gaelic tradition and cultures more familiar to a reader such as John Home. The dialogue between Ossian and St Patrick ('son of Alpin') is common in old Gaelic poetry; several of the pieces attributed to Ossian in *The Book of the Dean of Lismore* show St Patrick questioning the old bard about his memories of the Fiana.[34] As in Macpherson's poem, Ossian is generally portrayed as an unhappy old man, dwelling on the past and lamenting the passing of the heroes, although he retains his own proud spirit. The description of Dermid and Oscur (quoted above), for example, is much more like the heroic ballads in tone than the melancholy reflection, 'Why openest thou afresh the spring of my grief . . .' While Macpherson was drawing on the Gaelic tradition, he was also influenced by contemporary expectations of what ancient poetry should be like, and the most obvious and accessible example of an ancient text was the Bible.[35]

In addition to the Gaelic elements, many of the features of Hebrew verse discussed by Lowth appear in Macpherson's Ossianic poetry, which frequently recalls passages from the Old Testament. When Robert Fitzgerald analysed Macpherson's debt to the Gaelic ballads, he used his discoveries to counter the theory that Macpherson modelled his style on the Bible.[36] Given the obvious similarities between the Ossianic *Fragments* and the Old Testament, however, it seems more reasonable to suggest that Macpherson was drawing on more than one tradition. Indeed, he appears to have been using the Bible as a model, not only for imitation, but by which to judge the ballads of the Highlands.

Any features of Gaelic verse which appeared in the Hebrew poetry must surely be truly ancient, and could be part of Ossian's original style? Phrases such as 'sons of the mountains' (36) for deer are probably derived from the use of the genitive, so common in the Gaelic. But they could also be compared to the description of arrows as 'sons of the bow' in the Book of Job, which Robert Lowth had seen as a sign of the early bard's perception of a world in which everything was 'animated and informed with life, soul and passion'.[37]

The structure of Macpherson's prose paragraphs can also be seen as the result of Gaelic and Hebrew influences. The short exchanges between Oscur and Dermid (33) bear some resemblance to the presentation of dialogue in the Gaelic ballads, where speakers have alternate verses of four lines, and their conversation is made up of short, independent phrases. At the same time, the use of 'measured prose' rather than verse suggests the influence of Biblical patterns. Lowth had isolated the repetition of phrases or 'parallelism' as the guiding principle in the structure of Biblical verse, and the series of parallel images in the following passage suggests Macpherson's attempt to imitate the Hebrew style:

> He fell as the moon in a storm; as the sun from the midst of his course, when clouds rise from the waste of the waves, when the blackness of the storm inwraps the rocks of Ardannider. (31)

Parallelism was also a feature of the Gaelic ballads, as seen in the following poem from *The Book of the Dean*:

> Do-chonnaic mé teaghlach Finn,
> is níorbh é an teaghlach tim tréith;
> agus do-chonnaic mé sibh
> do mhuintir an fhir a ndé.
>
> Do-chonnaic mé teaghlach Airt,
> an fear lérbh ait duanna binn;
> fear as fearr ní fhaca mé:
> do-chonnaic me teaghlach Finn.
>
> (I have seen the household of Fionn, it was no faint nor feeble band; and I have seen you, I who am of the followers of the man of yesterday

I have seen the household of Art, the man who loved
sweet lays; a better man I never saw; I have seen the
household of Fionn.)[38]

Macpherson's use of the technique, however, is altogether more flowery and seems much more like the parallelism of the Psalms or The Song of Solomon. According to Lowth, the most common kind of parallelism was 'synonymous' (i.e. the repetition of the same idea in a slightly different form), and it is a common feature of Macpherson's style: 'They fought by the brook of the mountain, by the streams of Branno' (34), or 'And fallest thou, son of Morny; fallest thou by Oscur's hand!' (34). As in the Bible, the careful balance of phrases gives a sense of order and unity to Macpherson's apparently irregular prose, but avoids the sophistication or 'fetters' of formal verse.

One of the most striking examples of parallelism in 'The Death of Oscur' is the description of Dargo's daughter:

His daughter was fair as the morn; mild as the beam of night. Her eyes, like two stars in a shower: her breath, the gale of spring: her breasts, as the new fallen snow floating on the moving heath. The warriors saw her and loved; their souls were fixed on the maid.
(32)

In addition to the unifying effects of the Biblical parallelism, Macpherson was also making his own experiments with syllabic patterns. In the description above, the central passage is a series of fourteen-syllable units, which could be arranged with alternating lines of eight and six syllables, followed by a couplet of seven:

His daughter was fair as the morn;
Mild as the beam of night.
Her eyes, like two stars in a shower:
Her breath, the gale of spring:
Her breasts, as the new-fallen snow
Floating on the moving heath

Although there is no regular pattern to Macpherson's prose, the paragraphs can often be analysed in a similar way. The structure is barely perceptible; nevertheless it gives the verse an internal unity, without destroying the illusion that it is a spontaneous utterance.

The description of Dargo's daughter is also striking as an example of Macpherson's use of imagery. Figurative language was generally regarded as an essential part of ancient poetry, being further evidence of the primitive bard's strong feelings. Although the old Gaelic ballads include natural images, they are seldom grouped in this manner, so the sudden profusion of imagery again suggests Macpherson's debt to the Old Testament. Despite the Biblical style, the images are still drawn from a Highland landscape, just as Ossian himself is described as 'an ancient oak', blown by 'the wings of the north' (31). The description of Dargo's daughter shows not only Macpherson's careful blending of Biblical and Gaelic styles, but also his desire to make his translations beautiful. Robbed of their oral dimension, the Gaelic ballads might seem a little flat, so Macpherson embellished the narratives with passages like the one above. The sudden burgeoning of imagery stands out boldly against the simple prose, preventing the short sentences and monosyllables from becoming dull and lifeless. With the Bible as his authority, Macpherson would have felt justified in inserting such descriptions as part of his attempt to restore Ossian's work to its 'original purity'. In *The Highlander*, Macpherson had alluded to familiar epic poems to give his own Highland heroes added status, but now he was adopting a scriptural style, which conjured up associations of an even higher kind.

Macpherson appears to have drawn principally on ancient traditions, but it is also possible to find evidence of more modern influences. The opening lines of the poem, for example, ('My eyes are blind with tears, but memory beams on my heart' (31)), carry an odd echo of Milton's invocation in *Paradise Lost*, III, where the connection between blindness and inner light is explored. The simple diction of Macpherson's line makes it seem more ancient than Milton's, especially in the context of eighteenth-century theories of poetry. Although Macpherson robs the paradox of the rich Miltonic imagery, by grounding the ideas of blindness and inner light in normal human experience he achieves the highly-esteemed simplicity and concreteness of early verse. In *The Highlander* Macpherson had revealed his debts to *Paradise Lost* through the imitative style, but now he was trying to produce work that seemed more original than his source, while retaining the benefits of the dim, Miltonic allusions.

Despite the antique surface, 'The Death of Oscur' had as much in common with the poetry of the eighteenth-century as with that of any ancient bard, Hebrew, Gaelic or Greek. The very notion of being blinded by tears, for example, which could be interpreted as a sign of primitive passion, also suggests the contemporary emphasis on sensibility. Although Macpherson's bard was based on the traditional Gaelic character, the poet of the ballads has a much more heroic spirit as well as a lively sense of humour. Macpherson's solitary poet, while vaguely reminiscent of Homer or the Hebrew prophets, would not have seemed out of place in the reflective verse of the mid-eighteenth century. Just as Gray's 'Elegy' focused more on the poet than his subjects, so 'The Death of Oscur' has more to do with the narrator, Ossian, than with his son, Oscur. It is only through Ossian that our sympathies are drawn to Oscur rather than Dermid, since the young warriors themselves seem quite indistinguishable. At the same time,

The Death of Oscur

the presence of the speaker distances us from the violent action of the poem and imbues the main characters with a strange remoteness. While Oscur and Dermid seem truly ancient, Ossian, the reflective, melancholy poet seems closer to the modern world. Ossian hovers uncomfortably between two worlds, his heart with the dead, his body trapped with the living. While Ossian, the 'ancient oak' has his branches 'lopped away' and is left to 'moulder alone', the young warriors achieve perfect harmony with nature, through death:

> By the brook of the hills their graves are laid; a birch's unequal shade covers their tomb. Often on their green earthen tombs the branchy sons of the mountain feed, when mid-day is all in flames, and silence is over all the hills. (36)

There is a strong sense that those who have died are closer to nature and retain greater vitality than Ossian, who is at the mercy of hostile elements and seems impotent in his decay.

'The Death of Oscur' provides a foretaste of the themes Macpherson was to introduce in *Fragments of Ancient Poetry*, and then develop in *Fingal* and *Temora*. Despite its apparent simplicity, the poem is full of allusions, while the simple images are carefully chosen to develop the themes and contrasts. Although Macpherson appeared to be elevating the Highland poetry with his Biblical style and heroic warriors, the pervading tone was not of celebration, but despair. The death of the young warriors suggests that such heroism is doomed, while the presence of the ageing narrator places their actions firmly in the past. Ossian's lament for his son is filled with regret for the passing of a greater age and a sad sense of the inferiority of the present.

The 'sympathetick Bond' between James Macpherson and the ancient bard whose voice he was gradually adopting is already becoming plain.[39] Just as Ossian was lamenting the passing of the heroic age of Oscur and Dermid, so Macpherson was inspired by the growing awareness that the traditional world of the Highlands would soon have disappeared for ever. At the same time, Ossian's disgust at his present condition and idealisation of the past can be related to the more general anxieties about the progress of modern civilisation. Many eighteenth-century writers felt burdened by doubts about modern poetry and the pressure to be original but Macpherson's 'ancient poetry' both embodies the problem and attempts a solution. 'The Death of Oscur' was by no means a accurate translation of a Gaelic ballad, but a blend of traditional styles and modern preoccupations. As such, it was to appeal far more strongly to eighteenth-century readers than any literal translation could.

NOTES

1. See Lonsdale's introduction in *Gray, Collins and Goldsmith*, 1969, 492.
2. 'A Note from John Home', *Report*, App. 68–69.
3. See Saunders, *James Macpherson*, 64.
4. Home's Note, *Report*, App. 68–9.
5. Carlyle to Highland Society, January 1802, *Report*, App. 66. According to Carlyle, he visited Moffat on 2 October 1759.
6. Blair to Mackenzie, 20 December 1797, *Report*, App. 57.
7. Ibid.
8. See R. H. Carnie, 'Macpherson's *Fragments of Ancient Poetry* and Lord Hailes', *English Studies*, xli, 17–26.
9. Carlyle, *Anecdotes and Characters* . . ., 203.
10. 'Conversing with Mr Macpherson, Mr Home found that he was an exceedingly good classical scholar', *Report*, App. 68.
11. Letter, 18 January 1782, quoted in Laing ed. I, xv. For further information from Laurie see H. G. Graham, *Scottish Men of Letters in the Eighteenth Century*, (London 1901), 227–28.
12. Revised dissertation on *Temora, The Poems of Ossian*, translated by *James Macpherson*, 2 vols, (London 1773), II, 259.
13. John Clark to Highland Society, 1803, ADV MS 73.2. 15/ 11b.
14. *Report*, App. 57.
15. Clark, ADV MS 73.2.15 / 11b.
16. J. H. Delargy, 'The Gaelic Story Teller', *Proceedings of the British Academy*, xxxi, 1945, 177–221, 187. See also D. A. Macdonald & A. Bruford, *Memory in Gaelic Story-Telling*, (Edinburgh 1979).
17. Knott & Murphy, *Early Irish Literature*, 102.
18. *A Dictionary of the English Language*, (London 1755), Preface.
19. J. Locke, *An Essay Concerning Human Understanding*, 1690; ed. P. Nidditch, (Oxford 1975), 663–64.
20. Gallie to C. Mackintosh, 1801, *Report*, 44.
21. A. Grant, *Poems on Several Subjects*, (Edinburgh 1803), 364. Mrs Grant's authority was Ewan Macpherson, the Gaelic scholar who accompanied Macpherson for part of his Highland Tour, 1760.
22. 'Dedication of the Aeneis', *Essays of John Dryden*, ed. W. P. Ker, 1900, 1926; 2 vols, (New York 1961), II, 227. See also, J. Hollander, 'Versions, Interpretations, and Performances', *On Translation*, ed. R. A. Brower, (Cambridge, Mass. 1959), 205–31.
23. Dryden, ibid.
24. W. Dillon, Earl of Roscommon, *An Essay on Translated Verse*, (London 1685), 7.
25. See J. S. Smart, *James Macpherson, An Episode in Literature*, (London 1905), 91–3. The text of 'The Death of Oscur' is the one included in *Fragments of Ancient Poetry*, 1760; facsimile of 2nd edn, (Edinburgh 1970).
26. *An Introduction to the History of Great Britain and Ireland*, (London 1771), 6–7.
27. *Essays of John Dryden*, II, 228.
28. *De Sacra Poesi Hebraeorum Praelectiones Academicae Oxonii Habitae*, (Oxford 1753). Quotations are from Lowth, *Lectures on the Sacred Poetry of the Hebrews*, tr. G. Gregory, 2 vols, (London 1787), I, 79.
29. Adam Smith, *Lectures on Rhetoric and Belles Lettres* ed. J. M. Lothian, (London 1963), 134.

The Death of Oscur

30. Lowth, op. cit., I, 79.
31. 'The Progress of Poetry', 1757, lines 60–6l.
32. *Introduction à l'Histoire de Dannemarc*, (Copenhagen 1755). Quotations from *Northern Antiquities*, tr. T. Percy, 2 vols, (London 1770), I, 385.
33. Ibid.
34. See poems V and VI in *Heroic Poetry from the Book of the Dean*.
35. For the Bible in eigtheenth-century literature, see M. Roston, *Prophet and Poet, the Bible and the Growth of Romanticism*, (London 1965); D. B. Morris, *The Religious Sublime, Christian Poetry and the Critical Tradition in 18th-Century England*, (Kentucky 1972).
36. Robert P. Fitzgerald, 'The Style of Macpherson's Ossian', *Studies in Romanticism*, vi, 1966, 22–32.
37. Lowth, *Lectures on . . . the Hebrews*, I, 288–89.
38. Poem III, attributed to Oisean Mac Finn in *Heroic Poetry from the Book of the Dean*, 6–7.
39. Northrop Frye discusses Macpherson's 'psychological self-identification' in 'Towards Defining an Age of Sensibility', *ELH*, xxiii, 1956, 144–52.

Fragments of Ancient Poetry

> If you have seen Stonehewer he has probably told you of my old Scotch (or rather Irish) Poetry. I am gone mad about them. they are said to be translations (literal & in prose) from the Erse-tongue, done by one Macpherson, a young Clergyman in the High-lands. he means to publish a Collection he has of these Specimens of antiquity, if it be antiquity: but what plagues me is, I can not come at any certainty on that head. I was so struck, so *extasié* with their infinite beauty, that I writ into Scotland to make a thousand enquiries . . . this Man is the very Demon of Poetry, or he has lighted on a treasure hid for ages.
>
> Thomas Gray, Letter, 20 June 1760[1]

Fragments of Ancient Poetry, collected in the Highlands of Scotland, and translated from the Galic or Erse language was published in Edinburgh in June 1760. It was a flimsy production, containing a mere fifteen pieces of strange prose, most of which were untitled. The name of the translator remained a mystery and in the brief preface, the original poems were attributed to 'the Bards'. Despite its unassuming appearance, the pamphlet had an immediate success and by October a second edition was out.[2] By this time James Macpherson was well-known name in the literary circles of Edinburgh and, inspired by the enthusiastic response to his first translations, he had embarked on a far more ambitious project.

For Macpherson's patrons, *Fragments of Ancient Poetry* was only a foretaste of the great epic poem which was to appear in December 1761. Although the brief volume of 1760 has often been dismissed as being merely an introduction to *Fingal* and *Temora*, it was in many ways a more successful collection of poetry than the rambling epics which followed. It is also important as the work which first attracted the attention of the reading public, colouring their expectations of the nature of ancient Gaelic poetry. Anyone trying to understand the impact of Macpherson's *Fragments* should look at the original volume as a whole, considering not only the poetry but also the general presentation.

After Macpherson's initial introduction to the Edinburgh literati, the man who had the strongest influence on him was Hugh Blair. In

Fragments of Ancient Poetry   97

the autumn of 1759 Blair was working on his famous *Lectures on Rhetoric and Belles Lettres*, and as his biographer has suggested, 'Macpherson's stuff was meat for Blair's theories, and Blair's theories were . . . the food on which Macpherson's poetical efforts throve and fattened'.[3] It was Blair who persuaded Macpherson to publish the *Fragments* and who, with the translator's assistance, provided a preface for the work.

Blair's Preface gives important insights into the way in which both he and Macpherson regarded the *Fragments of Ancient Poetry*. Instead of following Jerome Stone's example and presenting the poems as works of primitive genius, Blair adopted an almost apologetic tone. He appears to have been influenced strongly by Macpherson's own distrust of the contemporary remains of Highland poetry:

> Though the poems now published appear as detached pieces in this collection, there is ground to believe that most of them were originally episodes of a greater work which related to the wars of Fingal. Concerning this hero innumerable traditions remain, to this day, in the Highlands of Scotland. (v)

Macpherson's notion that the ballads and stories still current in the Highlands were the corrupted versions of Ossian's original poetry accorded well with Blair's preconceptions about the epic. With Homer as the principal model for early poets, it seemed reasonable to suppose that epic poetry was a genre that came naturally to the primitive bard. Indeed, it had become commonplace to regard the earliest periods of society as providing the ideal conditions for the composition of epic poems.[4] Macpherson's short *Fragments* actually bore more resemblance to the genuine Gaelic ballads than did the longer structure of *Fingal* or *Temora*, but both Macpherson and Blair felt that the ancient poetry of Scotland *ought* to have been epic. Celtic society, in Macpherson's eyes, was very similar to that of Ancient Greece, so why shouldn't Caledonia have had her Homer?

Macpherson saw the inhabitants of North West Scotland as the direct descendants of the Celts, sharing their language and preserving the last relics of the ancient culture. It therefore seemed possible that an ancient epic poem, or at least part of it, could have survived in the areas furthest from southern influences. Throughout Blair's preface, the strong desire to retrieve a great epic poem for Scotland is obvious:

> Of the poetical merit of these fragments nothing shall here be said. Let the public judge, and pronounce. It is believed, that, by a careful inquiry, many more remains of ancient genius, no less valuable than those now given to the world, might be found in the same country where these have been collected. In particular

there is reason to hope that one work of considerable length, and which deserves to be styled an heroic poem, might be recovered and translated, if encouragement were given to such an undertaking (vii).

Rather than give a critical evaluation of the poems in the volume then, Blair concentrated on the hypothetical epic. A third of the preface is concerned with the subject and Blair even included a summary of the plot of *Fingal*, to whet the reader's appetite. The *Fragments* interested Blair chiefly as evidence that a true epic poem existed, which might give Scotland the literary stature of Ancient Greece.

But despite Blair's excitement about the possible discovery of a great, heroic poem, the preface concluded on a curiously flat note:

> The three last poems in the collection are fragments which the translator obtained of this Epic poem; and tho' very imperfect, they were judged not unworthy of being inserted. If the whole were recovered, it might serve to throw considerable light upon the Scottish and Irish antiquities.(viii)

Blair did not discuss the patriotic qualities of the legendary epic, nor its potential significance as literature. The imaginative appeal of the Ossianic poetry was played down, while the emphasis was laid on its historical importance.

Throughout the preface, Blair stressed that the value of the poems lay chiefly in their historical interest. It opens:

> The public may depend on the following fragments as genuine remains of ancient Scottish poetry. The date of their composition cannot be exactly ascertained. Tradition, in the country where they were written, refers them to an aera of the most remote antiquity: and this tradition is supported by the spirit and strain of the poems themselves; which abound with those ideas and paint those manners, that belong to the most early state of society. (iii)

Although Blair found Macpherson's antique style convincing, he was aware that less sympathetic readers might take a more sceptical line. Consequently he was at pains to present historical evidence for the antiquity of the poems, arguing that the absence of references to Christianity or the clan system proved that the *Fragments* antedated such institutions (iii–iv). Blair was presenting the *Fragments* not so much as literature, but as rare documents from an early period of man's history, adopting the tone of the philosophical historian rather than the critic.

The growing interest in early poetry as an expression of strong feelings and a powerful imagination can be seen partly as a reaction to the scepticism of the Enlightenment. Although primitive literature provided a welcome escape, however, academic writers such as Blair found it necessary to defend their interest in philosophical terms. Modern society could be explained by tracing its development from the earliest times, so any documents shedding light on these distant origins were valuable. Blair's own response to Macpherson's *Fragments* was essentially emotional and imaginative, but in his public presentation he adopted the voice of the philosopher: the poems were important because they belonged to 'the most early state of society' (iii).

Blair's defensive arguments were largely designed to fend off doubts about the authenticity of the *Fragments*, but a deeper anxiety was latent in the preface: the feeling that the value of poetry itself was under question. In 1820, Thomas Love Peacock was to survey the progress of poetry in comparison to the 'useful' pursuits of science and philosophy in his cynical essay, 'The Four Ages of Poetry':

> as the sciences of morals and of mind advance towards perfection . . . as reason gains the ascendancy in them over imagination and feeling, poetry can no longer accompany them in their progress, but drops into the background, and leaves them to advance alone.[5]

The cool, utilitarian attitude had been developing for at least a century before Peacock's provocative challenge was made. Despite the optimistic claims for Edinburgh being 'the Athens of the North', the literati were more remarkable for the production of histories and philosophical enquiries than for creative work.[6] When Blair wrote the introduction to his *Lectures*, he began by giving reasons for studying literature, which is indicative of his uneasiness about the status of poetry. In the preface to the *Fragments*, too, a similar lack of confidence is evident: the poetry seemed to require justification, so Blair added historical arguments.

Although Blair argued that early poetry should be read as an insight into early society, much of its appeal lay in the fact that there *were* no accurate historical records to contradict the accounts of the poets. Readers could therefore escape into a remote age, untroubled by the irritating questions of whether or not the events were true:

> Antiquity is favourable to those high and august ideas which Epic Poetry is designed to raise. It tends to aggrandise, in our imagination, both persons and events; and, what is still more material, it allows the Poet the liberty of adorning his subject by means of fiction. Whereas, as soon as he comes within the verge of real or authenticated history, this liberty is abridged.[7]

Similar considerations appear to have influenced William Wilkie, who selected ancient Greece as the setting for his own Scottish epic of the 1750s. In the preface to the *Epigoniad*, he wrote:

> there is in our minds a principle which leads us to admire past times, especially those which are most remote from our own. This prejudice is strong in us; and . . . forms in the mere vulgar of all countries, the most extravagant notions of the stature, strength, and other heroic qualities of their remote ancestors. This prejudice so favourable to poetical fiction, true history effectively destroys[8]

Any poet of the mid-eighteenth century who wanted to write about heroes or supernatural happenings was forced to turn to the past, where the imagination was still unhampered by empirical demands.[9] The tendency to confine the imagination to antiquity, however, brought with it a deep pessimism about the future of poetry, while even modern treatments of ancient themes were tinged with a despair quite alien to genuine early poetry.

The presentation of Macpherson's *Fragments* was thus complicated by the conflict between the imaginative and philosophical approaches to the poetry and, as a result, the volume was produced in the standard format of an eighteenth-century classical translation, suitably adorned by a Latin quotation. The Latin tag, taken from Lucan's *Pharsalia*, was particularly appropriate to Macpherson's *Fragments* (indeed, the title page of Macpherson's volume bore a strong resemblance to the standard translation of the *Pharsalia*, Dublin 1719). Lucan was regarded as a great epic poet and his lines about the Gallic bards seemed perfect as an introduction to the ancient verse of the Highlands:

> vos quoque qui fortes animas, belloque peremtas
> Laudibus in longum vates dimittitis aevum,
> Plurima securi fudistis carmina Bardi.   (I, 447–449)

The standard eighteenth-century translation of these lines by Nicholas Rowe read:

> You too, ye Bards! whom sacred Raptures fire,
> To Chaunt your Heroes to your Country's lyre;
> Who consecrate in your immortal Strain,
> Brave Patriot Souls in righteous Battle slain;
> Securely now the tuneful Task renew,
> And noblest Themes in deathless Songs pursue.   (I, 784–90)

Like the traditional songs of the Highland bards, the poems of the ancient Gauls were heroic, patriotic pieces, designed to inspire the audience to emulation. Unlike the uncertain, isolated modern poet, the ancient Bards were very much part of their society and had an important role to play.

The aptness of the allusion to Lucan was not confined to the superficial connections between the Gallic and Highland bards, however. The *Pharsalia*, which Blair admired greatly, was by no means a celebration of Roman virtue or the dignity of mankind.[10] Lucan's subject was Civil War:

> Emathian plains with slaughter cover'd o'er,
> And rage unknown to civil wars before,
> Establish'd violence, and lawless might,
> Avow'd and hallow'd by the name of right;
> A race renown'd, the world's victorious lords,
> Turn'd on themselves with their own hostile swords;
> Piles against piles oppos'd in impious fight;
> And eagles against eagles bending flight;
> Of blood by fiends, by kindred, parent, spilt,
> One common horror and promiscuous guilt;
> A shatter'd world in wild disorder tost,
> Leagues, laws, and empire in confusion lost;
> Of all the woes which civil discords bring,
> And Rome o'ercome by Roman arms, I sing. (Rowe, I, 1–14)

Although Blair was full of Lucan's genius, the theme of the *Pharsalia* points to rather more gloomy reasons for choosing it to introduce the *Fragments*. For Macpherson, who had witnessed the '45 and its aftermath, the allusion to Lucan's bloody epic must have seemed appropriate to the poetry of the Highlands. The overwhelming sense of a world in the process of disintegration which is conveyed in the *Pharsalia*, also emerged in the *Fragments*. Lucan dealt with Civil War, with conflicts within families, with human beings bent on death and with the destruction of an old order. His work was full of images of bloodshed and brutality, attended by grieving widows and mothers mourning their children. Although Macpherson's *Fragments* were much briefer and altogether more ephemeral, similar motifs recurred contributing to the general atmosphere of despair.

When Robert Graves edited the *Pharsalia*, he examined its fluctuating popularity in relation to changes in society, drawing an interesting parallel between Lucan's experience of Neronian Rome and the condition of England after the First World War:

> To poets whom loss of faith in their own national institutions, ethics, religion, and even in themselves, sends marching and counter-marching through the Waste Land, Lucan can be as much a 'standard-bearer' as he was for Piso's ill-considered conspiracy. His un-Virgilian rhetoric . . . impatience with craftsmanship, digressive irrelevancies, emphasis on the macabre, lack of religious conviction, turgid hyperbole, inconsistency,

appeal to violence, and occasional flashes of real brilliance – have been discovered by this new disagreeable world.[11]

Although one might argue with Graves' criticism of Eliot, the faults he discerned in Lucan were peculiarly relevant to Macpherson's work. The theory that such traits characterise the work of young poets whose world has suffered some violent change can easily be applied to the compositions of the eighteenth-century Highlander.

The experience of the Highlander, however, was only part of the wider social changes taking place in Britain, and the steady erosion of the traditional view of a universe controlled by God. The sense of hopeless despair was not peculiar to Macpherson's work, but emerged persistently in the literature of the period. Although *Fragments of Ancient Poetry* appeared to be a straightforward translation of traditional Gaelic verse, the underlying emotions can be discerned throughout. The very form (or formlessness) of the poetry, though apparently reflecting the unrestrained passions of primitive man, could in fact be seen as a disintegration of orderly Augustan verse. For Macpherson and Blair, the *Fragments* were not even complete poems, but the broken remains of 'a greater work': the dregs of a culture, rather than the essence. This very feeling, gave the volume of 1760 an ephemeral quality, which disappeared in the more substantial 'epics' that followed.

Fragments of Ancient Poetry consisted of a series of prose-poems recounting the deeds of ancient Highland warriors, each very similar to 'The Death of Oscur'. Throughout the volume, Macpherson employed the same quasi-Biblical style to give an antique atmosphere to his Scottish landscapes, although the overall effect was totally different from the Old Testament. The opening speech of the *Fragments*, for example, in which Vinvela describes her Highland lover, is strongly reminiscent of the Song of Songs:

> My love is a son of the hill. He pursues the flying deer. His gray dogs are panting around him; his bow-string sounds in the wind. Whether by the fount of the rock, or by the stream of the mountain thou liest; when the rushes are nodding with the wind, and the mist is flying over thee, let me approach my love unperceived, and see him from the rock. (9)

The Song of Songs, however, is a joyful celebration of love, using extravagant images of natural abundance and set in the spring. The story of Shilric and Vinvela, on the other hand, is far from happy and deals with the separation of the lovers when Shilric goes off to war. Vinvela, imagining that her lover has been killed, dies of grief so that when Shilric eventually comes home he is greeted only by a ghost. The echoes of the Song of Songs are thus grimly ironic, and serve to emphasise the misery and frustration of the Celtic heroes.

Macpherson's *Fragments* belong to the autumn. Throughout the volume there are references to autumn and the harvest, while the ubiquitous north winds suggest the onset, rather than the passing of winter. From the very first tale, the familiar association between the seasons and the cycle of life is made explicit, as the ghost of Vinvela is described by Shilric as 'bright as the moon in autumn' and proclaims herself to be 'alone in the winter-house' (14). The frequent references to the autumn in subsequent poems thus carry gloomy associations which increase with every new example.

The disintegration of Vinvela is characteristic of Macpherson's *Fragments*. She changes rapidly from a vigorous Highland maiden to the uncertain presence of a ghost:

> But is it she that there appears, like a beam of light on the heath? bright as the moon in autumn, as the sun in a summer-storm, comest thou lovely maid over rocks, over mountains to me? – She speaks: but how weak her voice! Like the breeze in the reeds of the pool. (14)

After a brief exchange, 'she fleets, she sails away; as grey mist before the wind!' (15). Vinvela's very existence seems doubtful. Has she really appeared? Or is it Shilric's distress, conjuring up images of the beloved in his mind?

Macpherson's uncertain world of ghosts and solitary speakers is very different from the sharp, concrete imagery of the Bible, or indeed of genuine Gaelic poetry.[12] Instead of the work of an ancient bard, it suggests the modern writer, moving back in time to a remote and indefinite period. The characters emerge with varying degrees of clarity and solidity through the mists of the Highlands, as if through centuries. The fragmentary form suggests glimpses of a distant age, which the writer is catching before it disappears completely. This lack of definition is essential to Macpherson's Celtic world, in which the reader is invited to become lost. Since the characters can hardly be distinguished as individuals, the reader seems to be responding to spirits rather than human beings. Even the settings are unspecific: the rocks, streams and hills could belong to any part of the Highlands.[13] With no familiar landmarks to guide us, we have to rely on the intangible speakers, piecing together the events from the enigmatic snatches and chants.

The consistency of the natural imagery made an important contribution to the atmosphere of the *Fragments*. In the longer *Poems of Ossian*, the repetition of the same simple images becomes rather tedious, but in the original *Fragments* the effect is strangely hypnotic. Macpherson's imitation of an early bard's limited vocabulary led to the constant use of certain stock features such as 'rock', 'deer', 'stream', 'mist', 'moon', 'sun', 'oak', 'wind', 'storm', 'grave' or 'cloud'. In 'The Death of Oscur' the language seemed plain and unsophisticated, but in the volume as a whole the simple words acquire almost symbolic significance, by being used and re-used in the different poems. For example, the associations between the strength of an oak tree and that of an heroic family which appeared in 'The Death of Oscur', recur throughout the *Fragments*. Fragment V includes the following lament for Connal: 'Thy family grew like an oak on the mountain, which meeteth the wind with its lofty head. But now it is torn from the earth' (24). The passing of Fingal's race is described in a similar manner: 'How hast thou fallen like an oak, with all thy branches round thee!' (37). Any analogy between a warrior and an oak tree is charged with ominous implications, through the cumulative associations.[14]

The gloomy atmosphere of the *Fragments* is also sustained through the plots of the poems. Some are straightforward elegies, such as Fragment III, where the aged Carryl laments the loss of Malcolm, 'the hope of the Isles'. Others, like 'The Death of Oscur', tell more complicated tales of tragic love affairs, involving the murder of close friends and family. In Fragment X, for example, a family feud obstructs the love of a nameless speaker for the warrior, Shalgar. When the Celtic Juliet discovers the bodies of Shalgar and her brother, slain in mortal combat, she raises a tomb and buries herself with them. A similar story is told in Fragment IX, which inspired the plot of John Home's play, *The Fatal Discovery*. This time the lovers are Rivine and Ronnan, while Rivine's brother, Connan, is a close friend of her lover. When Ronnan goes to war, he leaves his beloved under the protection of her brother, warning Connan about her other admirer, Durstan. When Ronnan is returning from battle, he is informed by a treacherous servant that Durstan plans to abduct Rivine that very night. The same servant also tells Connan this story, so that both heroes rush to the appointed place in order to save Rivine. In the dark they mistake each other for Durstan and begin to fight. Rivine arrives in time to find only the corpses of her lover and brother, so she promptly commits suicide.

Just as the imagery of the *Fragments* has a cumulative effect, so too the tragic plots build on each other. Gradually, it becomes possible to predict the outcome of the story as soon as the principle characters have been introduced. The speakers may vary, but each tale involves the frustrated love and ultimate death of all the major characters. The repetition of this pattern influences the reader's expectations, while the persistent fulfilment of these expectations gives a strongly fatalistic tone to the *Fragments*.

The pervading sense of doom is increased by the characteristic association between love and death. In Fragment V, Crimora is not prepared to sit at home like Vinvela or Rivine, while her lover goes to war, but dons a suit of armour and follows Connal into battle. Unfortunately her gesture is doomed to failure:

The daughter of Rinval was near; Crimora, bright in the armour of man; her hair loose behind, her bow in her hand. She followed the youth to the war, Connal her much-beloved. She drew the string on Dargo, but erring pierced her Connal. He falls like an oak on the plain; like a rock from the shaggy hill. What shall she do, hapless maid! – He bleeds; her Connal dies. All the night long she cries, and all the day, O Connal, my love, and my friend! With grief the sad mourner died.

Earth here incloseth the loveliest pair on the hill. The grass grows between the stones of their tomb; I sit in the mournful shade. The wind sighs through grass; and their memory rushes on my mind. Undisturbed you now sleep together; in the tomb of the mountain you now rest alone. (25)

Love seems unable to flourish in Macpherson's Caledonia. Instead of normal sexual activity, the lovers are united only in violent death, sleeping together not in bed, but in the grave.

The association between sex and death often emerges in the language of the violent death scenes. In Fragment XV, for example, Duchommar kills Cadmor in order to possess Morna, but is then slain by the lady in question.[15] As Duchommar breathes his last, he stabs Morna, who responds curiously: 'As she fell, she plucked a stone from the side of the cave, and placed it betwixt them, that his blood might not be mingled with hers.' (73). Both the stabbing of Morna and her resistance to mingling with Duchommar's blood have obvious sexual connotations. A similar situation occurs in Fragment VI, where a 'fair virgin' comes to Fingal for protection against the unwanted attentions of the Lochlin warrior, Ullin. Although the maid is protected by the Fein, Ullin's desire is such that he arrives alone, determined to achieve satisfaction.[16] Rather than abduct the woman, however, his lust takes a perverted form: 'He plunged his sword into the fair-one's breast. She fell as a wreath of snow before the sun in spring: Her bosom heaved in death; her soul came forth in blood' (28). Although the incident is disturbing in itself, Macpherson's treatment makes it more so. The lyrical description of the girl falling suggests a certain relish of the scene and total lack of feeling for the victim. The same uncomfortable sense of voyeurism emerges frequently in Macpherson's work: Ossian's own celebrated 'joy of grief' has a certain perverted quality. Although it appears to be the spontaneous response to emotional pain, there is also a brooding indulgence of morbid eroticism. Macpherson's 'ancient poetry' has a decadence which makes the regret about the passing of a truly ancient world more powerful.

Although the *Fragments* are tales about active young warriors, the speakers are invariably characters like Ossian, debilitated by grief or old age. The tension between the vigorous heroes and the impotent bards is an important part of the work:

> The wing of time is laden with care. Every moment hath woes of its own. Why seek we our grief from afar? or give our tears to those of other times? But thou commandest, and I obey, O fair daughter of the isles!
> Conar was mighty in war. Caul was the friend of strangers. His gates were open to all; midnight darkened not on his barred door. Both lived upon the sons of the mountains. Their bow was the support of the poor. (41)

The images of the strong, healthy warriors are always at one remove. They stand out sharply from the misty atmosphere of the *Fragments*, but their existence is reported only by bereaved wives and old men. The most immediate characters, the narrators, are passive figures who are unable to change their circumstances except through suicide.

The chorus of grieving women and bards is an important part of the *Fragments* and it is interesting to consider Lowth's interpretation of the Lamentations in this context.[17] The use of the widow as an image for the fallen Jerusalem ('She weepeth sore in the night, and her tears are on her cheeks: among all her lovers she hath none to comfort her') can be related to Macpherson's imagery.[18] The sorrowing women of Macpherson's Celtic world may be a similar expression of the disintegration of society; not only were the Highland communities in decay, but there was a pervading sense of the decline of modern civilisation. Macpherson's *Fragments of Ancient Poetry* can be read as eighteenth-century Lamentations, but the absence of God in the poems makes them particularly bleak.

The preponderance of widows lamenting their husbands is matched by the number of parents who have lost their children. Ossian is not the only father to outlive his son:

> Who on his staff is this? who is this, whose head is white with age, whose eyes are red with tears, who quakes at every step? – It is thy father, O Morar! the father of none but thee. He heard of thy fame in battle; he heard of foes dispersed. He heard of Morar's fame; why did he not hear of his wound? Weep, thou father of Morar! weep; but thy son heareth thee not. Deep is the sleep of the dead; low their pillow of dust. (58)

The theme reaches its most extreme expression in Fragment XI, where the cries of Armyn are reminiscent of those of Lear on the Heath:

> Rise, winds of autumn, rise; blow upon the dark heath! streams of the mountains roar! howl, ye tempests, in the top of the oak!

walk through broken clouds, O moon! show by intervals thy pale face! bring to my mind that sad night, when all my children fell; when Arindel the mighty fell; when Daura the lovely failed; when all my children died. (50)

The allusion to Lear is highly appropriate, recalling the horrifying transformation of the powerful ruler of Ancient Britain into a 'poor, infirm, weak and despis'd old man'. Of all Shakespeare's plays, the total disintegration of order is most pronounced in *King Lear*, while the themes of Civil War, family strife and murder are not unlike those of the *Fragments*. Lear's address to the elements as a poor substitute for his children is also an interesting parallel. The anthropomorphism in the passage above is typical of the *Fragments* and, at one level, can be seen as another attempt to use the techniques of early poetry. While the anthropomorphism of the Old Testament suggests the prophets' deep awareness of the presence of God, the effect in Macpherson's work is very different. Instead of contributing to the sense of harmony between man and nature, the personification of the natural world in the *Fragments*, as in *Lear*, tends to emphasise the isolation of the speaker.

Unlike James Thomson's natural world, which is presented as the language of God and an expression of divine order, Macpherson's Highland landscape is an uncontrolled and godless place. The Biblical language is therefore all the more disturbing, because the helpless speakers are at the mercy of nature, with no faith to sustain them. Although Blair's observation on the absence of religion in the *Fragments* was merely a point of historical evidence, Macpherson's ancient poetry demonstrates the horror of a world without God. Indeed, it is not difficult to relate the pervading despair of the *Fragments* to contemporary anxieties about the consequences of sceptical philosophy and the position of the aetheist in the world.

The image of the isolated speaker, pouring out a torrent of emotion to an empty landscape is perhaps the most memorable aspect of the *Fragments*. Voices play a prominent part in the work, and much of the distinctive style results from Macpherson's experiments with sound. Given the oral nature of the Gaelic tradition, it is not surprising that Macpherson should attempt to convey the dramatic aspect of Gaelic verse into his English versions. He obviously managed to convince Blair that his translation came close to the original because the preface includes the note that

> Rhyme is seldom used: but the cadence, and the length of the line varied, so as to suit the sense. The translation is extremely literal. Even the arrangement of the words in the original has been imitated; to which must be imputed some inversions in the style, that otherwise would not have been chosen. (vi)

The correspondence noted by Blair, between the cadence and the sense of Gaelic verse, is carefully recreated in Macpherson's *Fragments*. Thus when a battle is described, the verse is adapted accordingly:

> Swords sound on helmets, sound on shields; brass clashes, clatters, rings. Sparkles buzz; shivers fly; death bounds from mail to mail. As leaps a stone from rock to rock, so blow succeeds to blow . . . they leap, they thrust, they wound. (63)

The jerky rhythm, achieved through the series of short phrases, suggests the sound of blows and rapid movement. The passage makes an interesting comparison with the battle scenes of *The Highlander*, where the debts to Pope were so pronounced. Although the echoes of Pope are still evident, here the overall effect is quite different. *The Highlander* seemed derivative because the echoes were contained in heroic couplets, but the style of the *Fragments* suggests early poetry: again, Macpherson's antique style disguised the text on which it drew.

Although Macpherson's verse lacked the regularity of rhyme, it is nevertheless unified by the rhythm and the careful use of internal rhymes. The two 'sounds' in the first line suggest repeated blows, which are then echoed in 'death bounds from mail to mail', implying that death is the direct result of the sword's action. The effect of the combat is also created through the use of closely paired words, 'mail to mail', 'rock to rock', 'blow to blow', while the driving force of the warriors is conveyed through the active verbs, 'they leap, they thrust, they wound'.

Macpherson's careful use of vocal patterns contributes to the consistency of the *Fragments* in a manner similar to the repetition of imagery and plot. Often, the assonance and alliteration give the poetry a lyrical quality, as in Shilric's address to Vinvela, quoted above (p 103), where the alliteration and internal rhymes (appears, beam, heath, me, speaks, weak, breeze, reeds; light, bright, like; autumn, sun, summer, comest;) echo through the passage, linking words to produce a wistful, almost musical, effect.[19] At the same time, the assonance seems to hint at a regular rhyme scheme, and thus emphasises the absence of such an order. Comparison can be made with the poetry of Wilfred Owen, and the melancholy effects achieved through his experiments with vowel sounds. Dominic Hibberd has suggested that Owen's use of half rhyme is particularly suitable for war poetry: 'since they produce an effect of dissonance and failure; we expect the rhyme to be completed and it is not'.[20] Paradoxically, the free verse intended to recreate the sponataneity of the early bard could also give the impression of decay, and a world in the process of disintegration.

Macpherson's use of half-rhymes is an important feature of the

Fragments. Shilric's speech, on the verge of his departure, is full of internal echoes:

> What voice is that I hear? that voice like the summer-wind – I sit not by the nodding rushes; I hear not the fount of the rock. Afar, Vinvela, afar I go to the wars of Fingal. My dogs attend me no more. No more I tread the hill. No more from on high I see thee, fair-moving by the stream of the plain; bright as the bow of heaven; as the moon on the western wave. (10)

The negatives run through the passage, accumulating force with each repetition and producing a deep sense of emptiness and denial. The feeling is increased by the half-rhymes, 'Afar . . . afar . . . war . . . no more . . . no more', which link the words that emphasise the cause of the despair : Shilric's departure. The repetition of the key words makes the passage read like a chant, to be continued in Vinvela's reply:

> Then thou art gone, O Shilric! and I am alone on the hill. The deer are seen on the brow; void of fear they graze along. No more they dread the wind; no more the rustling tree. (10)

The echoes and refrains suggest an arrangement of music, corresponding to the emotions of the speakers. The lyrical chants have a semi-hypnotic effect, drawing the reader into the intangible landscape where the characters are insubstantial voices in the wind.

The idea of voice is crucial to the *Fragments*. Vinvela's dissolution into a spirit is marked by the change in her speech: 'She speaks, but how weak her voice! like the breeze in the reeds of the pool' (14). Noise, on the other hand, is associated with physical strength, as in the description of the mighty Connal, 'Louder than a storm was thy voice' (24). Oscur's arrival on the battlefield, too, is distinguished by its loudness:

> Oscur my son came down; the mighty in battle descended. His armour rattled as thunder; and the lightning of his eyes was terrible. There, was the clashing of swords; there was the voice of steel. (29)

These deafening passages stand out because so much of the text is attended by silence. The final image of Shilric shows him listening for Vinvela's ghostly tones, in the silence of his surroundings (9). Just as noise is a symbol of life and energy, so silence is associated with death and decay. When Armyn witnesses the death of his daughter, who is stranded on a rock in the sea, her gradual demise is conveyed through the weakening of her voice:

Frequent and loud were her cries; nor could her father relieve her. All night I stood on the shore. I saw her by the faint beam of the moon. All night I heard her cries. Loud was the wind; and the rain beat hard on the side of the mountain. Before morning appeared, her voice was weak. It died away, like the-evening breeze among the grass of the rocks. Spent with grief she expired. (53–54)

For the blind bard, Ossian, sound is the principal channel of communication with the outside world. Fragment VIII shows him listening to the 'voice of the north', and the river 'murmuring hoarsely': noises which prompt him to compose a poem. The river, brings back the memory of the past and the voice of Ossian's father, which only increases Ossian's melancholy:

Such, Fingal! were thy words; but thy words I hear no more. Sightless I sit by thy tomb. I hear the wind in the wood; but no more I hear my friends. The cry of the hunter is over. The voice of war is ceased. (40)

Ossian's words echo those of his fellow mourners, bringing together all the brief tragedies in the lament for the passing of the heroic age. Like so many of the speakers in the *Fragments*, Ossian is the last survivor of his race. Fingal, the symbol of courage, chivalry, generosity and strength, has vanished at last, leaving only memories in the mind of his son.

Although Ossian creates a song to preserve the voice of Fingal, his own isolation and age give the poetry an air of fragility. The theme of voices becoming weaker is embodied in the aged bards, who recall the heroic society of their youth but are acutely conscious of their own decay. Soon their own voices will be as silent as those that now exist only in their memories. With no children to remember them, or to continue the songs of the Fein, the age of Fingal will vanish for ever.

Ossian's attempt to preserve the words of Fingal can be related to Macpherson's own efforts in the *Fragments of Ancient Poetry*. Like Ossian and the bards, Macpherson had heard the 'voices' of the heroic age in the local recitations of Highland poetry. Just as Ossian knew that the age of his father had passed, so Macpherson was aware that the traditional heroic verse was in danger of extinction. By collecting the vestiges of the Fenian poetry, Macpherson was preserving the memory of Fingal, just as Ossian spent his days recreating the deeds of the heroes.

Although the bards of the *Fragments* are conscious of being the faded relics of an heroic age, they are given a more prominent role than the heroes themselves. Fingal, Oscar, Dermid and the other warriors belong to a greater age that has already disappeared, but

Ossian, Carryl and Alpin are left to witness the final extinction of their world. As a young man, Macpherson might be expected to identify with the energetic heroes, but instead his sympathies seem to lie with the old men.

The prominence of the declining speakers is symptomatic of Macpherson's own sense of malaise, as a Highlander and as a poet of the mid eighteenth century. As a Highlander, the regret caused by the destruction of his traditional society is obvious in the mournful elegies of the bards. As a modern poet, the relationship is less apparent, but the despair is equally profound. Just as the songs of the bards were memorials, inspired by the past, so Macpherson's creation was entirely backward looking. He had failed to find an original voice in the world of contemporary poetry, so his identity was now submerged in that of a bard who was long since dead. The contemporary pursuit of the past as an emotional outlet tended to result in work which lacked hope or vitality and Macpherson's attempts to restore the poetry to an 'original purity' were constantly undermined by his own sense of being the last in a line of Gaelic bards. Instead of purity, his work had a certain sterility, while the fragmentary form emphasised the decay.

Just as the bards were relics of a greater age, so the *Fragments* seemed to be the broken remains of the heroic tradition, through which the reader was invited to imagine the great original. Unlike the Romantic idea of poetry charged with 'something evermore about to be',[21] Macpherson's *Fragments* suggested that something greater had already been, which could not be redeemed. Although Blair praised the *Fragments* as examples of early verse, William Hazlitt's assessment of the Ossianic works as the 'old age' of poetry was rather more perceptive and sheds greater light on the popularity of *Ossian* in the latter half of the eighteenth century.[22]

NOTES
1. *The Correspondence of Thomas Gray*, ed. Paget Toynbee & L. Whibley, rev. edn, H. W. Starr, 3 vols, (Oxford 1935), II, 679–80.
2. Fragment XIII of the October edition had not appeared in June, and there were a few minor alterations which suggest an attempt to make the poems more 'poetical'. References are to the facsimile of the second edition, (Edinburgh 1970).
3. R. Schmitz, *Hugh Blair*, (New York 1948), 44.
4. See H. Blair, *Lectures on Rhetoric and Belles Lettres*, 2 vols, (London 1783), Lecture 37; J. Beattie, 'An Essay on Poetry and Music', 1762, *Essays*, (Edinburgh 1776), 64–5.
5. *Halliford Edition of the Works of Thomas Love Peacock*, ed. H. F. B.

Brett-Smith & C. E. Jones, 10 vols, (London & New York 1924–34), VIII, 11.
6. Cf. Hazlitt, 'Scotland is of all other countries in the world perhaps the one in which the question "What is the use of that?" is asked oftenest. But where this is the case, the Fine Arts cannot flourish', *Complete Works*, XVIII, 167. See also Adam Smith, *Lectures on Rhetoric*, 131.
7. Blair, op. cit., II, 417.
8. W. Wilkie, *The Epigoniad*, (Edinburgh 1757), vii–viii.
9. Cf. Collins 'Ode on the Popular Superstitions of the Highlands', Gray, 'The Bard'. See also P. Spacks, *The Insistence of Horror: Aspects of the Supernatural in Eighteenth-Century Poetry*, (Cambridge Mass. 1962).
10. Blair regarded Lucan as the third great poet of the classical world, coming after Homer and Virgil, op. cit., II, 451.
11. Lucan, *Pharsalia*, translated by R. Graves, (Harmondsworth 1956), 23–4.
12. Among the chief objections held by Celtic scholars against Macpherson is his introduction of the popular idea of the Celtic mind as 'mysterious and magical', K. H. Jackson, *A Celtic Miscellany*, rev. edn, (Harmondsworth 1971), 19.
13. The only reference to a recognisable location occurs in Fragment XI: 'Daura, my daughter! thou wert fair; fair as the moon on the hills of Jura' (51). The simile is obviously introduced because of the similarity between Daura and Jura.
14. See also 29, 38, 39, 50. Various natural objects acquire symbolic significance, e.g. the cairns which are associated with poetic memorials to the heroes.
15. The fragment is No XIV in the first edition. It was subsequently included in *Fingal*, 7–10.
16. The Fragment was incorporated into *Fingal*, 45–46. It was based on a traditional ballad, which survives in several of the Gaelic collections. See Thomson, *Gaelic Sources*, 29–31.
17. Lowth, *Lectures on . . . the Hebrew*, 138–39.
18. Lamentations, I, 2. On the recurrent image of the grieving woman in contemporary history painting, see Rosenblum, *Transformations in late Eighteenth-Century Art*, (Princeton 1967).
19. The effect was increased in the second edition by the addition of 'Comest thou lovely maid over rocks, over mountains to me?'
20. Wilfred Owen, *War Poems and Others*, ed. D. Hibberd, (London 1973), 34.
21. Wordsworth, *The Prelude*, 1805, VI, 542.
22. Hazlitt, *Complete Works*, V, 15–18.

The Highland Tours

> The Fragments, upon their first appearance, were so much approved of, that several people of rank, as well as taste, prevailed with me to make a journey into the Highlands and western isles, in order to recover what remained of the works of the old bards, especially those of Ossian, the son of Fingal, who was the best, as well as most ancient, of those who are celebrated in tradition for their poetical genius. – I undertook this journey, more from a desire of complying with the request of my friends, than from any hopes I had of answering their expectations. I was not unsuccessful, considering how much the compositions of ancient times have been neglected, for some time past, in the north of Scotland. Several gentlemen in the Highlands and Isles generously gave me all the assistance in their power; and it was by their means I was enabled to compleat the epic poem.
>
> James Macpherson, *Fingal*, preface

Macpherson's publication of the *Fragments of Ancient Poetry* met with immediate success. The ground had been well prepared by his influential patrons in Edinburgh, who had sent examples of the newly discovered poetry to various English writers, prior to publication. When the small volume actually appeared, the vague interest in Gaelic poetry turned into a warm enthusiasm, shared by academics and general readers alike. Extracts from the *Fragments*, together with Blair's preface, were published not only in the *Scots Magazine*, but also South of the border, in the *Gentleman's Magazine*. The popular response can be seen in the July editions of the journals, which included new versions of the *Fragments*, submitted by poets anxious to turn the simple measured prose of Macpherson's translations into poems with regular verses and rhyme schemes.[1] The *Fragments* were attracting attention throughout Britain, and with this success came the demand for more ancient poetry.

Nowhere was interest more intense than in Edinburgh. Not only did the *Fragments* show that Scotland had a literary heritage far more ancient than anything England could claim, but the preface hinted that, somewhere in the remote Highlands, the great national epic might be found.

Never could the idea of a Scottish epic have been more welcome than in 1760. The men who had first encouraged Macpherson to translate his Gaelic verse were in the forefront of a general drive to improve Scottish arts. John Home's controversial tragedy, *Douglas*, 1757, proclaimed the importance of Athenian 'learning, and the love of every art', and drew a direct parallel between Greece and Scotland.[2] This admiration for the multi-faceted genius of Athens was shared by David Hume and other members of the Select Society, who were all keen to promote improvements, both practical and cultural.[3] The desire to encourage Scottish literature, in particular, can be seen in projects such as the *Edinburgh Review*, a literary journal founded in 1755, which was designed to make Scotland 'distinguished for letters'.[4] The very purpose of the *Review*, however, reveals the deep sense of insecurity that undermined Scottish authors, even as it provided the challenge to 'improve'. Despite the apparent confidence of the literati, an uncomfortable feeling of literary inferiority to England, compounded by embarrassment about the Scottish language, prevailed in Edinburgh. The idea of a Scottish Homer, who might redeem the national poetry, was almost too good to be true.

The pervasive feelings of inferiority became particularly acute during the Seven Years War, as the Scottish people realised that they were now defenceless, and thus dependent on England for survival. Macpherson's *Fragments of Ancient Poetry* appeared in June 1760, only a few months after Admiral Thurot's alarming offensive on the West coast. The need for a national militia seemed desperate and it is perhaps not surprising to find that the men most anxious to establish Scotland's literary supremacy were also in the vanguard of the militia campaign.[5] Between 1757 and 1762 strenuous efforts were made to persuade the Government of the need for proper defences in North Britain. The Edinburgh literati formed a special society known as the Poker Club, 'to stir up' the issue, as well as devoting their energies to political satires such as *Sister Peg*, which attacked the defeat of the Militia Bill.[6] These were the men who were also closely involved with Macpherson's work: John Home, Adam Ferguson, Alexander Carlyle and David Hume.

By aggravating the sense of inferiority to England, the militia question provided an extra spur to literary activity: Macpherson's own 'epic', *The Highlander*, can be seen as a response to contemporary circumstances. Although *The Highlander* failed to attract the attention of the Edinburgh critics, the general need for a national epic can be seen in the enthusiasm that greeted William Wilkie's turgid effort, *The Epigoniad*, in 1757.[7] Wilkie was immediately hailed as the 'Scottish Homer' but his poem, set in ancient Greece and largely derived from Pope's *Homer*, could hardly satisfy the demands for a national epic. The sudden discovery that Scotland had her own ancient bard and that a true epic might still be recovered, filled the Edinburgh literati with a determination to find out more.

Blair's preface did much to excite interest in the Highland epic, but Macpherson also appears to have been voluble on the subject. One of David Hume's letters is full of a conversation he had had about the Gaelic poetry:

> I remember Mr Macpherson told me, that the heroes of this Highland epic were not only, like Homer's heroes, their own butchers, bakers, and cooks, but also their own shoemakers, carpenters, and smiths. He mentioned an incident which put this matter in a remarkable light. A warrior had the head of his spear struck off in a battle; upon which he immediately retires behind the army, where a forge was erected; makes a new one; hurries back to the action; pierces his enemy, while the iron, which was yet red-hot, hisses in the wound.[8]

Macpherson's vivid accounts of the Celtic warriors clearly succeeded in firing the imagination of Hume and his colleagues. He also convinced them that he knew people still living in the Highlands who could recite the heroic poetry from memory. Hume's letter contains an enthusiastic reference to an old surgeon in Lochaber:

> This surgeon has by heart the epic poem mentioned by Mr Macpherson in his preface; and as he is somewhat old, and is the only person living that has it entire, we are in the more haste to recover a monument, which will certainly be regarded as a curiosity in the Republic of Letters.[9]

Hume had caught not only Macpherson's enthusiasm about the poetry, but also his anxiety about its extinction. If the only people who could recite the epic were old men, there was no time to lose: it must be recovered before it vanished for ever.

Hugh Blair had been involved with Macpherson's work from the moment Home and Carlyle arrived in Edinburgh with the first translations. Once the *Fragments* appeared in June 1760, he wasted no time in urging Macpherson to set off on a journey through the Highlands and Islands in search of longer pieces and, in particular, the lost epic of Fingal.

This, surely, was the opportunity for fame and fortune that Macpherson had desired for so long? And yet, Blair's request met with a cool response. Rather than rush straight to Edinburgh to embark on the next venture, Macpherson remained in Balgowan where he was still working as a tutor, and sent the following reply:

> None would be more willing to undertake the work you and others, my friends, recommend, did it suit with my interests than I. I certainly admire the poetry of my country much; and would

> with eagerness seize on any opportunity to make its beauties known.
>
> But, Sir, a journey thro' the Highlands and Isles is attended with risque and Expence that are not proper for me to incur on my own Bottom.
>
> I would be obliged to throw up the business I pursue; devote myself for twelve month, at least to that work, and, besides my travelling expences, be obliged to gratify some persons who are in possession of the original poems.
>
> All which put together makes it too great a venture for me to go on such a design without some assistance and encouragement. Did all things answer I could make a large, and I hope valuable, collection of our ancient poetry; but as I cannot well spare the expence and time I must give over all thoughts of the matter.
>
> It were to be wished however that these remains of genius were not lost, And I am extreamly sorry it does not suit with my present circumstances to have the pleasure of preserving them.[10]

Macpherson's reason for objecting to Blair's scheme is obvious: he had no money. The idea obviously appealed to him, but he realised at once that such an extensive research project would involve a considerable financial outlay, which he was quite unable to make. It would also entail giving up his job and the small income he earned as a tutor.

Macpherson's letter was very effective. Blair grasped the problem at once and was determined not to be thwarted by mere financial considerations. He wrote immediately to David Dalrymple, who had shown great interest in the first Fragments, proposing that money should be raised for 'the making of a further Collection of Erse poetry and in particular for recovering our Epics'.[11] The call of the epic never failed to rally support, so Blair arranged a dinner party in Edinburgh, inviting Macpherson together with the men who were most anxious that the Scottish epics should be found. Everyone was happy to contribute 'a guinea or two guineas apiece' and eventually Macpherson agreed to accept the challenge.[12] Although raising money for the enterprise was a simple matter, the task of fulfilling the demands for an epic was to prove more difficult.

Macpherson set off on his journey in August 1760, accompanied for at least part of the trip by his kinsman, Lachlan Macpherson of Strathmashie. Strathmashie was an ideal travelling companion, being 'a gentleman of classical education, well known in the Highlands on account of his poetical genius and agreeable and polished manners'.[13] He was popular, charming, and could jot down poems from oral recitation as well as being able to help on the transcription of old Gaelic manuscripts. He also had a good reputation as a Gaelic poet, which would have made the two travellers especially welcome as they arrived in the remoter parts of the Highlands.[14] For James Macpherson, who was still only twenty three, Strathmashie must have provided conversation and general moral support on a journey that demanded great effort, both physical and psychological.

The aim of Macpherson's first trip was to travel through the Highlands to Skye and the Outer Hebrides, collecting poetry from oral recitals and in manuscripts. The Islands, being furthest from the contaminating influences of the Lowlands, were considered the home of the purest Gaelic, and the most likely place to find any ancient poetry that might still exist. Macpherson would almost certainly have been aware of the reference to 'antient Irish manuscripts' in Martin's description of Benbecula, and therefore keen to retrieve them if possible.[15] Benbecula was also the home of the MacMhuirichs, the last family of hereditary bards who were part of the Clanranald household and who would have passed traditional poetry down through many generations. In the Isle of Skye, too, Macpherson planned to visit his namesake, Dr John Macpherson of Sleat, who was a recognised authority on Celtic antiquities.

Although the exact itinerary of Macpherson's travels is difficult to ascertain, valuable details about the people and places he visited survive in the letters collected during the investigations into the authenticity of *Ossian*. We know, for example, that he visited the home of Donald Macleod, the minister of Glenelg, where he took down a 'description of Cuchullin's horse and car from Allan MacCaskie and Rory Macleod'.[16] Macpherson later described his venture as a 'peregrination of six months',[17] but during this period he made more than one tour.

The first, and most important journey, to the North West Highlands and Islands lasted about two months, because by 27 October 1760, Macpherson was back in Ruthven writing letters about his discoveries.[18] He was already planning a second trip to Mull and the coast of Argyll, but this was to prove disappointing. Apparently, Macpherson was unimpressed by the recitations he heard in Mull, and although a well known local poet was brought a considerable distance to entertain him, 'he was not at the trouble of committing to paper anything of what was recited to him'.[19] Since we do not know the dates of Macpherson's trip to Mull, it may have been the journey he made in the company of John Home, in June 1761. Home's excitement can be felt in the letter he wrote to Bute:

> I set out tomorrow with the highland bard to visit those regions that nursed the genius of Ossian and to gather if I can some of nature's gems, to adorn Rivine the daughter of Kew . . . I shall write to you my Lord from the top of Ardven and let you know how the oak flourishes in Morven and how fair the moon rises over the waves of Mologaichen.[20]

The journey was obviously intended to furnish Home with first-hand details for his own Ossianic tragedy, *The Fatal Discovery*. As *Fingal* was ready for the press by November, it seems unlikely that Macpherson collected any material for his first epic on the trip, although he may already have been working on *Temora*.

There is also evidence to suggest that at some stage, Macpherson went to visit Thomas Fraser, the Minister of Boleskine, on the shores of Loch Ness. Macpherson was introduced to the Minister through his old employer, Graham of Balgowan, and is said to have received a considerable collection of Gaelic poems from Fraser.[21] The collection was reputedly made by ancestors of the Fraser family, who had been Deans of the Isles, and it seems likely that Macpherson acquired the most important manuscript in his collection from Boleskine – *The Book of the Dean of Lismore*.[22]

The information that has survived about Macpherson's travels relates chiefly to his first journey to Skye and the Outer Hebrides. Although Macpherson is reported to have collected 'the bulk of his materials in the shires of Inverness, Perth and Argyll' before crossing to the Isles, he was still 'anxious to collect additional matter, and various editions of the same poems'.[23] As a consequence, he set off round Skye, interviewing anyone who could recite Gaelic poetry and persuading others to part with their manuscripts.

Once in Skye, Macpherson enjoyed great hospitality staying at homes such as that of Captain Morrison, who later described the manuscripts Macpherson had collected, venturing the opinion that they had come from Donald MacQueen, the minister of Kilmuir.[24] MacQueen's own account of Macpherson's visit includes no such evidence, but the Minister was nevertheless responsible for directing Macpherson to another important source – Alexander Macpherson, the blacksmith in Portree.[25]

Macpherson spent some four days with the blacksmith, a visit which made a considerable impact on his host family. The description left by Alexander's brother, Malcolm, gives us an invaluable glimpse of the translator at work. Apparently, Alexander had a thick manuscript, in quarto, full of Fingalian poems which he had picked up in Lochcarron. Once Macpherson knew of the manuscript and heard that Alexander knew the poems by heart, he lost little time:

> Mr Macpherson observed that, as the declarant's brother could repeat the whole of the poems contained in the said manuscript, he would oblige him if he would give him the said manuscript, for which he might expect friendship and future reward.[26]

Alexander promptly gave up the manuscript and never saw it again, a move that failed to impress his father. Malcolm's recollections of Macpherson's visit include the 'very severe reprimand' that his brother received from their father 'for spending so much time with Mr

Macpherson'. He also recalled Alexander's defence: 'that he found Mr Macpherson so very kind, and being a namesake, that he could not resist his solicitations'.[27]

Malcolm Macpherson's account helps to explain James' success as a collector: not only was he a Highlander (and in this case, of the same Clan), but he was also extremely persuasive. At this point, the experience of the nineteenth-century Gaelic collector, J. F. Campbell, is illuminating. In his introduction to the *Popular Tales of the West Highlands*, Campbell described the difficulties faced by strangers who wished to hear the stories of the Highlanders:

> Highland peasants and fishermen . . . are shy and proud, and even more peculiarly sensitive to ridicule than peasants elsewhere. Many have a lurking belief in the truth of the stories which they tell, and a rooted conviction that any one with a better education will laugh at the belief, and the story, and the narrator, and his language, if he should be weak enough to venture on English, and betray his knowledge of Sgeultachd and his creed. He cannot imagine that any one out of his own class can possibly be amused by his frivolous pastimes. No one ever has hitherto.[28]

Campbell found that the initial resistance could be overcome only through speaking Gaelic, which established confidence and encouraged the speaker. He was born in Islay in 1822, and attributed his own success as a collector to his background: 'I spoke Gaelic, and answered questions. I am one of themselves, so I got on famously'.[29]

Although Macpherson was not a native of the Isles, he was a Highlander and therefore in a good position to establish rapport with those he interviewed. As a Gaelic speaker, he mixed easily with the people he visited, so that they would feel no embarrassment about reciting poems for him. Indeed, he had been familiar with recitations of Gaelic verse since his childhood, so he knew how to listen attentively to the heroic tales. His own charisma and youthful enthusiasm also helped him persuade the Islanders to relinquish their manuscripts, while the pressure he was under from Edinburgh must have made him very persistent in his requests.

The novelty of Macpherson's mission intrigued the residents of the Scottish Islands and he attracted interest and generous assistance throughout his journey. He seems to have had little difficulty in persuading people to recite verse for him or, indeed, to copy down poems from Gaelic speakers on his behalf, as Colin MacFarquhar recalled:

> It is perfectly within my recollection, that about forty years ago . . . when I was living in the Highlands of Scotland, that the late Mr Macpherson, the reputed translator of Ossian's Poems, took a

tour then through the Highlands, with the professed design of possessing himself of as many of the Poems of Ossian as he could possibly find, and at the same time had applied to his friends in other parts, to assist him with as many of these poems as he could procure; among others, he accosted a co-presbyter of mine . . . who, knowing that a man of distinguished celebrity in that way, had resided in my congregation, he requested the favour of me, to have an interview with him, and to take down in writing, one or two of these poems from his lips; which I did; but cannot recollect, at this distance of time, the name of the Poems, though I well remember they were lengthy, and irksome to me to write, as it is difficult to spell the Gaelic, Celtic or Irish language, on account of the many mute or quiescent letters contained in almost every word.[30]

It is interesting to learn that J. F. Campbell experienced similar problems: 'It was easy to write English versions of the tales heard in Gaelic, but I wanted the Gaelic as it was told, and I had neither the time nor ability to write it down myself'.[31] Campbell's solution was to employ two reliable Highlanders to collect and transcribe the tales from native speakers. Where possible, Macpherson seems to have done the same, and the letter quoted above gives a good indication of how he made the most of his Highland connections.

Throughout his travels Macpherson received generous help from numerous friends and acquaintances. Colin MacFarquhar's contribution was probably only one of many and Macpherson had various travelling companions at different stages of his journey. Strathmashie was an invaluable colleague, but travelled with Macpherson only on the mainland. Once in Skye, Macpherson was lucky enough to run across Ewan Macpherson, a knowledgeable Highland scholar, who accompanied him for another three or four weeks.

Ewan Macpherson had been the tutor to Dr John Macpherson's sons and was visiting the family at Ostaig, on the Sleat peninsula, when James arrived.[32] Dr Macpherson gave the young translator a warm welcome and furnished him with a number of papers concerning the Celts.[33] He undoubtedly regaled Macpherson with his memories of the old bard, MacMhuirich, who had travelled through the Islands thirty years earlier, reciting Ossianic poems from an old Gaelic manuscript.[34] The Minister of Sleat was keen for Macpherson to visit the MacMhuirichs in Benbecula, and he also urged Ewan to join James, because of Ewan's superior knowledge of Gaelic orthography.

Although Ewan Macpherson had no particular desire to spend his summer tramping through the Highlands with James, he agreed to accompany him as far as Dunvegan. Once he had embarked on the journey, however, he found it difficult to extract himself from the enterprise:

The Highland Tours

when he reached that place (Dunvegan), he was in a manner compulsively obliged by Colonel Macleod of Talisker, and the late Mr McLean of Coll, to embark with Mr Macpherson for Uist on the same pursuit.[35]

Despite his reluctance, Ewan Macpherson made an extremely valuable contribution to Macpherson's work. During the month he spent travelling, Ewan took down poems from various speakers and gave the transcriptions to Macpherson, who 'was seldom present when they were taken down'.[36] Although they made extensive enquiries, however, and collected versions of various poems, Ewan recalled that they 'did not meet with any person capable of repeating much of them in a connected story'.[37]

When they finally reached Benbecula, the two Macphersons spent a week with the younger Clanranald, working on the old family manuscripts. According to Andrew Gallie, who assisted Macpherson with his materials when he returned to Badenoch in October, the visit to Benbecula was particularly rewarding:

> I inquired the success of his journey, and he produced several volumes, small octavo, or rather large duodecimo, in the Gaelic language and characters, being the poems of Ossian, and other ancient bards.
>
> I remember perfectly, that many of these volumes were, at the close, said to have been collected by Paul MacMhuirich Bard Clanraonuil, and about the beginning of the fourteenth century. Mr Macpherson and I were of opinion, that though the bard collected them, yet they must have been writ by an ecclesiastic, for the characters and spellings were most beautiful and correct. Every poem had its first letter of its first word most elegantly flourished and gilded; some red, some yellow, some blue, and some green; the material writ on seemed to be a limber, yet coarse and dark vellum: the volumes were bound in strong parchment: Mr Macpherson had them from Clanronald.[38]

There is some confusion over how many manuscripts Macpherson acquired in Benbecula, and Ewan Macpherson described only one in any detail.[39] In a letter of 1763, however, Angus MacNeill of South Uist described hearing Neil MacMhuirich repeat the 'whole of the poem of Darthula, or Clan-Usnoch' from a manuscript, as well as seeing the bard deliver four or five more manuscripts to James Macpherson.[40] When asked by the Highland Society in 1800, Lachlan MacMhuirich remembered his father being 'forced' by Clanranald to give Macpherson the 'Leabhar Dearg' (Red Book), which contained both Highland history and Ossianic poetry.[41] Although it is impossible to identify the actual manuscripts collected in Benbecula, Macpherson's visit there was evidently very profitable.

MacMhuirich's reference to his father being 'forced' to yield up his precious manuscript gives the impression that Macpherson was some sort of confidence trickster, obtaining manuscripts against the will of the owners. Before jumping to such conclusions, it is important to grasp the general attitude to old Gaelic books in the eighteenth century. After describing the collection of manuscripts his father had inherited from his ancestors, Lachlan MacMhuirich declared

> That none of these books are to be found this day because when they were deprived of their lands they lost their spirit and zeal – He is not certain what has become of the parchment but only thinks some of them were carried away by Alexander Macdonald . . . and others by Ranold Macdonald . . . and that he had seen one or two of them cut down by Taylors in order to make . . . measures with . . . that he himself had some of the skins or parchments in his custody after his father's death, but that because he had not been taught to read them, and had no cause to set any value on them, they were lost.[42]

The changes that had taken place in the Highlands meant that much of the traditional culture was threatened with extinction. With the collapse of the bardic order and the steady erosion of the Clan system, the practice of preserving history and poetry through generations of successive bards had disappeared. MacMhuirich's description of seeing ancient manuscripts being chopped up for tailors' measures highlights the importance of Macpherson's efforts at preservation. Although he was not at all scrupulous about returning the manuscripts to their owners, Macpherson undoubtedly saved many irreplaceable works from disappearing altogether. MacDonald of Clanranald, for example, admitted that Macpherson

> had the Gaelic manuscripts from him, and that he did not know them to exist, till, to gratify Mr Macpherson, a search was made among his family papers. Clanronald added that since Mr Macpherson's visit, more volumes were recovered.[43]

Without Macpherson's visit, these manuscripts might well have shared the fate of those described by MacMhuirich or of the Farquharson manuscript, which was full of Ossianic poems but fell into the hands of non-Gaelic speakers, and was used to kindle fires.[44]

Whatever charges can be levelled at Macpherson, then, his collection of Gaelic material was of great importance. Although some of the manuscripts collected by Macpherson may have been lost, nineteen were delivered to the Highland Society after his death.[45] Not only did he save a large number of manuscripts from destruction, but he also drew attention to the value of the ancient poetry. Suddenly people like Clanranald were aware that the old books that had been lying around the house for years had some importance and should not be

The Highland Tours 123

destroyed. Once the translation of Ossian was published, and the controversy over its authenticity ensued, both Highlanders and Lowlanders began to recognise the importance of the old Gaelic poetry and the manuscripts in which it was recorded.

Although Macpherson succeeded in gathering an extensive collection of Gaelic poetry, the business of selection and translation was by no means straightforward. He was a native speaker, but not a Gaelic scholar, and appears to have been largely ignorant of Gaelic orthography, so much of the manuscript material was completely inaccessible. Macpherson explained the problem in the letter he wrote to James Maclagan, thanking him for part of his collection:

> It is true, I have most of them from other hands, but the misfortune is, that I have found none expert in the Irish orthography, so that an obscure poem is rendered doubly so, by their uncouth way of spelling.[46]

Macpherson had returned to Badenoch with a large collection of almost unreadable manuscripts and numerous poems jotted down from the lips of Highland speakers. From this perplexing mixture of sources, he had now to recover the lost epic of Scotland.

Macpherson was not to be beaten, and he turned to his friend, the Revd Andrew Gallie, for help in tackling the problem. Macpherson's arrival at the Manse in Brae Badenoch made a considerable impression on the young Mrs Gallie, who could still remember it years later:

> Mr Macpherson returned to the Manse with two Ponies laden with old Manuscripts . . . Mr Gallie and he were employed in their perusal in study for six weeks during which period I seldom enjoyed the society of my husband.[47]

Later, Gallie himself wrote a series of letters describing the work which had taken place in his house in the autumn of 1760:

> At that time I could read the Gaelic characters, though with difficulty, and did often amuse myself with reading here and there in those poems, while Mr Macpherson was employed on his translation. At times we differed as to the meaning of certain words in the original.[48]

The translation appears to have been something of a corporate effort, because Strathmashie was also making contributions. According to Gallie, he was 'well known for an uncommon acquaintance with the Gaelic, and a happy facility in writing it in Roman characters', so he could give great assistance in the tricky task of transliterating the manuscripts.[49] As an accomplished poet, Strathmashie may also have been responsible for some of the embellishments which appeared in the final publication.[50]

The attitude towards James Macpherson which emerges in Gallie's letters is of particular interest. Gallie's admiration for his friend can be discerned clearly in his description of Macpherson's treatment of the seemingly incomprehensible manuscripts:

> I recollect (it was often matter of conversation), that by worm-eating, and other injuries of time, there were here and there whole words, yea lines, so obscured, as not to be read; and I, to whom this was then better known than to any one else, one excepted, gave great credit to Mr Macpherson; concluding, that if he did not recover the very words and ideas of Ossian that the substitution did no discredit to that celebrated bard, and this . . . I then considered as one of Mr Macpherson's chief excellencies.[51]

It is not difficult to imagine Macpherson piecing together his 'translation' with guesses and creative substitution, while his host applauded his inspirations. Gallie seems to have been more impressed by Macpherson's own contributions to the 'ancient' poetry than by the genuine Gaelic material.

Macpherson's own contempt for the existing remains of the heroic poetry could be seen in the earlier discussion of the *Fragments*. Gallie's description of the translator at work sheds further light on Macpherson's attitude to his manuscripts:

> I remember Mr Macpherson reading the MSS. found in Clanronald's, execrating the bard himself who dictated to the amanuensis, saying, 'D—n the scoundrel, it is he himself that now speaks, and not Ossian.' This took place in my house, in two or three instances: I thence conjecture that the MSS. were kept up, lest they should fall under the view of such as would be more ready to publish their deformities than to point out their beauties.
>
> It was, and I believe still is well known, that the broken poems of Ossian, handed down from one generation to another, got corrupted. In the state of the Highlands, and its language, this evil, I apprehend, could not be avoided; and I think great credit is due . . . to him who restores a work of great merit to its original purity.[52]

Macpherson's indignation at the bard's interpolations is somewhat ironic, considering his own treatment of the manuscripts. Gallie's anecdote nevertheless shows that Macpherson regarded the poems in the books he had collected as corrupt versions of ancient poetry. There is no suggestion that he regarded the manuscripts as being contemporary with Ossian, but rather that the poems, which had been transmitted through the oral tradition, were eventually committed to writing. Macpherson's anger was directed at the unknown bard who had dared to alter Ossian's poems, instead of preserving the original compositions. With such a view, he felt quite justified in his attempts at 'restoration', and in the dissertation on *Temora*, referred openly to his method of piecing together the Gaelic remains: 'The story of the poem, with which I had long been acquainted, enabled me to reduce the broken members of the piece in the order in which they now appear' (*Temora*, xviii).

Macpherson had already developed the style which he considered appropriate to ancient literature when working on the *Fragments*. The success of the volume reassured him that the quasi-Biblical diction was indeed the best for translating old Gaelic poetry, so he set about the new presentation using a similar style. He also had preconceived ideas about the genre of the new poem, influenced by the knowledge that his patrons were expecting him to have retrieved an epic. The fact that the poems he had collected were not epic in style or structure was only a minor stumbling block: they were, after all, the 'broken poems of Ossian'. As such, they could be refined, pieced together with connecting passages, and presented to the English-reading public in their 'original purity'.

Macpherson's treatment of the Gaelic material collected during his travels in the Highlands has been debated at great length. Almost as soon as *Fingal* appeared, the question of authenticity was raised and the subject has continued to provoke heated arguments ever since. The first really objective study was the *Report of the Highland Society's Committee* in 1805, which published information collected over several years from Gaelic scholars and residents of North West Scotland. The Highland Society announced to the sceptical world that Ossianic poetry not only existed in the Highlands, but was 'common, general, and in great abundance; that it was of a most impressive and striking sort, in a high degree eloquent, tender and sublime'.[53] Although the Committee had found poems which corresponded almost literally to passages in Macpherson's *Ossian*, however, they were unable to obtain 'any one poem the same in title and tenor with the poems published by him'. In conclusion, the Committee was

> inclined to believe that he was in use to supply chasms, and to give connection, by inserting passages which he did not find, and to add what he conceived to be dignity and delicacy to the original composition, by softening incidents, by refining the language . . . To what degree, however, he exercised these liberties it is impossible for the committee to determine.[54]

The Highland Society pointed out that the recent changes which had taken place in the Highlands had caused much of the traditional poetry to disappear, but the verdict was that Macpherson had altered and added passages according to his own taste in literature. The Gaelic poetry had been assembled into an epic structure, bowdlerised and refined for an English audience.

Half a century later, J. F. Campbell was to reach similar conclusions, though he expressed them in a rather less sympathetic way.

Campbell saw Macpherson's *Ossian* as similar to the works of John and Donald Smith, who used fragments of old Gaelic ballads to compose a new form of poetry.[55] Nevertheless, even Campbell admitted that although the Smiths 'worked up' the ballads into their own compositions, 'they believed their work to be genuine'.[56] Ideas of authenticity had changed since the 1760s and when Campbell set to work on the heroic ballads of the Highlands, his approach was totally different from Macpherson's. In *Leabhar na Féinne*, Campbell printed all the existing versions of different Gaelic poems which he found in the various collections. The published work thus enabled the reader to compare different versions of the same ballad, rather than having to accept an editor's decision on the quality of the poems.

While *Leabhar na Féinne* was an invaluable contribution to Gaelic studies, much of it remains inaccessible to the non-Gaelic speaker. Campbell himself was well aware of the popular appeal of Macpherson's *Ossian*, which he compared to a Greek hut, built from materials both ancient and modern:

> Macpherson's Ossian, like the Greek hut, is, in the main, composed of genuine materials, and a clever antiquary or a good critic, might yet pick out all the old fragments, and may be arrange them more scientifically . . . The Greek hut, with all its incongruities, dirt, discomfort, with its dress of shrubs and lichens, and utter disregard for the rules of architecture, is more likely to attract the painter's eye than the most symmetrical museum of antiquities, geology, and botany . . . and so Ossian has attracted the notice and the admiration of famous men, who would not have bestowed a thought upon popular tales and ballads separately arranged, and classed in due order, as I have striven to do with my stores.[57]

Campbell adopted the orderly methods of the scholar, but he could still recognise the popular appeal of Macpherson's more imaginative approach. Macpherson made no attempt to produce accurate transliterations of genuine Gaelic material, because the original ballads seemed to him crude and unsuitable for the delicate appetites of the Edinburgh literati. While the existence of variant versions seemed important to Campbell, for Macpherson, the variations indicated that all the existing poems were corruptions of Ossian's original. While Campbell printed each version in turn, Macpherson took only the gist of each tale, selecting passages from different sources according to his own judgement.

Campbell recognised that 'a clever antiquary or good critic' might be able to identify the genuine material in *Ossian*, but the task was not accomplished for almost a century. Ludwig Stern's vigorous attack drew attention to the genuine ballads at the turn of the century, but the full examination did not appear until 1952 when Derick Thomson published *The Gaelic Sources of Macpherson's Ossian*.[58] Thomson's conclusion was similar to those of the Highland Society and J. F. Campbell: Macpherson tended to use the story of a Gaelic poem, but adapted it freely to his own peculiar style. Thomson's work is very important in that it compares specific passages of Macpherson's *Ossian* with passages from the ballads in the Gaelic collections. In the discussion of *Fingal*, for example, he shows how Macpherson fused elements from the 'Garbh mac Stairn' and 'Magnus' ballads for the main plot, incorporating separate ballads such as 'The Maid of Craca' as episodes. In some cases, such as 'The Battle of Lora', Macpherson's plot comes close to the original, but Thomson points out that 'literal translation is never to be expected from Macpherson except in isolated phrases'.[59]

Although Thomson's approach is primarily that of a Celtic scholar, his work sheds light on Macpherson's general literary development. He draws an interesting parallel, for example, between Macpherson's description of Cuchullin's reply to Swaran in *Fingal*, and a similar passage in Stone's version of 'Magnus':

> But never shall a stranger have the lovely sun-beam of
> Dunscaich, or ever deer fly on Lochlin's hills before
> the nimble footed Luath.   (*Fingal*, 26)

> Choidhe cha tugamsa mo Bhean
> Do dh'aon neach a ta fuidh'n Ghrein
> 'S cha mho mheir mi Bran gu brath
> Gus an teid am Bas 'na Bheil.

> (Never shall I give my wife to any man under the sun,
> nor shall I ever give away Bran until death comes to
> him.)[60]

Although it is impossible to make absolute judgements about Macpherson's use of material gathered from oral sources, the difference between his prose and the Gaelic ballad in Stone's collection is quite plain. The terse statement of the Gaelic poem has become softened in Macpherson's version, with the description of Cuchullin's wife as 'the lovely sun-beam of Dunscaich' and of his dog as 'nimble-footed'. Instead of a simple statement that the dog will not be given away, Macpherson conjured up an image of deer flying on Lochlin's hills as a consequence of the dog becoming Viking property. Throughout his translations, Macpherson introduced a vein of sentimentality and wistful lyricism that is not to be found in the original Gaelic.

When Macpherson altered the actual plots of the Gaelic poems, he showed a similar tendency to romanticise the events. Fingal's visit to Norway (*Fingal*, III) resembles accounts which occur in two ballads from the collections of MacNicol and Fletcher.[61] The ballads describe

Finn's invitation to Norway from the King of Lochlin's daughter, and the great feast he attends there. He and his men are then ambushed, but they manage to overthrow their treacherous host and take him back to Ireland as a prisoner. In Macpherson's version of the story, the King's daughter, Agendecca, falls in love with Fingal and warns him that he will be attacked while out hunting. Fingal is therefore prepared for the attack, defeats his assailants and returns to the King's hall safely. The angry King turns on his daughter and has her put to death, so when Fingal eventually returns home he takes only the corpse of Agandecca.

In Macpherson's hands the story has become a romance, with additional motifs such as the picturesque hunting scene. The principal alteration is the development of Agandecca's passion: an adaptation strongly resembling the sentimental plots of the *Fragments* and Macpherson's own early poetry. The princess's death is a characteristic piece:

> She came with the red eye of tears. She came with her loose raven locks. Her white breast heaved with sighs, like the foam of streamy Lubar. Starno pierced her side with steel. She fell like a wreath of snow that slides from the rocks of Ronan; when the woods are still and the eccho deepens in the vale. (*Fingal*, 38)

The combination of violence, frustrated love and family conflict expressed in lyrical, alliterative prose is only too familiar.

Macpherson was not writing his 'translations' for a Gaelic audience. His work was aimed at English-speakers and, in particular, at the literary circles of Edinburgh, so he was anxious to give them what they wanted. The Gaelic names seemed too harsh, so he softened them, the stories were too simple and terse, so he made them more romantic. Above all, he 'restored' the entire collection of broken poetry, making it into the epic that his patrons were expecting.

After a few weeks at Brae Badenoch, struggling over the Gaelic manuscripts with Gallie and Strathmashie, Macpherson returned to Edinburgh. He rented lodgings below Hugh Blair's house in Blackfriar's Wynd and continued to work on the translations under the enthusiastic eye of his patron.[62] The sight of the old manuscripts filled Blair and his friends with hope and Macpherson was often invited to dinner to give a progress report on the work.[63] Blair had provided a preface for the first collection of *Fragments*, but now he was undoubtedly supplying Macpherson with ideas and critical opinions on the great epic. The Highlands and Islands might have furnished Macpherson with the raw material for his work, but the final publication was very much a product of Edinburgh.

The Highland Tours

NOTES

1. *Scots Magazine*, xxii, 1760, 335–36, 360–62; *Gentleman's Magazine*, xxx, 1760, 287–88, 335–36.
2. J. Home, *Douglas*, 1757, ed. G. D. Parker, (Edinburgh 1972), 17. The words were included in the prologue 'spoken at Edinburgh', but not in the London version.
3. See R. Sher, *Church and University* . . .; McElroy, *Literary Clubs* . . . .
4. *Edinburgh Review*, i, 1755, preface, ii.
5. See Chapter Four, note 38.
6. *The History of the Proceedings in the Case of MARGARET, Commonly called PEG, only lawful Sister to John Bull, esq.*, (London 1761). The pamphlet has traditionally been attributed to Adam Ferguson, but see also David Raynor's edition, *Sister Peg: A Pamphlet hitherto unknown by David Hume*, (Cambridge 1982), and Sher's reply, op. cit., 230.
7. See e.g. Hume to Minto, 2 July 1757, *The Letters of David Hume*, ed. J. Y. T. Grieg, 2 vols, (London 1932), I, 255.
8. Hume to Dalrymple, 16 August 1760, ibid, I, 330–31. Hume had also discussed the poetry with Adam Smith, ibid, 329.
9. Ibid, 330.
10. The letter, dated Balgowan, 16 June 1760, is published in Robert Hay Carnie's 'Macpherson's *Fragments of Ancient Poetry* and Lord Hailes', *English Studies*, xli, 1960, 17–26.
11. Blair to Dalrymple, 23 June 1760, ibid 21–2.
12. Hume *The Letters*, I, 330. There appear to have been two subscriptions, one collected by Dalrymple, (Carnie, op. cit., 24), the other by Robert Chalmers, (*Report*, App. 58).
13. Bishop Alexander Macdonell's memorandum, see P. Macgregor, *The Genuine Remains of Ossian*, (London 1841), 39–40. See also Strathmashie to Blair, 22 October 1763, 'In the year 1760, I had the pleasure of accompanying my friend Mr Macpherson, during some part of his journey in search of the poems of Ossian, through the Highlands. I assisted him in collecting them; and took down from oral tradition, and transcribed from old manuscripts, by far the greatest part of these pieces he has published', *Report*, App 8.
14. MacBain believed that Strathmashie 'finds an honourable place among the minor Highland bards, and his Gaelic is as classical as any of his time', 'The Gaelic Dialect of Badenoch', *TGSI*, xviii, 1891–1892, 80. Examples of his work can be found in T. Sinton, *The Poetry of Badenoch*, (Inverness 1906); *TGSI*, xxiii, 1898–1899, xxiv, 1899–1901.
15. Martin, *A Description of the Western Islands* . . . , 89.
16. Macleod to Blair, 26 March 1764, *Report* App. 29.
17. *The Works of Ossian, the Son of Fingal*, 2 vols, (London 1765), xxii. This so-called 'Third Edition' included an appendix by Blair with information on the authenticity of the poems, supplied by residents of North-West Scotland.
18. Macpherson wrote to Revd J. Maclagan, saying that he had 'transversed most of the Isles and gathered all worth notice in that quarter' but was still anxious to see Maclagan's own collection, *Report*, App. 176.
19. A. McArthur to H. Mackenzie, Mull, 2 October 1797, ADV MS 73.2.13/24. According to Captain Morrison, however, Macpherson

did receive some manuscripts in Mull, 'likely from the Fletchers of Glenforsa', *Report* App. 176.
20. Home to Bute, Edinburgh, 12 June 1761, published by R. George Thomas, 'Lord Bute, John Home and Ossian. Two Letters', *MLR*, li, 1956, 73–5.
21. John Sinclair's *Prospectus of the Intended Publication of Ossian's Poems in the Original Gaelic*, (London 1804), 6–7 notes that Macpherson was introduced to Fraser of Boleskine by George Fraser, friend of Graham of Balgowan, and that the manuscripts were collected during his 'Northern tour'. See also ADV MS 73.2.24/39 on Macpherson's association with the Frasers.
22. The transmission of *The Book of the Dean* has been discussed by various writers – see Ronald Black's *Catalogue of Gaelic manuscripts in the National Library of Scotland*, ADV MS 73.1.37. See also D. T. Mackintosh, 'James Macpherson and the Book of the Dean of Lismore', *TGSI*, xxxvii, 1936, 347–65; *SGS*, vi, 1949, 11–20, for the theory that the book came from the blacksmith in Portree.
23. According to Ewan Macpherson, James' companion in Skye and the Outer Hebrides, *Report* App. 97.
24. Morrison stated that 'he gave him some, which he afterwards translated and published; together with fingalian or old heroic poems, not published in his translations, one of them Dargo', 7 January 1801, *Report* App. 176.
25. MacQueen to Blair, Kilmuir, 25 October 1763, ADV MS 73.2.12/2; 17 April 1764, *Report* App. 32–35. See also Malcolm Macpherson's evidence, *Report* App. 93–4.
26. Malcolm Macpherson, 5 September 1800, *Report* App 93.
27. Ibid.
28. J. F. Campbell, *Popular Tales*, I, xiv.
29. Ibid, xix.
30. McFarquhar to P. Bond, 6 January 1806, in J. Sinclair, *An Account of the Highland Society of London, from its Establishment in May 1778 to the Commencement of the Year 1813*, (London 1813), 74–5.
31. Campbell, op. cit., I, xvii.
32. Ewan's recollections: *Report* App. 94–98 and ADV MS 73.2.12/55. Later, he taught Gaelic to Mrs Grant of Laggan who recorded further details of the tour with Macpherson, Grant, *Poems on Various Subjects*, 362–63. See also ADV MS 73.2.15/7 where she described Ewan as 'a Man of Primitive notions, Evangelical Piety and held in Veneration for his integrity by every one who knew him'.
33. ADV MS 73.2.14/76 contains a request that the papers should be returned. In 1768, Dr Macpherson's *Critical Dissertations on the Origin, Antiquities, Language, Government, Manners and Religion of the Ancient Caledonians* was published, a work expounding views very similar to those of James Macpherson (see Chapter Nine).
34. See John Macpherson to Blair, 27 November 1763, 'I have seen a Gaelic manuscript in the hands of an old bard, who travelled about through the Highlands and Isles about thirty years ago, out of which he read, in my hearing, and before thousands yet alive, the exploits of Cuchullin, Fingal, Oscar, Ossian, Gaul, Dermid,and the other heroes celebrated in Mr Macpherson's book', *Report* App. 10.
35. *Report* App. 95.
36. Ibid, 96.

The Highland Tours

37. ADV MS 73.2.12/55.
38. Gallie to Mackintosh, 12 March 1799, *Report* 31.
39. 'a common-place book, which contained some accounts of the families of the Macdonalds, and the exploits of the great Montrose; together with some of the poems of Ossian', *Report* App. 96–97. Ewan also stated that Macpherson 'obtained an order from Clanranald senr. on a Lieutenant Donald Macdonald at Edinburgh, for a Gaelic folio manuscript belonging to the family, which was called the Leabhar Dearg'.
40. MacNeill to Blair, 23 December 1763, *Report* App. 20.
41. Lachlan MacMhuirich's declaration was made in Barra, 9 August 1800, when he was 58, ADV MS 73.2.12/66. A slightly altered version appears in *Report* App. 38–51.
42. ADV MS 73.2.12/66.
43. Gallie, 12 March 1799, *Report*, 36.
44. ADV MS 73.2.11/76. For correspondence relating to the Farquharson manuscript see Sinclair's edition of *Ossian*, 1807, I, 40ff.
45. See R. Black, 'The Gaelic Academy: The Cultural Commitment of the Highland Society of Scotland', *SGS*, xiv, Pt ii, 1986, 1–38.
46. Macpherson to Maclagan, 16 January 1761, *Report* App. 155.
47. R. Lingle, 'The Ossianic Manuscripts: A Note by Gordon Gallie Macdonald', *BNYPL*, xxiv, 1930, 79–81.
48. Gallie to Mackintosh, 12th March, 1799, Report, 31.
49. Ibid, 33. Although Strathmashie is not named here, he was identified in a subsequent letter, *Report*, 43.
50. Gallie included an extract 'taken out of a manuscript' by Strathmashie, *Report*, 32–3. According to Skene, an early draft of the Gaelic *Temora*, VII, was found among Strathmashie's papers after his death in 1767, T. McLauchlan, ed., *The Dean of Lismore's Book*, lvii. Irvine, who searched Strathmashie's papers in 1808, wrote to Sinclair, 'Alas! they contained not a hint of Ossian', ADV MS 73.2.14/76. Strathmashie was generally associated with the translation, however, and Macdonell observed that 'it was the general opinion of those who were best acquainted with both James Macpherson and Strathmashie, that the former was incapable of doing justice to the original; and that whatever merit the translation may possess, it is owing to Strathmashie', Macgregor, *The Genuine Remains of Ossian*, 40.
51. *Report*, 34; cf. Mackintosh to Mackenzie, 30 November 1798, 'Mr Gallie added that the Poem of Fingal was not perfectly compleat in the MS and that in his opinion the greatest merit Mr Macpherson had was in correcting the detached parts and supplying some little deficiencies so as to make the whole a regular connected poem', ADV MS 73.2.13/57.
52. *Report*, 44.
53. Ibid, 151.
54. Ibid, 152.
55. J. F. Campbell, *Leabhar na Féinne*, xxix. Campbell compared Donald Smith's 'Comparison of Passages' in the *Report* App. 190–260, with John Smith's *Galic Antiquities* (Edinburgh 1780) and Macpherson's *Ossian*.
56. Ibid, xxx. See also D. S. Thomson, 'Bogus Gaelic Literature'.

57. J. F. Campbell, *Popular Tales* . . ., iv, 228–29; cf. A. Grant, *Poems on Various Subjects*, 365.
58. L. Stern, 'Ossianic Heroic Poetry', tr. J. L. Robertson, *TGSI*, xxii, 1897–1898, 257–325.
59. Thomson, *Gaelic Sources*, 42.
60. Ibid, 22. In the ballad, the request is sent to Finn, not Cu Chulainn.
61. Ibid, 28–9. The ballads are printed in *Leabhar na Féinne*, 83–4.
62. *Report* App. 59. Macpherson appears to have left Badenoch by January 1761, because a letter to Maclagan is headed 'Edinburgh, 16 January 1761'.
63. Blair 'saw him very frequently', *Report*, 59; but Macpherson also received visits from Adam Ferguson, *Report* App. 59, 63; and John Ramsay : 'he had a small room at the back of the Guard that was filled with books and MSS. Some of the latter bore marks of the rust of antiquity. One of them was, he said, a book on medicine by an ollah or Highland doctor', Ramsay, *Scotland and Scotsmen*, I, 549.

7. Trenmor and Inibaca (by Angelica Kauffman)

8. Ossian Evoking Spirits on the Banks of the Lora (by Gerard)

9. Apotheosis of Napoleon's Generals (by Girodet)

10. The Dream of Ossian (by Ingres)

CHAPTER EIGHT

Fingal

> Thence issued forth, at great Macpherson's call,
> That old, new, epic pastoral, Fingal.
> Churchill, *The Prophecy of Famine*, 1763[1]

Almost as soon as Macpherson arrived in Edinburgh with his exciting stores of Highland poetry, plans for the publication of the great epic were underway. By February, Macpherson found himself on his way to England, bearing letters of introduction from his Edinburgh patrons to prospective publishers in London.[2] Little information has survived concerning Macpherson's first trip to the capital, although we know he was accompanied by Robert Chalmers who had organised the subscription for financing the Highland tours. According to Ramsay of Ochtertyre, who met Macpherson shortly before his journey south, 'he was a plain-looking lad, dressed like a preacher. What he said was sensible, but his manner was starch and reserved'.[3] It is hard to imagine such a figure making much impression on the busy social scene of London in the 1760s, but within a year, Macpherson was a well known personality, being invited for dinner by people such as Elizabeth Montague, 'Queen of the Blue Stockings'.[4] By then, he was famous as the 'translator' of *Fingal*.

When he arrived in the Capital, however, Macpherson was neither well-known nor well-heeled. In an angry letter, provoked by Macpherson's *History of Great Britain*, 1775, Sir Hew Dalrymple claimed that when Macpherson had first come to London, he had attempted to secure financial independence through marriage:

> The leanness of your circumstances in those days pointed out to you the paths of oeconomy: in that path, you got acquainted with the jolly Buxsom widow of a cheesemonger. The husband being dead . . . three months, you made your address to her but she, never fixing on her commodity by the eye, but by lack of —, proposed a month's triall of your person before she would make over lands and tenements to you.[5]

Apparently Macpherson objected to the widow's terms at first, because he had already accepted an offer of ten shillings a week from a

Bookseller 'to transcribe and compose bloody murders and sovereign intelligence to be called about the streets'.[6] The buxsom widow was obviously quite taken with the young Scot, however, as she then offered twice as much money for a weekly wage, plus room and board, and even threw in her husband's clothes. Macpherson, however, was not cut out for life as a cheesemonger and according to Dalrymple, his contract was rapidly terminated.

Although it would be a mistake to make too much of a gossipy anecdote, Dalrymple's story nevertheless casts interesting light on Macpherson's position. After the publication of *Fingal*, his success was rapid, but until it appeared in December 1761, Macpherson had to struggle to support himself. His initial reservations about Blair's project must have come to mind frequently as he tried to survive in London, working as a popular hack or even as a shop assistant. In such circumstances, it is hardly surprising to find him exploiting his connections and paying court to George III's influential Scottish minister, the Earl of Bute.

Macpherson was almost certainly introduced to Bute through John Home. In the spring of 1761, Home was working on his new play, *The Fatal Discovery*, which was based on the story of Ronnan and Rivine, from Macpherson's *Fragments of Ancient Poetry*. Home's patron was the Earl of Bute, so it seems highly likely that he would have introduced Macpherson, whose work had provided him with such inspiration and who was about to reveal the lost epic of Scotland to the English-speaking world. The letter Home sent to Bute, when he set off for the Highlands with Macpherson in June, certainly suggests that his patron was already acquainted with the young 'highland bard'.[7] Macpherson's enterprise was certain to attract the attention of Bute, who had a strong interest in the arts and particularly in Scottish writers. Although it is difficult to trace the Minister's involvement with the publication of *Fingal*, Macpherson's reference to the 'generosity of a certain noble person' in the list of acknowledgements is undoubtedly addressed to Bute.[8] When *Temora* appeared in 1763, it was explicitly inscribed to 'the Earl of Bute, in obedience to whose commands, they were translated . . . by his Lordship's most obedient, and most obliged, humble servant, James Macpherson'. The 1765 edition was even more fulsome in its gratitude though Macpherson was obviously aware of his patron's lack of popularity: 'I throw no reflexions on this age, but there is a great debt of fame owing to the EARL of BUTE, which hereafter will be amply paid'. Ironically, Bute's assistance was to prove something of a mixed blessing for Macpherson and *The Poems of Ossian*. In 1761, however, for an impecunious young man from the Highlands, the patronage of one of the most influential men in Britain must have seemed welcome indeed.

The patronage of Bute, like that of the Edinburgh literati, also increased the pressure on Macpherson. The more attention he sought, the greater the expectations of the imminent publication. Certainly Macpherson had wasted little time on his task, because less than eighteen months after his initial sortie into the Highlands in August 1760, the first volume of Ossianic poetry had gone to press.

In December 1761, the fruits of Macpherson's labours were presented to an eager public as *Fingal, an Ancient Epic Poem, In Six Books: Together with several other Poems, composed by Ossian the Son of Fingal.* The impressive, quarto volume could hardly have been more different from the humble pamphlet that had appeared in Edinburgh the year before. Unlike the anonymous *Fragments*, there was no doubt about the identity of the translator of *Fingal* and James Macpherson's name was printed under the title in bold, red capitals. These were not fragments, but an 'epic poem, in six books', complete with annotations and lengthy dissertations by the learned translator.

While the *Fragments* had only Blair's diffident preface as an introduction, *Fingal* had all the trappings of a classical text. The decoration on the title page was an engraving of the Celtic bard, Ossian, posing with the rapt expression and flowing robes of the traditional Hebrew prophet, his long white beard also reminiscent of Blackwell's image of Homer. Indeed, both the bard and his attendant lady (presumably Ossian's daughter-in-law, Malvina), in their flimsy robes and sandals would have looked more at home in a Mediterranean climate than in the chilly hills of Caledonia. Their surroundings, however, were essentially Scottish, with the river and distant crags, the oak tree with the clarsach hanging in its boughs and the cloud of ghostly warriors overhead. From the very first page of *Fingal*, Macpherson's intentions were plain: determined to raise the poetry of the Highlands to the highest status, he alluded constantly to the Bible and the classics in his presentation of Scottish material.

In *Fingal*, Macpherson had to fulfil not only the expectations of his sponsors. Anyone who had read the *Fragments*, or indeed the extracts which had been published in the periodicals, knew what to expect. Blair's preface had concentrated chiefly on the great epic and even included the following plot summary:

> The subject is, an invasion of Ireland by Swarthan King of Lochlyn; which is the name of Denmark in the Erse language. Cuchulaid, the General or Chief of the Irish tribes, upon intelligence of the invasion, assembles his forces; councils are held; and battles fought. But after several unsuccessful engagements, the Irish are forced to submit. At length, Fingal, King of Scotland . . . arrives with his ships to assist Cuchulaid. He expels the Danes from the country; and returns home victorious.
> (*Fragments*, vii–viii)

When he produced *Fingal*, Macpherson retained this basic narrative, but extended it to six books by incorporating numerous shorter tales as episodes. But the great epic poem demanded more than a mere development of the plot promised in the preface to the *Fragments*. An epic poem should deal with noble themes and characters: it was the highest form of literature and must contain heroes, battles, supernatural beings and conform to a host of literary conventions. At the same time, Macpherson's epic must be close enough to the style of the *Fragments* to seem convincing as the great original from which the shorter pieces had been broken.

Fingal follows good Horatian principles by beginning *in medias res*:

> Cuchullin sat by Tura's wall; by the tree of the rustling leaf. – His spear leaned against the mossy rock. His shield lay by him on the grass. As he thought of mighty Carbar, a hero whom he slew in war; the scout of ocean came Moran the son of Fithil.
>
> Rise, said the youth, Cuchullin, rise; I see the ships of Swaran. Cuchullin, many are the foe: many the heroes of the dark-rolling sea. (*Fingal*, 1–2)

Thus the reader is plunged straight into the action, with the appearance of the enemy ships in the Irish sea. For those familiar with the *Fragments*, the opening lines of *Fingal* would have been recognisable as 'Fragment XIV', although the Danish leader 'Garve', who appears in the genuine ballads as 'Garbh mac Stairn' had now become 'Swaran'.[9] Anyone unacquainted with Macpherson's earlier production, could refer to the copious footnotes on Cuchullin's ancestry and character. Already Macpherson was combining the style of the *Fragments* with the solid appearance of a classical text.

Although Macpherson incorporated several of the Fragments into *Fingal*, he generally revised the earlier pieces. The opening lines, though very similar to 'Fragment XIV', had various amendments, such as the replacement of the original 'as a grey cloud upon the hill' (*Fragments*, 66) with the more lyrical 'like a cloud of mist on the silent hill' (*Fingal*, 2). Similarly, the address of the Lochlin chief was made more rhetorical as 'The king of the Desert of hills alone can fight with Garve' (67) became 'None can meet Swaran in the fight, but Fingal, king of stormy hills' (3).[10] The simple diction of the *Fragments* was turning into the lofty style of an epic poem, as Macpherson introduced more lyrical epithets and rhetorical flourishes.

The epic conventions developed from classical models also inspired Macpherson to employ numerous epic similes, such as this:

> Thou hast seen the sun retire red and slow behind his cloud; night gathering round on the mountain, while the unfrequent blast roared in narrow vales. At length the rain beats hard; and thunder rolls in peals. Lightning glances on the rocks. Spirits ride on beams of fire. And the strength of the mountain-streams

Fingal

> comes roaring down the hills. Such was the noise of battle, maid
> of the arms of snow. (*Fingal*, 58–59)

Macpherson's imitations of *The Iliad* and *The Aeneid* were not merely stylistic, and throughout *Fingal* he made explicit allusions to classical predecessors.[11]

Echoes of Homer, Virgil and Milton could be heard faintly in the *Fragments*, but in *Fingal* the debts were more pronounced. The first description of Swaran, for example, is strongly reminiscent of Satan, as he appears in *Paradise Lost*, I, 284–294: 'His spear is like that blasted fir. His shield like the rising moon. He sat on a rock on the shore: like a cloud of mist on the silent hill' (*Fingal*, 2). As in the *Fragments*, the images are pared down to the most direct analogies, in an attempt to suggest the work of a primitive bard. But at the same time the powerful Miltonic associations give extra weight to Macpherson's villain. Indeed, it is tempting to search for consistency in Macpherson's allusions, promoting Swaran to a type of Satan, but in 'Carric-Thura', the description of Fingal himself recalls Milton's arch-fiend: 'His blue arms were on the hero; like a gray cloud on the sun, when he moves in his robes of mist, and shews but half his beams' (*Fingal*, 194).[12] Rather than seek an allegorical dimension in *Fingal*, then, each allusion should be considered in its own context. In most cases, Macpherson alludes to Homer, Milton or Virgil in an attempt to enrich his unfamiliar Celtic heroes with classical associations and elevate his own, rather insubstantial work.

Malcolm Laing spent eight years tracing such echoes in order to prove Macpherson a plagiarist, finally producing an edition of *Ossian* annotated with parallel passages from Virgil, Homer and Milton.[13] But the translator himself made no secret of his debts to earlier epics. In fact, he emphasised the similarities, often inviting the reader to compare a particular passage of Fingal with a classical source. In *Fingal* II, for example, Cuchullin is described in the following manner:

> But Cuchullin stood before him like a hill, that catches the clouds of heaven. – The winds contend on its head of pines; and the hail rattles on its rocks. But, firm in its strength, it stands and shades the silent vale of Cona. (*Fingal*, 28)

At the foot of the page, Macpherson included this note:

> Virgil and Milton have made use of a comparison similar
> to this; I shall lay both before the reader, and let
> him judge for himself which of these two great poets
> have best succeeded.
>
> Quantus Athos, aut quantus Eryx, aut ipse coruscis,
> Cum fremit ilicibus, quantus gaudetque rivali

> Vertice se attollens pater Appeninus ad auras.

> Like Eryx or like Athos great he shews
> Or father Appenine when white with snows;
> His head divine obscure in clouds he hides,
> And shakes the sounding forest on his sides.
>
> DRYDEN.

> On th' other side Satan, alarm'd,
> Collecting all his might, dilated stood
> Like Teneriff or Atlas unremov'd:
> His stature reach'd the sky.
>
> MILTON.

Although the reader is only explicitly invited to compare Virgil with Milton, the footnote implies that the question should also include Ossian. Macpherson never disguised the similarities between *Fingal* and the classical epics because he intended Ossian to be seen as a rival to Homer, Virgil and Milton.

A few pages earlier, Macpherson had deliberately drawn attention to the Virgilian passage which must have inspired his own description. Although he was undoubtedly using a certain amount of traditional Gaelic material in his epic, passages such as the appearance of Crugal's ghost owed more to his classical education:

> My hero saw in his rest a dark-red stream of fire coming down from the hill. Crugal sat upon the beam, a chief that lately fell. He fell by the hand of Swaran, striving in the battle of heroes. His face is like the beam of the setting moon; his robes are of the clouds of the hill: his eyes are like two decaying flames. Dark is the wound of his breast . . .
>
> Dim, and in tears, he stood and stretched his pale hand over the hero. – Faintly he raised his feeble voice, like the gale of the reedy Lego. (*Fingal*, 22)

The resemblance to the scene in which Hector's ghost appears before Aeneas is striking, and Macpherson actually included the relevant passage from the Aeneid (II, 270–80), together with Dryden's translation in the footnotes. Again, he was capitalising on his readers' familiarity with the classics. Crugal, who had not appeared in the opening book, is immediately elevated through the parallel with Hector, while Swaran's character gains further power from the implicit association with Achilles. At the same time, the evocation of Virgil's Troy, rather than Homer's, gives an ominous undertone to the Celtic war: despite Fingal's epic victory, the underlying notes of despair are never completely silenced.

Although Macpherson was drawing partly on the Gaelic tradition and partly on the classical, the final product was still distinguished by his own peculiar voice. Despite the parallels between Crugal's ghost and the spirit of Hector, the differences between the two passages are equally revealing. Hector's ghost is a horrifying spectre, still disfigured by his humiliating defeat:

> squalentem barbam et concretos sanguine crinis
> vulneraque illa gerens quae circum plurima muros
> adcepit patrios.
>
> His hair and beard stood stiffen'd with his gore,
> And all the wounds he for his country bore (Dryden)
>
> *(Fingal,* 22)

Macpherson chose to present Crugal in very different terms: the soft language diffusing any horror and making the apparition uncertain and ethereal. The voice of the Celtic warrior is 'feeble', his face 'dim' and 'pale', his eyes no longer fires, but 'decaying flames'. Unlike the strong, physical presence of Hector, Crugal is on the verge of dissolving into the Highland landscape: 'his face is the beam of the setting moon; his robes are the clouds of the hill'.

Crugal's appearance may be less dramatic than Hector's, but it is certainly more ghostly, and this ethereal quality is perhaps the most distinctive aspect of Macpherson's work. Crugal's ghost is the most clearly realised apparition in the whole poem because in most cases, the spirits of the dead appear only dimly through the Highland storms and mist:

> Trenmor came, before mine eyes, the tall form of other years. His blue hosts were behind him in half distinguished rows. Scarce seen is their strife in mist, or their stretching forward to deaths. I listened, but no sound was there. The forms were empty wind.
>
> *(Temora,* 161)

This other-worldly atmosphere was inherited directly from the *Fragments,* where the lost voices had drifted vaguely in their mountain settings. The dialogue between Shilric and Vinvela, for example, which had set the tone of the *Fragments,* was now adapted as a song in 'Carric-thura', introducing the same intangible quality to a so-called heroic poem.[14] While such passages had seemed peculiarly appropriate to the detached remnants of ancient poetry, their contribution to the epic was not always beneficial, and all too often uncertainty becomes confusion.

The presentation of *Fingal* as an epic poem raised certain expectations in the reader and among these was the demand for a continuous narrative. The brief romantic tales which had appeared as *Fragments* in 1760 were now being forced into longer poems as 'episodes'. Macpherson's penchant for the macabre had emerged plainly in the earlier volume and he was obviously not prepared to abandon the successful formula in his epic. The bloody tale of Duchommar and Morna, which had originally taken the form of a dialogue in 'Fragment XV', was thus introduced into *Fingal* I as an anecdote.[15] Although Morna's lover has now become Cathbat rather than Cadmor, the story is the same, while Macpherson's treatment is even more extravagant:

> She came, in all her tears, she came, and drew it from his breast. He pierced her white side with steel; and spread her fair locks on the ground. Her bursting blood sounds from her side: and her white arm is stained with red. Rolling in death she lay and Tura's cave answered her sighs. (*Fingal*, 9)

While such an episode did not seem out of place in the *Fragments*, it causes a considerable disruption to the narrative flow in the longer poem. Macpherson's attempt to integrate it into the main story, by including the tale when Cuchullin passes Cathbat's grave, fails because it is completely unconnected with the plot of the epic. Having plunged his readers into the dramatic opening situation, with the news of the Viking invasion, Macpherson dissipates any tension by dwelling on this irrelevant story of a broken romance. His obvious relish for the tale makes matters worse, since Duchommar and Morna seem as important as Cuchullin, so the reader is diverted from the principal character before he has even had a chance to develop. After repeated digressions of this sort, the story of Fingal's victory is completely lost.

The confusion is compounded by Macpherson's tendency to diffuse scenes of high drama by the use of refined aesthetic effects. The battle in *Fingal* I, for example, remains a generalised description, with little power to move the reader:

> Chief mixed his strokes with chief, and man with man; steel, clanging, sounded on steel, helmets are cleft on high. Blood bursts and smoaks around. – Strings murmur on the polished yews. Darts rush along the sky. Spears fall like the circles of light that gild the stormy face of the night. (*Fingal*, 12–13)

The concentration on the picturesque qualities of the scene diffuses the drama in much the same way as the horror was removed from the vision of Crugal. While such a technique is eminently suitable for ghosts, it is less successful in the portrayal of an epic battle. Although the battle is the main incident in the plot of the first book of *Fingal*, Macpherson gave greater emphasis to the digressional tale of Morna and Duchommar so the reader moves on to Book II in a somewhat bewildered state.

On the whole, *Fingal* tends to leave the reader uncertain as to which characters have actually appeared in the main action and which survive only in the memories of the protagonists. The problem is not confined to the 'epic' but also occurs in the 'other poems' in the volume. In 'The Death of Cuchullin', for example, Bragela is supposed to be a living contemporary of Ossian, but she seems no more distinct than the dead Cuchullin whom she describes in her song (*Fingal*, 143–145). The uncertainty is increased by the fact that the entire poem is being sung by Ossian, who seems to make little distinction between the living and the dead.

The development of Ossian was perhaps the most important difference between *Fingal* and the *Fragments*. The earlier collection had been attributed to an anonymous body of 'Bards', but when *Fingal* appeared, there was no question about the identity of the author: Ossian, the son of Fingal. An epic poem required an epic poet, so Ossian, who had appeared in the *Fragments* as a character, was now placed firmly in the tradition of Homer and Milton as the blind bard of the Highlands. Macpherson's concentration on the isolated poet owed as much to the literature of the mid-eighteenth century as to the classics. Despite its epic pretensions, *Fingal* is a sprawling work, held together not by unified action or theme, but by the presence of the narrator. As in Sterne's contemporary novel, *Tristram Shandy*, a baffling series of recollections is made coherent only through the development of the narrator as the focal point.

Despite its antique style, *Fingal* reflected the preoccupations of the eighteenth century, and Macpherson's obsession with memory accorded well with the contemporary interest in psychology. Ossian's invocations, for example, suggest a certain awareness of the workings of the mind:

> As flies the unconstant sun, over Larmon's grassy hill; so pass the tales of old, along my soul by night. When bards are removed to their place; when harps are hung in Selma's hall; then comes a voice to Ossian, and awakes his soul. It is the voice of the years that are gone: they roll before me, with all their deeds. I seize the tales as they pass, and pour them forth in song. (*Temora*, 211)

Macpherson's favourite metaphor for inspiration was of light dawning: 'Let the light of Ossian's soul arise' (*Fingal*, 209), 'The song rises, like the sun, in my soul' (*Fingal*, 104), an idea strikingly similar to those of the contemporary aesthetician, Edward Young. In his *Conjectures on Original Composition*, 1759, Young examined the predicament of the modern poet and discussed the idea of genius rising from within the poet's mind 'as the sun from chaos'.[16] Young's *Conjectures* reflected the mid-eighteenth century tendency to replace the traditional notion of divine inspiration with a new investigation of man's psyche. For Young, self-analysis offered enormous potential for artistic expression and, despite his attack on the mediocrity of contemporary poetry, the *Conjectures* were essentially optimistic.

The increasing interest in man as an individual rather than man in relation to an omniscient God, however, was not always greeted with enthusiasm. Martin Battestin has explored some of the more alarming aspects of Lockean epistemology in his discussion of *Tristram Shandy*, where 'not Nature, not Nature's God, but the self is the hub of the universe'.[17] Tristram Shandy can be seen as a representative of modern man, isolated within his own perceptions and released only by his imagination, through which he can share the emotions of others. Ossian is isolated in a similar manner and there is no God in his lonely Celtic world.[18] It is only by conjuring up the memories of those he has loved that he can achieve any happiness in his sterile universe:

> My soul is often brightened with the song; and I remember the companions of my youth. – But sleep descends with the sound of the harp; and pleasant dreams begin to rise. Ye sons of the chace stand far distant, nor disturb my rest. The bard of other times converses now with his fathers, the chiefs of the days of old. – Sons of the chace, stand far distant; disturb not the dreams of Ossian. (*Fingal*, 110)

The growing idea of the poet as an independent genius, faced with the struggle against the isolation that such independence brings, sheds interesting light on the personality of Macpherson's ancient bard. His preoccupations and helpless melancholy belonged more to the eighteenth century than to the third.

Ossian, like the rest of Macpherson's work, was a curious blend of the traditional and the contemporary. The character of the ancient bard was derived from a variety of sources, old and new, epic and lyrical. Oisin is a distinctive figure in the genuine Gaelic tradition, and his habit of looking back to the days of the Fiana is well documented in a number of poems in *The Book of the Dean of Lismore*:

> Anbhfann anocht neart mo lámh,
> ní fheil mo choimhghein ar lár;
> ní h-iongnadh dhomh bheith brónach,
> im ghiobal truagh seanórach . . .
>
> (Feeble tonight is the strength of my hands; there is not on earth my fellow in years; it is no wonder that I am sad, a pitiful, worn-out rag of an old man)
>
> Fá mé an comhairleach cródha
> don Fhéin i gcath Crunmhóna;
> iomdha neach gan aithne ann:
> dá n-aithle atáim go h-anbhfann
>
> (I was the Fian's valorous counsellor in the battle of

Crunnmhoin. Many a one was slain there, after whom I am left feeble.)[19]

Macpherson's ancient bard clearly owes much to the genuine Gaelic ballads and would have been recognisable to Highlanders familiar with the old heroic poetry.

At the same time, Ossian fitted neatly into the classical tradition of the blind poet/prophet, with which Milton had aligned himself in *Paradise Lost*:

> Blind Thamyris, and blind Maeonides,
> And Tiresias and Phineus prophets old.　　　　(III, 35–36)

Unlike these poets, however, there is little sense that Ossian has been compensated for his loss of sight by the ability to sing. His blindness is part of his general decay and the memory of his former prowess only emphasises the decline:

> Myself, like a rock, came down, I exulted in the strength of the king. Many were the deaths of my arm; and dismal was the gleam of my sword. My locks were not then so gray; nor trembled my hands of age. My eyes were not closed in darkness; nor failed my feet in the race.　　　　(*Fingal*, 44).

For Milton, the question of blindness was ambivalent: while his inner 'celestial light' was a blessing, there was also a dim sense that his blindness was a punishment for poetic aspiration, especially since Homer and Thamyris were said to have suffered for similar reasons. The conflict between artistic aspiration and obedience to God is never resolved in *Paradise Lost* and for readers of the late eighteenth and early nineteenth centuries, it became crucial to the poem. Ossian, however, is no rebel, and although he rails against the degeneration of the present age, his only solution is to retreat into the safety of the past. His blindness is not the result of over ambition: it is not a Fall, but a misfortune. Ossian is no tragic hero, but a mid-eighteenth-century innocent, whose suffering is unjust and whose disability increases the pathos.[20]

The tradition of the blind epic poet caused various difficulties for writers of the eighteenth century. By retaining the Miltonic motif, Macpherson was in danger of robbing his poet of imagination, according to contemporary theories. Once people believed knowledge to be rooted in the senses, sight became essential to the formation of ideas and the imagination largely dependent on vision. In his influential essay on the imagination, Addison had argued that sight is 'the most perfect and delightful of all our Senses' and the one which 'furnishes the Imagination with its Ideas'.[21] With this empirical approach, the loss of sight became a serious disability for the poet, especially since divine inspiration now seemed unacceptable for similar reasons. For Ossian, inspiration was a kind of memory: the light rising in his soul had its source in people and events of the past. Unable to receive fresh impressions of the external world, his poetry depended on the repetition of the 'tales of the times of old', so the general monotony and lack of definition in his poems seemed appropriate to the ramblings of a blind old man.

The association between blindness and poetry continued to attract interest in the mid-eighteenth century. Discussions of the Scottish poet, Thomas Blacklock (1721–1791), frequently focused on the fact that he had been blind from infancy: where did the images in his poetry come from?[22] Whatever the source of Blacklock's imagery, critics were in agreement about his character, which John Home considered to be 'endued with the most exquisite feelings . . . tremblingly alive all over'.[23] Instead of tackling the embarrassing problem of divine inspiration, readers of the mid eighteenth century seized upon sensibility as the new compensation for a poet's loss of sight.

James Beattie, in his 'Epistle to Blacklock' (235–40), listed Resignation, Melancholy, Fortitude and Thought as virtues belonging to the blind poet and all these traits are to be found in *Ossian*. The most prominent characteristic of Macpherson's bard was melancholy, but this above all was seen as a sign of fine feeling. Alexander Gerard at Aberdeen suggested that melancholy stemmed from 'quick sensibility, the common attendant of a lively fancy and delicate taste, too strongly affected by the gloomier views of human life',[24] and Ossian's own 'joy of grief' seemed to derive from similar causes. In *Fingal*, Ossian's impulse to create poetry invariably comes from his emotions. The old man reflects on his miserable condition but is then moved to creativity by the contrasting memories of past joys:

> When shall Ossian's youth return, or his ear delight in the sound of arms? When shall I, like Oscar, travel in the light of my steel? – Come, with your streams, ye hills of Cona, and listen to the voice of Ossian! The song rises, like the sun, in my soul; and my heart feels the joys of other times. (*Fingal*, 104)

Ossian's blindness, then, led not to epic investigations of poetic aspiration and divine inspiration, but to the melancholic isolation of the mid eighteenth century. Indeed, the closest literary parallel for Ossian is not Homer, Milton or the Oisin of Gaelic tradition, but the fictional contemporary created by Thomas Gray. Gray's Bard had been launched on the public in July 1757:

> On a rock, whose haughty brow
> Frowns o'er old Conway's foaming flood,
> Robed in the sable garb of woe,

With haggard eyes the poet stood;
(Loose his beard and hoary hair
Streamed like a meteor, to the troubled air)
And, with a master's hand and prophet's fire,
Struck the deep sorrows of his lyre. (15–22)[25]

Although Macpherson's was a Highland bard, rather than Welsh, the first description of Ossian, which had appeared in 'Fragment VIII' bore strong similarities:

> By the side of a rock on the hill, beneath the aged trees, old Oscian sat on the moss; the last of the race of Fingal. Sightless are his aged eyes; his beard is waving in the wind. Dull though the leafless trees he heard the voice of the north. Sorrow revived in his soul: he began and lamented the dead. (*Fragments*, 37)

Gray's Bard, who stands as a representative for the traditional poetry of Wales, had obvious relevance to Macpherson's concern with Highland poetry, especially as the last lines show the Bard plunging to death in the face of an invading English army.

Despite the obvious similarities between Gray's Bard and Ossian, however, there are also significant differences which, as usual, reveal more about Macpherson. Originally, Gray had envisaged his poet sitting down, but in the final version of the poem, the Bard stands defiantly on the edge of a precipice. Ossian, on the other hand, sits helplessly beneath an 'aged tree', surrounded by moss. The tone is quite different and while Gray offers a stirring portrait of the doomed Bard, Macpherson's description is wistful and unornamented. Ossian, unlike the Bard, seems a very old man.

One of the principal differences is the narrative framework. While the speech and actions of Gray's Bard are reported by a modern poet, in *Fingal* Ossian speaks in the first person. The distancing effect of a narrator is thus removed and the reader feels closer to the ancient Scottish poet. Gray's Bard embodies the very heroic spirit that Ossian is constantly lamenting, and not only places a bloody curse on the English king, but eventually plunges to a violent death. He is a true Ancient: remote, vengeful and unmoved by the 'shrieks of an agonizing King!' Despite the violence, Gray presents the Bard's power as something attractive, and as something which had been lost in the process of civilisation. The primitive Bard's faith in the spirit of poetry is undermined by the ominous fading of his vision: 'And distant warblings lessen on my ear That lost in long futurity expire. (133–34). The future of poetry hardly seems secure, and the reader is left with the words of the modern narrator, describing the death of the heroic Bard.

A similar sense of the shortcomings of the modern world pervades

Fingal, but here the position of the 'ancient' bard is less clear cut. Although Ossian, as the son of Fingal, is presented as part of the heroic world of the ancient Celts, the character who emerges in the poems seems to lack all the traditional energy of primitive man. Throughout *Fingal* and the accompanying poems, there is a strong sense that the true heroic age has already passed and that Ossian himself is part of a newer, inferior society:

> Often have I fought, and often won in battles of the spear. But blind, and tearful, and forlorn, I now walk with little men. O Fingal, with thy race of battle I now behold thee not. The wild roes feed upon the green tomb of the mighty king of Morven.
>
> (*Fingal*, 48)

To the blind poet, the present is sterile and meaningless, so he turns constantly to the past for emotional relief.

The dominance of the past pervades every aspect of *Fingal*, and even the ghosts are part of the same preoccupation. Although the spirits fulfil the need for 'machinery' in the academic epic formula and provide the thrill of the unknown for the popular reader, they are above all representives of the heroic past. In 'The War of Caros', Oscar calls out to his ancestors for inspiration:

> Come, ye dim ghosts of my fathers, and behold my deeds in war! – I may fall; but I will be renowned like the race of the ecchoing Morven. (*Fingal*, 102)

For Ossian, however, the inspiration of the ghosts is double-edged. Although his poetry stems from the inspiration of the past, the very memory of the bold heroes emphasises his own inadequacy. Ossian sings about the battles of his father, but there is no hope of the heroic age of Fingal being revived, because Ossian's own son, Oscar, is dead:

> And art thou fallen, Oscar, in the midst of thy course? the heart of the aged beats over thee! He sees thy coming wars. The wars which ought to come he beholds, but they are cut off from thy fame. When shall joy dwell at Selma? When shall grief depart from Morven? My sons fall by degrees: Fingal shall be the last of his race. The fame which I have received shall pass away: my age will be without friends. I shall sit a grey cloud in my hall: nor shall I hear the return of a son, in the midst of his sounding arms. Weep, ye heroes of Morven! never more shall Oscar rise!
>
> (*Temora*, 15)

Oscar's death makes the passing of Fingal's world complete.

The theme of the parent outliving the child, which had recurred in the *Fragments*, emerged in an even more disturbing way in the new volume. In 'The War of Caros', Lamor's nameless son fails to achieve fame in battle, so the aged Lamor takes his own father's sword to execute his child (*Fingal*, 100). The obsession with the superiority of the past thus becomes a destructive force, denying the young any opportunity to develop their own potential. The pessimism of the *Fragments* continued to pervade *Fingal* and *Temora*, just as the tales of surviving parents, suicide or broken romance were incorporated into the new epics.

The Poems of Ossian are marked by the absence of children and the preponderance of old men. Even Fingal himself is portrayed as a rather elderly father-figure:

> Fingal himself was next to the foe; and listened to the tales of the bards. His godlike race were in the song, the chiefs of other times. Attentive, leaning on his shield, the king of Morven sat. The wind whistled through his aged locks, and his thoughts are of the days of other years. (*Fingal*, 44)

Although age carries authority and wisdom, throughout Ossian's songs, it is associated with physical decay and approaching death. Even the famous Ossianic landscape could be seen as a symbol of degeneration. In *The Sacred Theory of the Earth*, Thomas Burnet had described mountains as the 'Ruins of a broken World', regarding them as the direct result of the Deluge, which had disfigured the smooth face of the Earth.[26] Although the new, Romantic attitude towards mountains was already developing by the middle of the eighteenth century, the traditional view of mountains as symbols of corruption and decay has obvious relevance to Macpherson's work.

Ossian's own preoccupation with ruins emerges explicitly in 'Carthon', where he describes the fallen Balclutha:

> I have seen the walls of Balclutha, but they were desolate. The fire had resounded in the halls: and the voice of the people is heard no more. The stream of Clutha was removed from its place, by the fall of the walls. – The thistle shook, there, its lonely head: the moss whistled to the wind. The fox looked out, from the windows, the rank grass of the wall waved round his head. – Desolate is the dwelling of Moina, silence is in the house of her fathers. – Raise the song of mourning, O bards, over the land of strangers. They have but fallen before us: for one day, we must fall. (*Fingal*, 132)

The idea of a ruined world was a literary commonplace of the late eighteenth century, inspiring both poets and prose writers with thoughts of mortality and the collapse of Empires. In *Fingal*, too, the choice of Virgil's 'fortia facta patrum' ('the brave deeds of the forefathers') as a Latin tag had ominous undertones. The words come from the gold plate at Dido's banquet in *The Aeneid*, I, 641, and with them come ominous thoughts of the death of Dido and the ultimate ruin of Carthage.

Macpherson's *Ossian*, then, though based on traditional materials and aspiring to antiquity, was very much a product of the mid-eighteenth century. The heroic world of the Celts was not constructed with the accuracy of an archaeologist, but with the imagination of an eighteenth-century poet. It appealed to the contemporary interest in the antique by conveying not only an idealised Ancient World, but also the sense of the modern inferiority to that world.

On one level, Ossian can be seen as a symbol of the traditional Highland poetry Macpherson had collected and claimed to be translating. Just as Highland culture was revered for its antiquity but was nevertheless in danger of extinction, so Ossian was respected for his wisdom and poetic gifts, but had no natural successor. Ossian was representative of the oral tradition of Celtic poetry, his gradual decline serving as a comment on the erosion of the Gaelic in the eighteenth century. Unlike Gray, who treated similar ideas with the spirit of an antiquarian, Macpherson could identify closely with the situation of Ossian, having witnessed for himself the recent changes in the Highlands. Despite his ancient weeds, Ossian voiced the feelings of many eighteenth-century Highlanders.

Ossian's appeal, however, was not limited to Northern Scotland, and indeed found many of its most ardent enthusiasts elsewhere. The discovery of a new 'ancient bard' attracted many readers, who turned to Macpherson's work as they turned to Homer: eager for the 'fire' of primitive society. Ossian could be admired as an original genius and provide a hitherto unknown source of inspiration to future poets, in much the same way as Homer or Virgil. But although Ossian remembers the days of Fingal personally, his own sense of being part of a newer, inferior society seemed to set him apart from the age of heroes. His very consciousness of the Ancient World being something great but remote was, in fact, very modern. Ossian is, in a sense, caught between two worlds and is a symbol of the Modern poet just as much as the Ancient. The idea of an old man representing modern poetry can be related to *The Battle of the Books*, where the Moderns claim to be 'much the more Antient of the two'.[27] Swift's paradox has been illuminated by reference to Francis Bacon:

> And to speak truly, *Antiquitas saeculi juventus mundi*. These times are the ancient times, when the world is ancient, and not those times which we account ancient *ordine retrogrado*, by a computation backward from ourselves.[28]

There is a sense then, in which eighteenth-century poets could see themselves as 'ancient' because their age was the oldest: it was an age worn out, with nothing new to say. The growing emphasis on originality tended to equate genius with the earliest stages of society, thus increasing the modern sense of inferiority. The classics were admired not only for their antiquity, but because they possessed the energy of an early world, unhampered by literary predecessors. While this would be true of a third-century Ossian (and, indeed, accounts for much of the acclaim which met *Fingal*), Macpherson's bard, who remembers a vigorous past but remains doomed to an impotent present, was symptomatic of the mid eighteenth century.

The modern problem of equalling the past and wrestling with the debilitating notion that everything had been said before was particularly acute in Scotland. The self-consciousness about the Scottish language meant that many writers sheltered behind imitations of English masters, just as Macpherson had in his earlier attempts at poetry. Past masters could provide inspiration, but they could just as easily lead to depressing feelings of inadequacy. The image of the decrepit bard decaying slowly in his ruined world casts interesting light on the anxieties of the eighteenth-century poet, and Hazlitt's comments on Ossian are extremely revealing:

> As Homer is the first vigour and lustihed, Ossian is the decay and old age of poetry. He lives only in the recollection and regret of the past. There is one impression which he conveys more entirely than all other poets, namely, the sense of privation, the loss of all things, of friends, of good name, of country – he is even without God in the world. He converses only with the spirit of the departed; with the motionless and silent clouds . . . The feeling of cheerless desolation, of the loss of the pith and sap of existence, of the annihilation of the substance, and the clinging to the shadow of all things as in a mock-embrace, is here perfect . . . If it were indeed possible to show that this writer was nothing, it would only be another instance of mutability, another blank made, another void left in the heart, another confirmation of that feeling which makes him so often complain, 'Roll on, ye dark brown years, ye bring no joy on your wing to Ossian!'[29]

NOTES
1. *The Poems of Charles Churchill*, ed. J. Laver, 1933; (London 1970), 216.
2. See Hume's letter to William Strahan, 9 February 1761, *The Letters of David Hume*, I, 342-3.
3. Ramsay, *Scotland and Scotsmen*, I, 549.
4. Elizabeth Montagu, *The Queen of the Bluestockings, Her Correspondence from 1720-1761*, ed. E. J. Climenson, 2 vols, (London 1906), II, 267-68.
5. SRO GD 110/1171, Hamilton/Dalrymple of North Berwick Muniments.
6. Ibid.
7. Home to Bute, 12 June 1761, R. George Thomas, 'Lord Bute, John Home and Ossian', 73.

8. *Fingal*, Advertisement: 'the translator yet avoids to name him, as his exalted station as well as merit has raised him above the panegyric of one so little known.'
9. *Fragments*, 66. For the correlation betwen *Fingal* and the Gaelic ballads, see Thomson, 'The Gaelic Sources . . .'
10. In the 1773 edition, the line was further embellished to 'Who can meet Swaran in the fight? Who but Fingal, king of Selma of storms?' (1773, 1, 221).
11. For a detailed study of the parallels between *Fingal* and the *Iliad*, see J. Bysveen, *Epic Tradition and Innovation in James Macpherson's Fingal*, (Uppsala 1982).
12. Cf. *Paradise Lost*, I, 595. See also *The Highlander* where Macpherson used allusions to *Paradise Lost*, I, 192–196, for both Magnus (II, 243) and Indulph (VI, 179).
13. Laing suggested his notes would 'form no unnecessary commentary, to point out the real originals from which the poems were derived', Laing ed., 1805, I, vi.
14. *Fragments*, 9–12, cf. *Fingal*, 195–98.
15. *Fragments*, 69–73, cf. *Fingal*, 8–9.
16. E. Young, *Conjectures on Original Composition*, 1759, ed. E. J. Morley, (Manchester 1918), 24.
17. M. Battestin, *The Providence of Wit*, (Oxford 1974), 243.
18. Macpherson's own views on the replacement of divine intervention by human endeavour can be seen in *Fingal*, x–xi, see below, Chapter Nine.
19. From Ballad VIII, *Heroic Poetry from the Book of the Dean*, 37–39. See also Ballad IV, 9–11.
20. Vickers regards the 'concept of suffering innocence' as crucial to Mackenzie's *The Man of Feeling*, 1771, (Oxford 1967), xvii. On Ossian's blindness, see N. Drake, 'On the Blindness of Homer, Ossian and Milton', *Evenings in Autumn*, 2 vols, (London 1827), II, 1–23, 170–96, 252–86.
21. *The Spectator*, No 411, 1965, III, 535–37. Cf. David Hartley on the senses of sight and hearing being the 'principal Storehouse of the Fancy or Imagination', *Observations on Man, his Frame, his Duty and his Expectations*, 2 vols, (London 1749), I, 235.
22. See *Poems of Thomas Blacklock*, 2nd edn., (Edinburgh 1756).
23. Quoted in H. Mackenzie, *An Account of the Life and Writings of John Home, esq.*, (Edinburgh 1822), 131.
24. Gerard, *An Essay on Genius*, (London 1774), 416.
25. Gray's inspiration for the description came from paintings of Old Testament prophets: *Correspondence*, 1935, II, 476–477.
26. T. Burnet, *Telluris Theoria Sacra*, (London 1681). On Burnet's theory and the changing attitudes towards mountains in the eighteenth century, see M. H. Nicolson, *Mountain Gloom and Mountain Glory*, (New York 1959); D. G. Charlton, *New Images of the Natural in France*, (Cambridge 1984), 41–52.
27. J. Swift, *The Tale of a Tub and The Battle of the Books*, 1710, ed. A. C. Guthkelch & D. Nichol Smith, 2nd edn. (Oxford 1958), 227.
28. Ibid. The reference is from *The Advancement of Learning*, I, v, i.
29. Hazlitt, *The Complete Works*, V, 18.

Macpherson's Vision of Celtic Scotland

> Methinks I hear the *Grecian* Bards exclaiming,
> (The *Grecian* Bards, no longer worth the naming),
> In song the Northern tribes so far surpass us,
> One of their *Highland-hills* they'll call PARNASSUS:
> And from the sacred Mount *decrees* shall follow,
> That Ossian was himself the TRUE APOLLO.
>   D. Erskine Baker, *The Muse of Ossian*, 1763[1]

Fragments of Ancient Poetry had been presented to the public with no editorial comment, few notes and only Blair's brief preface to serve as an introduction. When it came to *Fingal*, Macpherson's approach was very different. His new production was the first English version of an ancient Celtic epic and had to be displayed with the appropriate trappings. Macpherson's models were works such as Duncan's translation of *Caesar* or Sale's edition of the *Koran*, both of which were prefaced by a discourse on the society of the classical author. *Fingal* must, therefore, begin with a preliminary dissertation on the ancient Celts.

The dissertation on *Fingal* may have seemed rather dry to Romantic readers of *Ossian*, who turned to the poetry for emotional rather than antiquarian reasons, but it nevertheless provides invaluable information for anyone trying to understand Macpherson. After publishing *The Works of Ossian*, 1765, Macpherson more or less abandoned poetry, moving instead to history and politics, but it is clear from the essays on *Fingal* and *Temora* that his more mature interests were already developing in the early 1760s. When *Temora* appeared in 1763, Macpherson observed, 'what renders Temora infinitely more valuable than Fingal, is the light it throws on the history of the times' (*Temora*, xviii) and the same historical emphasis eventually led to Macpherson's final contribution to Celtic studies, his three-hundred-page history, *An Introduction to the History of Great Britain and Ireland*, 1771.[2] Both the dissertation on *Temora* and the later *Introduction* concentrated largely on the knotty problem of the origin of the Scots, which was being hotly debated by Irish and Scottish antiquaries of the time. Macpherson refused to accept that the Scots were originally inhabitants of Ireland, despite the evidence of seventeenth-century historians, and the debate raged throughout the eighteenth century.[3] Since the question is hardly relevant to *Ossian*, this chapter focuses chiefly on the dissertation on *Fingal*, which was the first and most illuminating of Macpherson's prose works on the Celts.

Although Macpherson suggested that his epic was 'the genuine history of Fingal's expedition, embellished by poetry' (*Fingal*, preface), he was fairly evasive about the early history of Scotland in his first essay. In fact the dissertation begins by emphasising the absence of historical records concerning the Celts, attributing this loss to the impermanence of their oral tradition. It was, of course, advantageous to Macpherson as a creative writer: the Celts were a vanished people, whose greatness was magnified by the mystery surrounding them. At the same time, Macpherson's imagination was unhampered by inconvenient facts: his conjectural history was really a personal view of the Ancient World which he wished others to share.

Although Macpherson's dissertations were highly idiosyncratic, he made some use of the sources available and on this particular point, both *Temora* and the *Introduction* are helpful. In the dissertation on *Temora*, for example, Macpherson refers to various historians, including Fordun, Buchanan, Keating and O'Flaherty, but only in order to reject their accounts as misguided and inaccurate.[4] He then describes Sir James Ware's *De Hibernia* in more favourable terms, but still does not appear to have been greatly influenced by the work.[5] When we come to the *Introduction*, we find that the main source cited is Dr John Macpherson's *Critical Dissertations on the Origin, Antiquities, etc of the Caledonians*, (*Introduction*, 152). Although the work was not published until 1768, it bears a certain resemblance to the dissertations on *Fingal* and *Temora*, which suggests that Macpherson's views on Celtic Scotland may well have developed during his visit to Dr Macpherson in Skye. The Minister of Sleat was a recognised authority on Celtic antiquities and Macpherson's admiration for him was unreserved:

> His observations are so judicious, and his arguments so conclusive . . . that to give him the merit of being the best antiquary that has ever treated of the origin of the Scots, is too small a tribute to his memory. (*Introduction*, 45–6)[6]

Macpherson's view that the Scots had not originated in Ireland probably derived from Dr John Macpherson, which would account for his dogmatic rejection of any historian who failed to concur. There is, however, a possibility that James himself had a hand in the preparation of the *Critical Dissertations on the Caledonians*, as seen from a letter to the publisher, Thomas Becket, written by Dr Macpherson's son: 'The Errors which have been objected to can have little weight, I see many of them with my own eyes and our friend Mr Macpherson is so friendly as to undertake the revisal of the proof sheets. It is unnecessary to say that a few strokes of his pen will throw a lustre over the whole performance.'[7] The resemblances between the two works may thus have stemmed from James' amendments rather than from the Doctor's original ideas.

The second major source cited by Macpherson in his *Introduction*, though non-literary, was by far the most interesting. In addition to Dr Macpherson's history, James drew directly on his own knowledge of Highland society:

> The opinions of our forefathers ought to be traced among those of their posterity, whom their situation excluded from any considerable commerce with strangers; such, till of late years, were the inhabitants of a part of Wales, and such are some Irish tribes, and the natives of the mountains of Scotland.(*Introduction*, 152)

Macpherson believed that the only way to understand the Celts was through a study of contemporary Scottish Highlanders, whom he regarded as a rare example of a race which had survived uncorrupted by outside influences since the third century:

> If tradition could be depended upon, it is only among a people from all time, free of intermixture with foreigners. We are to look for these among the mountains and inaccessible parts of a country: places, on account of their barrenness, uninviting to an enemy or whose natural strength enabled the natives to repel invasions. Such are the inhabitants of the mountains of Scotland. We, accordingly, find, that they differ materially from those who possess the low and more fertile part of the kingdom. Their language is pure and original, and their manners are those of an antient and unmixed race of men.   (*Temora*, ii)

In Macpherson's eyes the Highlanders were direct descendants of the ancient Caledonians, who had remained undefeated by the Romans and all subsequent invasions. They seemed to be living representatives of an early society, free from the corrupting influences of civilisation and retaining the virtues of their heroic ancestors. Therefore, 'by applying the accounts of the ancients to the criterion of the living manners and indigenous opinions of an unmixed race of men' (*Introduction*, 153), Macpherson thought he could reconstruct the society of the ancient Celts.

The reference to 'the accounts of the ancients' recalls the classical bias of Macpherson's education at Aberdeen. It was not difficult to imagine the young Highland student identifying with the societies portrayed in Blackwell's *Homer* or Duncan's *Caesar* and when Macpherson came to writing about the Celts, he made the most of the parallels between his native society and the Ancient World. Macpherson's vision of Celtic Scotland was heavily indebted to Tacitus,

Strabo, Caesar, Pliny, Livy, Diodorus Seculus and Pomponius Mela and references to these sources appear in the margins of his dissertations, just as the poems are annotated with classical poetry. Macpherson could find many familiar features in the classical accounts, which stressed the energy and hardiness of the primitive races. As we saw in Chapter Two, ancient German society had much in common with the eighteenth-century Highlands and Macpherson drew a direct parallel in his discussion of the Celtic oral tradition:

> All the historical monuments of the old Germans were comprehended in their ancient songs; which were either hymns to their gods, or elegies in praise of their heroes, and were intended to perpetuate the great events in their nation which were carefully interwoven them (sic). (*Fingal*, xii–xiii)

The similarities between the Highlanders and the ancient people described by classical authors was designed to prove Macpherson's theory that they were the direct descendants of the Celts, while the learned references had the added benefit of bolstering the impression of scholarship.

Macpherson's references to the Germans were not merely intended to prove the antiquity of the Highland people. In the passage on the oral tradition, he also referred to the Spartans and the Incas: both races which were now extinct, but still carried strong associations for the eighteenth-century reader. While the Spartans were renowned for their austerity, courage and military zeal, the Incas evoked thoughts of a great civilisation destroyed by foreign conquest. The Germans themselves were thought to be remarkable for their vigour, social feeling and primitive virtue and in works such as Tacitus' *Germania*, they represented a strong contrast to the corrupt society of Imperial Rome. It is not difficult to see Macpherson's idealised picture of the ancient Celts as a similar expression of dissatisfaction with the dominant civilisation of Britain.[8]

By the mid eighteenth century, the complacent parallels between modern Britain and Augustan Rome were being undermined by the growing emphasis on the decline of the Roman Empire. Macpherson's interest in the Celts can be seen partly as a reaction against out-worn classicism; as far as he could see, the 'unrivalled fame' of the Greeks and Romans depended not so much on their actions as on the classical historians who recorded these actions (*Fingal*, ii). Although the Celts had once been as powerful as the Greeks or Romans, the absence of written records meant that their fame had vanished with their race. In Macpherson's eyes, the lost Celtic heroes far surpassed many of the Romans whose names had survived as a result of their national literacy:

> no dignity of character, no greatness of soul, can rescue the

prince from the oblivion which must involve his unpolished and illiterate people. Fingal passed away unnoticed in Caledonia, at the time that Heliogabalus employed the page of the historian at Rome. (*Introduction*, 202).

In a sense, Macpherson's own Ossianic poems, with their lengthy historical essays, were an attempt to redress the balance.

Throughout Macpherson's work there is a strong desire to establish an alternative to the familiar societies of ancient Greece and Rome. The fact that neither the Celts, the Spartans, the Germans nor the Incas had recorded their deed in writing, did not preclude them from being great races. Indeed, Macpherson associated the development of letters with a degeneration from the earliest stages of society, when mankind is at its most active: 'British nations, till of late years, were more remarkable for the performance of great actions in the field, than for recording them with dignity and precision in the closet' (*Introduction*, 4). Despite the benefits of literacy, the very act of writing could be seen as inferior to the original experience which it recorded. The anxieties of Blackwell and Reid appear to have had far-reaching effects on their student. Macpherson's account of the Celts was the complete antithesis of their gloomy concern with the isolating effects of modern academic life. The oral tradition was part of a closely-knit community where all news was passed on through the personal medium of speech. Although the memory of great deeds then died out with the race, the active, primitive society had retained something that vanished with the development of the arts of civilisation.

Poetry was a vital element of the primitive races, and in Macpherson's Caledonia, the Bards played an important role in their society. Not only did they provide essential channels of communication, but they also contributed to the moral education of the people:

> They could form a perfect hero in their own minds, and ascribe that character to their prince. The inferior chiefs made this ideal character the model of their conduct, and by degrees brought their minds to that generous spirit which breathes in all poetry of the times. The prince, flattered by his bards, and rivalled by his own heroes, who imitated his character as described in the eulogies of his poets, endeavoured to excel his people in merit, as he was above them in station. This emulation continuing, formed at last the general character of the nation, happily compounded of what is noble in barbarity, and virtuous and generous in a polished people. (*Fingal*, x–xi)

In early society, poetry was not the 'mere private art' which it seemed to have become in eighteenth-century Britain. The songs of the bards inspired the Celtic chieftains and their men, thus encouraging the development of a 'noble . . . virtuous . . . and generous' race. Blackwell's concern about the 'unnatural separation of *Learning* from *Life*' had no place in the society of Macpherson's Celts. As the influence of the bards made people strive to become 'perfect heroes', so the efforts of the people, in turn, inspired the bards to compose further poetry:

> When virtue in peace, and bravery in war, are the characteristics of a nation, their actions become interesting, and their fame worthy of immortality. A generous spirit is warmed with nobleactions, and becomes ambitious of perpetuating them. This is the true source of that divine inspiration, to which the poets of all ages pretended. (*Fingal*, xi)

Macpherson's portrait of the Celts and their Bards is insistently human. The tradition of the divine afflatus has no place in Morven, where poetry depends on the reciprocal inspiration of the Bards and their society. Indeed, Macpherson was careful to point out the absence of the divine in Celtic poetry:

> That race of men carried their notions of martial honour to an extravagant pitch. Any aid given their heroes in battle, was thought to derogate from their fame; and the bards immediately transferred the glory of the action to him who had given that aid.
> Had Ossian brought down gods, as often as Homer hath done, to assist his heroes, this poem had not consisted of eulogiums on his friends, but of hymns to these superior beings.
>   (*Fingal*, v–vi)

The mythological elements of classical literature caused considerable problems for sceptical readers of the eighteenth century, but Macpherson rejected them for a specific reason: the presence of the deities in *Homer* reduced the status of the human characters.[9] As a result, his Celtic world was a Romantic one, filled not with gods, but with 'godlike' heroes. The demand for epic machinery could be fulfilled by the introduction of ghosts, which still sustained the emphasis on the human rather than the divine.

A complete absence of religion would not have pleased all Macpherson's patrons. The essay on *Fingal* includes the following comment, presumably for the benefit of readers such as Blair who regretted the lack of religion in *Ossian*: 'To say, that a nation is void of all religion, is the same thing as to say, that it does not consist of people endued with reason' (*Fingal*, vi). The absence of Christianity was necessary to suggest that the poems antedated the era of conversion, but Macpherson also avoided any discussion of Celtic theology. The poems include no evidence of Ossian believing in anything other than his father's memory and indeed, the only passages concerned with Celtic religion concentrate on the role of the priesthood in society, in terms which are far from complimentary.

Rather than speculate on the beliefs of the Druids, Macpherson attacked their abuse of power:

> Their pretended intercourse with heaven, their magic and divination were the same. The knowledge of the Druids in natural causes, and the properties of certain things, the fruit of the experiments of ages gained them a mighty reputation among the people. The esteem of the populace soon increased into a veneration for the order; which a cunning and ambitious tribe of men took care to improve, to such a degree, that they, in a manner, ingrossed the management of civil, as well as religious, matters.
>
> (*Fingal*, iv)

Macpherson's attitude to the Druids is similar to that of John Toland, who portrayed them as cunning manipulators in *A Critical History of the Celtic Religion and Learning: containing an account of the Druids* (London 1740), but the attack on clerical power also had a certain relevance to contemporary Scotland, where the Presbytery enjoyed such authority. For Macpherson, the Druids were a restrictive force, who governed 'through the channel of prejudice and ignorance', while the Bards were concerned with the true 'moral character' of the nation (*Introduction*, 198–99), a distinction which would undoubtedly have appealed strongly to the moderate intellectuals of Edinburgh. Some five years before the publication of *Fingal*, Macpherson's most enthusiastic patrons, Blair, Ferguson, Carlyle and Hume, had been deeply involved in the controversy surrounding John Home's tragedy, *Douglas*.[10] In the debate between the Moderates and the austere Kirk, similar questions about the moral influence of the arts and the narrow attitudes of the Presbytery had been raised, so Macpherson's image of the Celts, whose morality came from the poets rather than the priests, would have given his sponsors considerable satisfaction.

The influence of Macpherson's patrons is difficult to determine absolutely, but both internal evidence and information concerning the composition of *Fingal* suggest that the views of both Hugh Blair and Adam Ferguson have a certain relevance. We know that Macpherson's lodgings in Edinburgh were directly beneath Blair's and that he was seeing Blair regularly, during the composition of *Fingal*. Blair had written the preface for the *Fragments* and now his enthusiasm for the poetry of early societywas a driving force behind *Fingal* and *Temora*. Another regular visitor, whose views appear to have been equally influential, was the moral philosopher, Adam Ferguson.

While Macpherson was busy assembling *Fingal* and the 'Other Poems' in 1760-1761, Ferguson was throwing his energies into the campaign for the Scottish Militia. It is not difficult to imagine the two men discussing Ferguson's military ideals, which included courage, patriotism, camaraderie, loyalty to one's leader, and the unselfish pursuit of virtue for the benefit of the country.[11] Such ideals accorded well with Macpherson's opinions of the Scottish Highlanders and his Celtic heroes could be seen as an embodiment of Ferguson's 'martial spirit'. Just as the ancient Bards had inspired the Celtic warriors, so Macpherson's *Ossian* should stir up Scottish readers of the 1760s.[12]

Ferguson's relevance to *Ossian* does not consist solely in his military interests. Of all the Edinburgh literati, he was probably the most interested in the progress of society, publishing his *Essay on the History of Civil Society* in 1767. It is possible that Ferguson's attitude to early man was influenced by Macpherson, but equally likely that Macpherson's ideas were affected by his conversations with the Highland philosopher who was thirteen years his senior.[13] Whatever the source of the ideas, Macpherson's sketch of the history of civilisation has much in common with Ferguson's views:

> There are three stages in human society. The first is the result of consanguinity, and the natural affection of the members of a family to one another. The second begins when property is established, and men enter into associations for mutual defence, against the invasions and injustice of neighbours. Mankind submit, in the third, to certain laws and subordinations of government, to which they trust the safety of their persons and property. As the first is formed on nature, so, of course, it is the most disinterested and noble. Men, in the last, have leisure to cultivate the mind, and to restore it, with reflection, to a primaeval dignity of sentiment. The middle stage is the region of compleat barbarism and ignorance.   (*Temora*, xii)

Although the division of society into stages was commonplace in the eighteenth century, Macpherson differed from many of his contemporaries, including Hugh Blair, by ignoring the issue of subsistence.[14] Rather than emphasise the difference between societies based on hunting, pasturage, agriculture or commerce, Macpherson stressed the importance of property and its effect on morality. The idea of property as a factor in social change can be traced back to the works of John Locke, Samuel Pufendorf and Hugo Grotius, but of contemporary writers, Macpherson's scheme has most in common with Ferguson.[15]

Like Macpherson, Adam Ferguson was deeply concerned with the moral implications of progress and the dangers of corruption in a civilised state. In his *Essay on the History of Civil Society*, Ferguson divided society into the three stages of 'savagery', 'barbarism' and 'civilisation', which bears close resemblance to Macpherson's scheme. Although the *Essay* is altogether more subtle and objective than Macpherson's work, it is possible to relate Ferguson's views on the 'Corruption incident to polished nations' to observations such as this:

Luxury grows with the increase of the arts of civil life, rapacity treads close on its heels; and then, for the first time, the check of law and regulation becomes necessary to the welfare, if not to the very being of the community.   (*Introduction*, 229–230)[16]

While Ferguson merely pointed out the dangers of progress, Macpherson saw luxury (and therefore corruption) as the inevitable consequence of civilisation.

Despite his reservations about civilisation and admiration for the virtues of early man, Ferguson was by no means a primitivist and constantly stressed man's progressive nature.[17] Macpherson, on the other hand, maintained an unqualified preference for the earliest stages of society as 'the most disinterested and noble'. While Ferguson, like most of his contemporaries, was aware of the less attractive features of savage society, Macpherson saw no disadvantages.[18] Neither Thomas Hobbes's view of the 'state of nature' nor the Calvinist idea of man being corrupted through Original Sin had any bearing on Macpherson's vision. According to Macpherson, 'man is by nature just' (*Introduction*, 236), while 'vice is not natural to man' (*Introduction*, 198). Such a view can be seen as part of the optimistic tradition of Shaftesbury and Hutcheson, but the conclusions drawn by Macpherson were profoundly pessimistic.

Unlike Ferguson who defined the 'state of nature' as being anywhere that 'this active being is in the train of employing his talents', Macpherson imposed a historical pattern on his view of human nature.[19] His equation between early society and natural man led to the corresponding association between modern society and corrupt man. As a consequence, the moment when Ossian was alive to compose his songs, at a point of transition from the earliest to the second stage of society, was a moment of degeneration. The heroic age of Fingal was the ideal – the earliest stage based on nature – so its passing marked the beginning of a steady decline.

Macpherson applied his theoretical scheme to the history of Scotland, correlating the second stage with the departure of the Romans and the establishment of government in the Lowlands (*Temora*, xiv) . Above all, it was the period in which transactions with the Saxons began. Macpherson describes the ancient Caledonians retreating into the mountains, forming clans and living in ideal rural societies, self-sufficient and autonomous, while the people of the Lowlands declined steadily into a modern, commercial state. Macpherson's attitude towards the Saxons as a malignant influence is highly significant. His view of human nature as innately good led to the tendency to blame corruption on external influences. A society could retain its original virtue as long as it remained unconquered and free from communication with foreign, more advanced (ie more corrupt) civilisations. His view of Scottish history isolated the Highlanders as just such a community, untainted by commerce or conquest since their original settlement.

Macpherson's views help to explain his deep anxiety about the 1707 Union with England and the changes that were taking place in the Highlands in the eighteenth century. His ostensibly historical dissertation on *Fingal* concluded not with remarks on the ancient Celts, but with a discussion of the contemporary Highlanders:

> The genius of the highlanders has suffered a great change within these few years. The communication with the rest of the island is open, and the introduction of trade and manufactures has destroyed that leisure which was formerly dedicated to hearing and repeating the poems of ancient times. Many have now learned to leave their mountains, and seek their fortunes in a milder climate; and though a certain *amor patriae* may sometimes bring them back, they have, during their absence, imbibed enough of foreign manners to despise the customs of their ancestors. Bards have been long disused . . . consanguinity is not so much regarded.
>
> (*Fingal*, xv)

Macpherson's description of the contemporary Highlands is in sharp contrast to his vision of Celtic Scotland. He was acutely conscious of the steady integration of the Highlands into the rest of Britain, seeing himself as a witness to the final collapse of a society which had remained uncorrupted for over two thousand years. Instead of expressing anger over the events of the '45, he observed factors which were to have far more permanent effects on the Highlands. Communication with Lowland Britain brought commercial products and trade to the Highlands, while the wealth of the South drew the inhabitants away from their homes. The erosion of the Gaelic language was another important factor in the disintegration of Highland culture, breaking down the close communities and destroying the memories of their ancestors. Macpherson's own emphasis on poetry as a moral guide suggested that the disappearance of the oral tradition threatened the very virtues of the Highlanders. Thus he saw his own collection of Gaelic poetry as a hopeless gesture towards the preservation of Celtic Scotland. He could identify only too closely with Ossian as the last of the heroic race. The age of Fingal had vanished, but at least the memory of a greater society could be carried into the degenerate civilisation of eighteenth-century Europe.

NOTES
1. D. Erskine Baker, *The Muse of Ossian*, (Edinburgh 1763). The British Library's copy includes John Wilkes' note, 'The Muse of Ossian is a vile Scottish jade'.

2. *An Introduction to the History of Great Britain and Ireland*, (London 1771); 2nd edn, enlarged, 1772; 3rd edn, 1773. References are to the first edn. Macpherson was prompted to revise his work by a rival historian: 'A Dull Scotch Presbyterian Parson having come up to town the month of October last with two immense quartos on the origin and antiquities of the British nations, I was induced to furbish up my dissertations on that subject – and to add as many more in order to get the start of the heavy rogue and behold some copies are herewith sent. One copy is my present to you – or if you please – all are mine to be given away to as many friends as you chuse; or to be used in a Madras little house for I believe the paper is of deliberate softness', James to John Macpherson, 25 March 1773, IO MS Macpherson, 122.
3. See M. V. Hay, *A Chain of Error in Scottish History*, (London 1927). See also G. Menzies, *Who are the Scots?* (London 1971).
4. John of Fordun, *Chronica Gentis Scotorum, Gesta Annalia*, c. 1380; G. Buchanan, *Rerum Scoticarum Historia*, 1582; R. O'Flaherty, *Ogygia; seu, rerum Hibernicarum Chronologia*, 1685; G. Keating, *Foras Feasas ar Eirinn*, 1629.
5. Macpherson may have been influenced by the preface to the English translation of *De Hibernia*: 'The Writers of the History of Ireland, for the most part utterly ignorant or negligent of the Genuine Remains of Antiquity, have obtruded on the World a multitude of uncouth, incoherent and ridiculous Fables and Legends instead of Authentic Relations of Matters of Fact', *The Antiquities and History of Ireland*, (London 1705). Macpherson's historical sources have been examined in detail by I.Haywood, 'The Making of History: A Study of the Literary Forgeries of James Macpherson and Thomas Chatterton in Relation to Eighteenth-Century Ideas of History and Fiction', (unpublished doctoral dissertation, University of London, 1983).
6. Cf. Gibbon, 'In the dark and doubtful paths of Caledonian antiquity I have chosen for my guide two learned and ingenious Highlanders, whom their birth and education had peculiarly qualified for that office. See Critical Dissertations on the Origin, Antiquities, etc, of the Caledonians by Dr John Macpherson, London 1768, in 4to; and Introduction to the History of Great Britain and Ireland by James Macpherson', *The Decline and Fall of the Roman Empire*, 1776–1778; ed. J. B. Bury, 7 vols, (London 1896–1900), III, 41.
7. John Macpherson offered the manuscript of his late father to Becket for publication in December 1766, BL MS ADD 40166 f104. There is no indication of how many strokes of James Macpherson's pen were needed or supplied.
8. See H. N. Fairchild, *The Noble Savage*, (New York 1928); A. Pagden, 'The Savage Critic: Some European Images of the Primitive', *The Yearbook of English Studies*, xiii, 1983, 32–45.
9. Cf. O. Goldsmith & J. Newbury, 'the aid which Homer attributes to the gods, is often to the disadvantage of his own heroes, I mean the Grecian chiefs; for it is no wonder that those should fight bravely, and betray no symptoms of fear, who are assur'd of the protection of heaven, and have armour formed by the celestial powers to render them invincible; tho' the great Ajax, has, I think, no supernatural aid, and may therefore be deemed a greater hero than

Achilles', *The Art of Poetry on a New Plan*, 2 vols, (London 1762), II, 214–15.
10. On the *Douglas* controversy see Sher, *Church and University . . .*, 74–93; E. C. Mossner, Hume and the Scottish Shakespeare, *Huntingdon Library Quarterly*, iii (4), 1940, 419–41; *Scots Magazine*, xix, 1757, passim.
11. Ferguson's ideals were expressed in his *Reflections Previous to the Establishment of a Militia*, (London 1756) and his *Essay on the History of Civil Society*, 1767, ed. D. Forbes, (Edinburgh 1966).
12. See Sher, op. cit.; Sher, 'Those Scottish Imposters and their Cabal: Ossian and the Scottish Enlightenment', *Man and Nature, Proceedings of the Canadian Society for Eighteenth-Century Studies*, i, ed. R. L. Emerson, (London & Ontario 1982), 55–63.
13. Many of Ferguson's ideas had been developing for several years before the publication of the *Essay*, G. Bryson, *Man and Society. The Scottish Inquiry of the Eighteenth Century*, (Princeton 1945), 30.
14. Blair, *A Critical Dissertation on the Poems of Ossian*, (London 1763), 16–17. The various divisions of society by Kames, Smith, Dalrymple etc. are discussed by R. Meek, *Social Science and the Ignoble Savage*, (Cambridge 1976).
15. Meek, ibid., 14ff. The emphasis on family and the effects of property also find parallels in Rousseau (see Meek, 115). Macpherson's own division is discussed by M. M. Rubel, *Savage and Barbarian, Historical Attitudes in the Criticism of Homer and Ossian in Britain, 1760–1800*, (Amsterdam 1978), 34.
16. Cf. Ferguson, *Civil Society*, 248–61.
17. Ibid, 6–7.
18. Ferguson saw pride, vanity, gambling, revenge and idleness as characteristics of uncivilised nations, Ibid, 76, 93, 101.
19. Ferguson, op. cit., 8.

The Response to Ossian

> Ossian, sublimest, simplest bard of all,
> Whom English infidels, Macpherson call.
> Churchill, The Prophecy of Famine, 1763

If *Fragments of Ancient Poetry* had captured the attention of the British reading public, *Fingal* and *Temora* were to make Ossian famous throughout the world. By 1763 the Abbe Cesarotti had translated *Fingal* into Italian, and from here, the vogue for *Ossian* spread across Europe and even to America, as the poems were published in Swedish, German, French, Spanish, Danish, Russian, Dutch, Bohemian, Polish and Hungarian.[1] Suddenly everybody was talking about the lonely hills of Morven and the publicity campaign planned by the Edinburgh literati seemed to have been a huge success. Or had it?

Today *The Poems of Ossian* are known principally as a forgery, but this prejudice against Macpherson's work is by no means new. As soon as the *Fragments* appeared doubts were raised about their authenticity, and the controversy has rumbled along ever since. Thomas Gray's response is an interesting example of the conflicting feelings that Macpherson provoked. As one of the first to be exposed to the Gaelic translations, Gray's initial reactions were uninfluenced by the numerous arguments put forward after the publication of *Fingal* and *Temora*. Nevertheless, even in the summer of 1760 Gray was torn between his delight in the poetry and his doubts about its authenticity:

> The Erse Fragments have been publish'd five weeks ago in Scotland . . . I continue to think them genuine, tho' my reasons for believing the contrary are rather stronger than ever: but I will have them antique, for I never knew a Scotchman of my own time, that could read, much less write, poetry; & such poetry too![2]

Though thrilled by the imaginative power of the poetry, as an antiquarian and scholar of the eighteenth century Gray's scepticism was also aroused. His initial reaction to the *Fragments* was twofold: 'I was so struck, so *extasié* with their infinite beauty, that I writ into Scotland to make a thousand enquiries'.[3] From the beginning, Macpherson's work provoked both enthusiasm and enquiry, with readers divided between admiration for the poetry and suspicion about its antiquity. Gray's remarks about the 'Scotchman' are also indicative of the nationalistic prejudices which were to affect the fortunes of *Ossian* in the eighteenth century. Gray's ironic mockery was light-hearted enough, but for many readers *Ossian* was a symbol of Scotland, and attitudes towards the poems were a point of national pride. Not surprisingly, the readers who were quickest to find fault with Macpherson's work came from outside Scotland.

Interest in the ancient poetry of Wales was already flourishing by the 1760s, so the discovery of Celtic poetry from the North aroused considerable discussion. The general attitude of the Welsh antiquaries was one of scepticism. Lewis Morris, who had studied the Welsh tradition, greeted Macpherson's *Fragments* with scorn: 'to me it appears, and also from his own words in the preface, to be entirely his own invention'.[4] Ironically, it was not the poetry itself but the observations in Blair's preface that provoked Morris's attack. To the Welsh scholar, as indeed to many fellow readers, the idea that Ossian's poetry should have survived unaltered since the third century seemed decidedly implausible: 'If they were handed down by illiterate shepherds or minstrels, without rhyme or numbers, pray what was the *bondage* that kept the words together?'[5] Like many contemporary readers, Morris showed a strong distrust of the oral tradition. His observation that if the poems had been handed down by Bards, 'they must be in MS',[6] was typical of the criticism that was to be levelled at Macpherson for the next century.

Macpherson did little to help his own reputation, and Morris's opinion probably owed as much to the translator's attitude as to the published volume. In February 1761, Lewis Morris wrote indignantly:

> I have seen a letter of his lately wherein he says that he could soon make himself master of the Welsh tongue, so as to translate any pieces *if there be anything worth translating* out of it, and he says it is an easy matter for a person acquainted with one of the dialects of Celtic (the Erse for example) to understand the rest. This is a little flashy and romantic, I think, or else I am exceedingly dull.[7]

Remarks such as these did little to endear Macpherson to non-Scottish readers, and especially not to those who had spent years on the study of Celtic literature and history. Indeed, some of the most vigorous attacks on *Ossian* came from Ireland.

Just as Lewis Morris had taken exception to the preface to the *Fragments*, so the Irish scholars fell upon the dissertations on *Fingal* and *Temora*. One of the first full-length criticisms to appear was

Ferdinando Warner's *Remarks on the History of Fingal and Other Poems of Ossian*, (London 1762).⁸ Warner was actually an admirer of the Ossianic poetry:

> If the Epic Poem had not a single Word of True History for its Foundation – and indeed it has very little – it would . . . be just as good a poem as tho' it were all genuine History: and I believe Mr Macpherson has done much Justice to the Original in his Translation as an English Dress is capable of. (*Remarks* . . ., 12)

What he found intolerable, however, was Macpherson's attempt to present himself to the world as a scholarly editor and learned historian. Warner demonstrated how Macpherson had appropriated the old Irish heroes to Scottish soil, and confused the chronology of the legends by making Fingal and Cuchullin contemporaries. Despite his criticisms, Warner was prepared to accept that *Fingal* was based on genuine Celtic tradition, but that it was a *poetic* tradition and not historically accurate. The Irish heroes had long been part of Highland culture, while the confusion of stories from the Ulster and Fenian cycles of literature had taken place in the oral tradition many years before Macpherson began his work. In early Irish literature, Cuchullin appears in stories from the first-century Ulster cycle, while Finn and his followers were part of the third-century Fenian cycle, but as Macpherson was drawing on his own knowledge of the Highland legends, he was probably unaware of any error. Warner, however, was not questioning Macpherson's use of genuine Gaelic poetry. His objections were directed towards the presentation of *Ossian* as history, but the exposure of Macpherson's errors opened the way to further onslaughts.

Other Irish historians were rather less polite about Macpherson's efforts, especially after the publication of *Temora*. In the essay that prefaced the second epic, Macpherson made sweeping condemnations of the Irish writers Keating and O'Flaherty, while criticising John Fordun (somewhat ironically) for deriving historical facts from the 'improbable fictions' of the Irish bards. The Celtic scholars rallied to the defence of Irish history and in 1764, Macpherson's remarks were refuted boldly in *Fingal, King of Morven, a Knight-Errant*, 1764. Vigorous attacks on Macpherson's 'Forgeries, Omissions and Misplacings' were also made by Charles O'Conor in the appendix to his *Dissertations on the History of Ireland*, 1766.⁹

The sentiment shared by almost all the Celtic scholars who attacked *The Poems of Ossian* had been expressed in the anonymous pamphlet, *Fingal Reclaimed*, (London 1762): 'I cannot help wishing that Mr Mc—N had produced these Poems without Notes' (7). The scholarly dissertations and copious footnotes, so carefully designed to impress an English-reading public, had brought Macpherson more abuse than praise. Without the pretentious notes, Macpherson's adversaries would have had less ground on which to base their criticisms and might have been more inclined to accept the poems as works of art. As it was, Macpherson's translations were seized upon as historical documents, the dissertations were dismembered and the accusations of fraud followed.

Just as the Welsh and Irish scholars were goaded by patriotic pride, so the responses of English readers tended to be coloured by nationalistic feelings. Gray's ironic remarks about the 'Scotchman' reflect the uneasy relationship between Scotland and the rest of Britain in the mid eighteenth century. By the early 1760s the perennial rivalry had reached a peak. Although the Jacobite threat had largely disappeared after the '45, the antagonism between the 'united' countries was aggravated during the Seven Years War by the Militia question. By 1762, the threatening image of the Scots had been fuelled once again, this time by the sudden rise to power of the Earl of Bute.

The publication of *Fingal* coincided with Bute's rapid ascent in the British Government and many of the earliest attacks on Macpherson were, in fact, political. As Hume observed in November, 1762: 'Fingal is not much heard of at present. The English were exceedingly fond of it at first but hearing that it was Scotch, they became jealous and silent.'[10] 1762 saw the appearance of works such as *Gisbal, An Hyperborean Tale: translated from the Fragments of Ossian the Son of Fingal*, a Biblical parody describing the successes of Gisbal the 'mighty man from the North'. Although the attack was primarily on Bute and his intimacy with the Princess of Wales, Macpherson's work also came under fire. Bute's patronage of Macpherson made *Fingal* the perfect butt for any writer bent on exposing the unpopular Minister. In John Wilkes' satirical journal, *The North Briton*, the sarcasm was particularly heavy:

> I am happy to find that the *English* are not so sparing and penurious to us, both of money and praise, as they used to be. We are certainly growing into fashion. The most rude of our bards are admired; and I know some choice wits here, who have thrown aside *Shakespeare*, and taken up *Fingal*, charmed with the variety of character, and richness of imagery.[11]

Wilkes's close friend and co-editor, Charles Churchill, was hardly less damning in his 'Scots Pastoral', *The Prophecy of Famine*:

> Now be the Muse disrobed of all her pride,
> Be all the glare of verse by Truth supplied,
> And if plain nature pours a simple strain,
> Which Bute may praise and Ossian not disdain,
> Ossian, sublimest, simplest Bard of all,
> Whom English infidels Macpherson call,

Then round my head shall honour's ensigns wave,
And pensions mark me for a willing slave. (265–72)

Bute's patronage may have helped Macpherson financially, but it did little to enhance his reputation as a writer.

Contemporary political prejudices were not always adverse, however, and the most enthusiastic review of *Fingal* appeared in the Tory journal *The Critical Review*. Smollett, whose journal *The Briton* was being satirised by Wilkes' *North Briton*, was a staunch supporter of both the Bute government and *The Poems of Ossian*. In his novel *Humphry Clinker*, the Bramble family travel wearily through the fashionable resorts of Britain in search of health, arriving at last in the refreshing air of Northern Scotland. Smollett's idealised portrait of the uncorrupted Highlands includes the following eulogy:

> These are the lonely hills of Morven, where Fingal and his heroes enjoyed the same pastime: I feel an enthusiastic pleasure when I survey the brown heath that Ossian wont to tread; and hear the wind whistle through the bending grass – When I enter our landlord's hall, I look for the suspended harp of that divine bard, and listen in hopes of hearing the aerial sound of his respected spirit – The Poems of Ossian are in every mouth – A famous antiquarian of this country, the Laird of Mackfarlane, at whose house we dined a few days ago, can repeat them all in the original Gaelick. (240)

Smollett's defence of *Ossian* revealed a certain patriotism typical of Scots in the mid-eighteenth century. Similar zeal can be discerned in the critical dissertations works of Blair and Lord Kames and, more obviously, in the indignant replies to Dr Johnson's famous attack on Macpherson. The very fervour of the *Ossian* supporters tended to increase the doubts over the authenticity and, as early as 1763, David Hume was beginning to question his own desire to accept Macpherson's work as genuine. He expressed his concern about the widespread allegations of forgery in a letter to Blair:

> I often hear them totally rejected with disdain and indignation, as a palpable and most impudent forgery. This opinion has indeed become very prevalent among the men of letters in London, and I can foresee, that in a few years the poems, if they continue to stand on their present footing, will be thrown aside, and will fall into final oblivion. It is in vain to say, that their beauty will support them, independent of their authenticity: No; that beauty is not so much to the general taste to ensure you of this event; and if people be once disgusted with the idea of a forgery, they are thence apt to entertain a more disadvantageous notion of the excellency of the production itself. The absurd pride and caprice of Macpherson himself, who scorns, as he pretends, to satisfy

any body, that doubts his veracity, has tended much to confirm this general scepticism: and I must own, for my own part that, though I have had many particular reasons to believe these poems genuine, more than it is possible for any Englishman of letters to have, yet I am not entirely without my scruples on that head. You think that the internal proofs in favour of the poems are very convincing; so they are; but there are also internal reasons against them, particularly from the manners, notwithstanding all the art, with which you have endeavoured to throw a varnish on that circumstance: and the preservation of such long, and such connected poems by oral tradition alone, during a course of fourteen centuries, is so much out of the ordinary course of human affairs, that it requires the strongest reasons to make us believe it.[12]

Although Hume had originally been an enthusiastic supporter of Macpherson's enterprise, he was now aware of the embarrassing situation that he and his colleagues would face, should *Fingal* prove a fake. Now that the doubts had been raised in England, Hume's own scepticism was roused by certain features of the poems, such as the civilised manners of Macpherson's Celts. He also shared Lewis Morris' doubts about the validity of the oral tradition, finding it hard to accept that poems as long as *Fingal* and *Temora* could have survived from the third century.

The empirical philosopher could not be satisfied by mere arguments, so Hume's letter continued with a demand for testimonies to the authenticity of the poems. Although he was as anxious as Blair to uphold the honour of *Ossian* (and the Edinburgh literati), he could no longer accept Macpherson's claims without independent evidence. Accordingly, he urged Blair to write to ministers in the Highlands, in the hope of obtaining proof of *Ossian*'s authenticity to convince the English:

> Let the clergymen have the translation in their hands, and let them write back to you, and inform you, that they heard such a one (naming him) living in such a place, rehearse the original of such a passage, from such a page to such a page of the English translation, which appeared exact and faithful. If you give to the public a sufficient number of such testimonies, you may prevail.[13]

Blair co-operated promptly, seeking opinions of Macpherson's work throughout the Highlands. In the 1765 edition of *The Works of Ossian*, the results of his investigations were published as an appendix, in which Blair presented the public with an impressive catalogue of Highlanders, who all concurred 'in testifying that Mr Macpherson's collection consists of genuine Highland poems; known to them to be such, both from the general report of the country where they live, and from their own remembrance of the originals'.[14]

Despite Blair's triumphant tone, a careful reading of the letters he received reveals that Macpherson's translation met with a mixed reception in the Highlands. Though quick to defend the existence of Ossian's poetry, the men interviewed by Blair were by no means united in their attitude to Macpherson. Dr John Macpherson emphasised the enormous variations among different versions of the same poem, and thought that Macpherson was well within his rights as an editor to have selected the best of each version, 'when he found the original text corrupted by all rehearsers'.[15] The general reaction, however, was one of disappointment. Many of the Highlanders objected to Macpherson's anglicisation of the traditional names, feeling that Ossian should still be called Oisin, or Inistore should be Inistork.[16] Even Blair was prepared to admit that it appeared, from the letters he had received, that Macpherson had 'not been able to attain the strength and sublimity of the original which he copied'.[17] Most of the Gaelic speakers preferred to dwell on the beauties of the original poetry rather than on Macpherson's version, and Ewan Macpherson voiced what appears to have been a common belief:

> no man, excepting Ossian himself, was ever capable of making such Gaelic poetry as Ossian's, which has a sublimity and nervousness that cannot be equalled, nor successfully imitated: Nor can the Gaelic of Ossian be rendered by the ablest translator into any other language, with an elegance suitable to the grandeur of the original.[18]

The Highland readers recognised the familiar heroes, events and stories in Macpherson's *Ossian*, but were not always impressed by his presentation. Although it took outsiders years to analyse Macpherson's method of adapting his sources, Donald MacQueen realised at once that in order to construct his epic, Macpherson had 'tacked together into the poem, descriptions, similes, names &c, from several detached pieces'.[19] Above all, it was the pseudo-epic form that most disappointed the Highlanders. Even James Macdonald, who admired *Fingal* and *Temora* greatly, wished that 'Mr Macpherson had not given them in that form for it is not the natural dress of Ossian' and the same objection has always been raised by any reader familiar with the genuine Gaelic ballads.[20]

Hugh Blair, however, who was confident that the epic genre was not only the highest literary form, but also the most suitable for an ancient bard, was not interested in the critical opinions of his Highland correspondents. The object of his enquiry had been to find out whether Macpherson's collection consisted of genuine Highland poems and he was therefore happy with the results. There now seemed no doubt about the existence of Ossian's poetry, nor that James

Macpherson had made an extensive collection. The only quibbles were over the quality of the translation but Blair, the Professor of Rhetoric and Belles Lettres, felt competent to judge the poetry for himself. As the new, collected edition of *Ossian* was published, Blair wrote to Hume to let him know that he had managed to silence 'all infidelity and even scepticism concerning Fingal in the Appendix'.[21]

But David Hume, like many other readers, remained unconvinced. While his colleagues continued their patriotic defence of *Ossian*, Hume felt embarrassed that nationalistic prejudices could influence any search for truth. Although he refrained from making his doubts public, he later felt moved to write a brief but forceful essay, in which he condemned *Ossian* as a 'tiresome, insipid performance . . . which has been puffed with a zeal and enthusiasm that has drawn a ridicule on my countrymen'.[22]

Despite Blair's confidence, the doubts about Macpherson's work never really subsided and the controversy continued to rage well into the nineteenth century, flaring up whenever new scholars turned their attentions to *Ossian*. The debate was at its most heated during the two decades following the first publication and Hume's essay on *Ossian* was prompted by the observations made by Johnson in his *Journey to the Western Isles*, 1775. Part of the purpose of Johnson's famous trip had been to get to the bottom of the *Ossian* mystery and Johnson had no qualms about making his conclusions public: 'I believe they never existed in any other form than that which we have seen' (98). Although some of Johnson's observations on Macpherson's use of 'wandering ballads' were reasonably astute, his refusal to believe in the existence of Gaelic manuscripts and the references to 'Caledonian bigotry' did little to increase his popularity North of the Border.

Johnson's attack provoked an equally spirited reply from Donald McNicol (and friends) in 1779,[23] while one of Johnson's supporters, William Shaw, fuelled further debate with the publication of *An Enquiry into the Authenticity of the Poems ascribed to Ossian*, 1781. Shaw's work provoked a diatribe from Macpherson's old friend, John Clark, in *An Answer to Mr Shaw's Enquiry*, 1781, but Shaw was unwilling to admit defeat and promptly parried with his *Reply to Mr Clark's Answer*, 1782. In the meantime another independent investigator, Thomas Hill, was busy conducting his own enquiries in the Highlands. Despite his ignorance of Gaelic, Hill succeeded in collecting several ballads from Highland speakers, which he then published in the *Gentleman's Magazine* together with parallel translations, for readers to compare with Macpherson's *Ossian*.[24]

And so Macpherson's work has continued to attract both supporters and sceptics. The question of whether or not Macpherson was regarded as a forger has depended largely on the definition of forgery, since his practice of blending genuine material with his own creations

The Response to Ossian   171

has been known since the Highland Society's *Report* of 1805. Apart from the political attacks, Macpherson's most vehement critics have always been Gaelic scholars, enraged by his falsification of the true Celtic voice. Although Macpherson's work spawned a number of spurious Ossianic pieces, he nevertheless gave Gaelic scholarship a timely boost. His foresight attracted public attention to the importance of the Gaelic tradition and the danger of it becoming extinct. Whatever the shortcomings of his translation, he was a pioneer and the fine work of later scholars such as J. F. Campbell was largely inspired by Macpherson, even if only by the desire to correct his faults.

The sentimental vein in Macpherson's work is always going to irritate true Celtic scholars, but few of his original readers would have found it offensive. Indeed, for many readers of the late eighteenth and early nineteenth centuries, the whole question of authenticity was irrelevant. As George Chalmers observed in 1805:

> Pray, does anybody at Edinburgh trouble himself about Ossian except Mr Laing? Except the Bible and Shakespeare, there is not any book that sells better than Ossian. This sale seems to me to arise from the intrinsic merit of the book, and not from the talk about it.[25]

Despite the critical attention which Macpherson received from scholars and antiquarians, most of the enthusiasm for *Ossian* came from readers who were quite unconcerned about the sources of the work. They sought ancient literature not for historical or philological reasons, but as an escape from the advancing civilisation of eighteenth-century Europe. Indeed, most of the continental readers came to Ossian through Cesarotti's version – through a translation of a translation – and for them, authenticity was not an issue.

Macpherson succeeded in producing work that struck a deep, emotional chord in readers of the latter half of the eighteenth century. Most would have agreed with the *Critical Review*, that *The Poems of Ossian* had the power to 'wake the soul to sensibility', even though they still felt obliged to mention the historical importance of the work.[26] Thomas Sheridan, for example, announced that the Ossianic poems were 'a great discovery', shedding light 'into the history of mankind', but his observation was very much an afterthought.[27] His real interest had little to do with the antiquity of the poems, as Boswell shows:

> Erskine came in, and he and Sheridan talked very well upon the poems of Ossian, whom Sheridan said he preferred to all the poets in the world, and thought he excelled Homer in the Sublime and Virgil in the Pathetic. He said Mrs Sheridan and he had

fixed it as the standard of feeling, made it like a thermomemeter by which they could judge of the warmth of everybody's heart; and that they calculated beforehand in what degrees all their acquaintances would feel them, which answered exactly. 'To be sure,' said he, 'except people have genuine feelings of poetry, they cannot relish these poems.'[28]

The response belongs to the 'age of sensibility', when judgement of both the work of art and the critic depended on the degree of emotion stirred. Macpherson had provided Mr and Mrs Sheridan with a moral thermometer for gauging the sensitivities of their friends and acquaintances.

Even writers who claimed to have a more philosophical approach to *Ossian* tended to reveal a similar emotionalism in their responses. The antiquary William Stukeley, who was apparently using *Fingal* as documentary evidence to prove his theories on Ancient Britain, still admitted that he 'took more pleasure in reading the poem of Ossian than any other person can'.[29] Hugh Blair, too, though adopting the voice of the philosophical historian, was still attracted primarily by the imaginative power of Macpherson's work.

Blair's *Critical Dissertation on the Poems of Ossian*, 1763, is the best example of the contemporary approach to *Ossian* as literature. It begins:

> Among the monuments remaining of the ancient state of nations, few are more valuable than their poems or songs. History, when it treats of remote and dark ages, is seldom very instructive. The beginnings of society, in every country, are involved in fabulous confusion; and though they were not, they would furnish few events worth recording. But, in every period of society, human manners are a curious spectacle; and the most natural pictures of ancient manners are exhibited in the ancient poems of the nations. These present to us, what is much more valuable than the history of such transactions as a rude age can afford, The history of human imagination and passion.

Despite the stuffy tone, Blair's emphasis on the historical significance of Ossian's poems was not that of the archaeologist. He was not seeking details of social history, or information about important events, but 'the history of human imagination and passion'. In the poetry of early man, he hoped to find emotion in its most natural form, undisguised by the sophistications of civilised life. Blair saw early society as an innocent Golden Age, peopled by men who responded to their environment with a childlike delight:

> the beauties of nature are their chief entertainment. They meet with many objects, to them new and strange; their wonder and surprize are frequently excited; and by the sudden changes of

fortune occurring in their unsettled state of life, their passions are raised to the utmost. Their passions have nothing to restrain them: their imagination has nothing to check it. They display themselves to one another without disguise; and converse and act in the uncovered simplicity of nature. (2)

Blair appears to have turned to *Ossian* for much the same reason that Wordsworth was to seek 'low and rustic life', forty years later. Indeed, his essay continued with the assertion that poetry was the spontaneous expression of feeling: 'as their feelings are strong, so their language, of itself, assumes a poetical turn' (2). And the place to find this ideal expression of strong passion was in the pages of Macpherson's *Ossian*:

> His poetry, more perhaps than that of any other writer, deserves to be stiled, *The Poetry of the Heart*. It is a heart penetrated with noble sentiments, and with sublime and tender passions; a heart that glows and kindles the fancy; a heart that is full, and pours itself forth. Ossian did not write, like modern poets, to please readers and critics. He sung from the love of poetry and song. (21)

Despite Blair's belief in Ossian's noble motivation, the poems were perfectly suited for pleasing both readers and critics. Blair himself had supplied Macpherson with his preconceived notions about what the poetry should be like, so it was hardly surprising that the published poems of Ossian should fulfil his expectations. *Fingal* had all the primitive passion Blair craved:

> Voices of ecchoing Cona! he said, O bards of other times! Ye, on whose souls the blue hosts of our fathers rise! strike the harp in my hall; and let Fingal hear the song. Pleasant is the joy of grief! It is like the shower of spring, when it softens the branch of the oak, and the young leaf lifts its green head. Sing on, O bards!
>
> (*Fingal*, 194)

Here was powerful emotion issuing forth in music and poetry. The simple style offered no disguise to the feelings, while the strong imagination of the ancient bard created metaphors drawn from the natural world. For Blair, figurative language was a vital part of primitive poetry and much of his dissertation was devoted to Ossian's similes, which were evidence of a 'lively imagination' and 'a mind under the dominion of strong passion' (66). Above all, Ossian was the poet of the Sublime:

> The works of Ossian . . . abound with examples of the Sublime. The subjects of that author and the manner in which he writes, are particularly favourable to it. He possesses all the plain and venerable manner of the antient times. He deals in no superfluous or gaudy ornaments; but throws forth his images with a rapid

conciseness, which enables them to strike the mind with the greatest force. Among poets of more polished times, we are to look for the graces of correct writing, for just proportion of parts and skilfully conducted narration. In the midst of smiling scenery and pleasurable themes, the gay and the beautiful will appear, undoubtedly to more advantage. But amidst the rude scenes of nature and society, such as Ossian describes; amidst rocks and torrents, and whirlwinds, and battles, dwells the Sublime; and naturally associates itself with that grave and solemn spirit which distinguishes the author of Fingal.[30]

'Sublimity' was a word constantly associated with *Ossian*, and the *Annual Register*, for example, saw *Fingal* as a sublime poem, with a 'rare and irresistable union of the pathetic and terrible'.[31] Burke had pointed seekers of the Sublime towards storms, whirlwinds, vast cataracts and gloomy mountains, so the Ossianic landscape was an obvious hunting ground. In his classic discussion of the development of new ideas of freedom in eighteenth-century art, Samuel Monk observed that 'the sublime, from the first friendly to greater freedom of expression, became the natural domain of this new freedom, justified in theory by Young, Blair and Duff, in actuality, by *Ossian*.'[32] The new taste for storms, mountains and blasted heaths was part of the desire for powerful emotional experience, which could not find an outlet in comtemporary literature. *The Poems of Ossian*, with their wild landscape and irregular structure, seemed to promise the imaginative release that was so desperately needed.

The sudden yearning for the Sublime can be related to the growing uncertainties about the existence of God. Blair's own lecture on Sublimity is very revealing, since it follows Burke's method of using Biblical illustrations. Blair quotes from the poetical books of the Bible to demonstrate that the Sublime originates in the grandeur of God in exactly the same way as he quotes from *Fingal*. Although the connection between the dark mystery of *Ossian* and the Christian God was probably unconscious, the idea is latent throughout the essay. Although it would be absurd to suggest that the Ossianic poems were some sort of substitute for God, the overwhelming emotions sought by readers of *Fingal* certainly had something in common with religious enthusiasm. The vogue for *Ossian* can be seen as part of a subconscious reaction against the scepticism of David Hume and the French *philosophes*, which seemed to threaten the traditional frameworks of belief. The world of *Ossian* was remote and mysterious, haunted by ghosts and surrounded by mists and darkness. It was the complete antithesis of the Enlightenment.

Blair's own search for sublimity was bound up with his sense of the inadequacy of contemporary civilisation:

> I am inclined to think, that the early ages of the world, and the

rude unimproved state of society, are peculiarly favourable to the strong emotions of Sublimity . . . In the progress of society, the genius and manners of men undergo a change more favourable to accuracy, than to strength or sublimity.[33]

Just as Pope had searched for spirit and fire in *Homer*, so Blair turned to *Ossian* for the 'vehemence and fire, which are the soul of poetry'.[34] Blair saw *The Poems of Ossian* as reservoirs of the vitality and imaginative power that had drained out of the modern world.

Macpherson's Celts were far more suited to Blair's sentimental image of primitive man than any truly ancient poetry could be. Blair's *Critical Dissertation* included 'Lodbrog' as an example of poetry composed by a 'barabarous nation', but despite his admiration for the 'ferocious spirit' of the Scandinavian, Blair's preference was for *Fingal*:

> when we open the works of Ossian, a very different scene presents itself. There we find the fire and the enthusiasm of the most early times, combined with an amazing degree of regularity and art. We find tenderness, and even delicacy of sentiment, greatly predominant over fierceness and barbarity. Our hearts are melted with the softest feelings, and at the same time elevated with the highest ideas of magnanimity, generosity, and true heroism. When we turn from the poetry of Lodbrog to that of Ossian, it is like passing from a savage desart, into a fertile and cultivated country.[35]

For Blair, early poetry was good by definition, but an idealised form of early verse was even better.

Despite his reservations about contemporary society, Blair was as much a mid-eighteenth-century reader as anyone else. The Ossianic poetry had more than strong emotions and original genius to recommend it to the man of taste. Although Blair isolated sublimity as one of the most important features of *Ossian*, the other quality he admired was that of 'tenderness'. One of the main difficulties faced by critics in search of Original Genius was, after all, the lack of refinement in much of the poetry they wished to elevate. Alexander Gerard, for example, though a great admirer of Homer, was also a firm believer in 'refinement of taste', and the two ideals were not always easy to reconcile.

Gerard's observation that 'even Homer admits images in some degree coarse and indelicate' was characteristic of the mid-eighteenth-century critic.[36] The Homeric heroes, for all their fighting spirit and unfailing courage, were nevertheless ruthless barbarians, who failed to meet eighteenth-century demands for virtuous behaviour: Achilles's treatment of Hector's corpse did not quite measure up to the sentimental standards of morality.

In *Fingal*, however, the actions of the heroes were very different. Although the Celts displayed the necessary courage and resolution, they tempered it with benevolence, pity, generosity and tenderness. Eighteenth-century aestheticians, therefore, seized on *Fingal* as the ideal example of ancient poetry, stressing the fine feelings of the Celts in their comparisons between Homer and Ossian. Lord Kames was particularly struck by the noble characters of Macpherson's epics:

> In Homer's time, heroes were greedy of plunder; and, like robbers, were much disposed to insult a vanquished foe. According to Ossian, the ancient Caledonians had no idea of plunder; and as they fought for fame only, their humanity overflow'd to the vanquished . . . Agreeable to the magnanimous character given by Ossian of his countrymen, we find humanity blended with courage, in all their actions: 'Fingal pitied the white-armed maid; he stayed the uplifted sword. The tear was in the eye of the King, as bending forward he spoke: King of streamy Sora fear not the sword of Fingal: it was never stained with the blood of the vanquished; it never pierced a fallen foe'.[37]

Fingal had as much in common with the heroes of Mackenzie and Sterne as with those of the Homeric epic. His tears were not a sign of weakness, but an expression of undisguised sympathy and, therefore, moral virtue. Macpherson's Celts were remarkable not only for their primitive energy, but also for their 'humanity'.

The emphasis on refinement and good taste also affected the form of Macpherson's work. As soon as the *Fragments* appeared he had been put under pressure to polish his raw materials into a more acceptable genre, but even the elegant epics he produced were not sufficiently refined for some of his readers. It was Lord Kames who encouraged Macpherson to produce a new and 'improved' translation of *The Poems of Ossian* in 1773, as he explained to Mrs Montagu:

> I have also suggested to him some amendments of the style; for though the composition on the whole is excellent, yet many passages are capable of higher polish, without losing in point of strength. Mr Macpherson has embraced my hint more readily than I expected.[38]

When the new edition appeared, the poems were arranged in chronological order, while many of the epithets were replaced by more elegant phrases: 'golden mist' becoming 'sun-streaked mist', 'heath' becoming 'ridge of rocks'.[39] Despite the initial excitement over the Ossianic poems as spontaneous effusions of a primitive bard, the eighteenth-century emphasis on improvement and refinement could not be quelled. For Kames, *Fingal* required further 'amendments', while other readers sought to re-write the poems in more acceptable forms. Although the measured prose and loose structure suggested the great antiquity of Ossian, new translations were quickly produced in which Macpherson's work was transformed into regular blank verse or rhyming stanzas. The desire for refinement is as characteristic of the period as the wistful yearning for the past, and it is remarkable that Macpherson should have produced a work which could satisfy these apparently contradictory impulses.

Despite the grumblings of Dr Johnson and the Herculean efforts of Malcolm Laing, Macpherson's work continued to gain in popularity for at least half a century after its first publication. Throughout Europe and America, *The Poems of Ossian* provided inspiration to poets, playwrights, artists and musicians, as well as popular entertainment to the growing reading public. In his study of *Scotland in Music*, Roger Fiske claims that during the fifty years when Macpherson's 'reputation abroad was at its zenith, he was far more highly regarded than Shakespeare or any other British writer'.[40] The claim may seem extravagant until one starts counting up the number of paintings, plays, poems and musical compositions with Ossianic titles, let alone the numerous pieces which show the general influence of Macpherson.

One of the best examples of Macpherson's influence is in Goethe's early novel, *Die Lieden des jungen Werthers* (The Sorrows of Young Werther), 1774, which caused a sensation across Europe, taking *Ossian* with it. Napoleon, who was an avid reader of Goethe's novel, is said to have taken a copy of *Ossian* with him on all his campaigns, as well as inspiring the Swedish Royal Family to adopt the name 'Oscar'. Buonaparte was not the only statesman to be enchanted by *Ossian* and in America, Thomas Jefferson considered Macpherson's 'rude bard of the north the greatest poet that has ever existed'.[41]

In Britain, all the great Romantic poets came under Macpherson's spell to a greater or lesser degree. Blake was a great enthusiast ('I own myself an admirer of Ossian equally with any other Poet whatever') and Macpherson's influence can be seen in early works such as 'Gwin, King of Norway' as well as in the free verse and strange names of the prophetic books.[42] Coleridge, too, composed imitations of *Ossian* in 1793 and three years later, he was contemplating the possibilities of writing 'Carthon, an Opera'.[43] Although Wordsworth came to reject Macpherson's *Ossian* as bogus, he wrote a number of pieces on the subject and it is not difficult to trace an unacknowledged influence in several of his poems.[44] In Byron's poetry, the echoes are everywhere and Macpherson's work seems to have affected him as strongly as it affected Hazlitt, who placed Ossian beside Homer, Dante and the Bible.[45]

Ossian was a herald of the Romantic Movement. For readers who were not entirely satisfied by the prevailing attitudes of the Enlightenment, Macpherson offered emotional and imaginative release. His Celtic world was remote and mysterious, its heroes ideal, magnificent and yet intangible. The dark scenery and the supernatural elements appealed strongly to Gothic tastes, as well as to those readers seeking the Sublime. Ossian's poetry burst straight from the overpowering emotions of the ancient bard and was lost in the 'sublime' landscape of mountains and storms. As such, it offered an exciting alternative to the familiar classical models, and *Ossian* rapidly became a symbol for the literature of the North.

At the same time, Macpherson's vision of Celtic society accorded well with the ideals of Rousseau and his followers. In Ossian's age of heroes, men were free from the burden of property and unrepressed by Church or State. There were no class barriers: Fingal was a leader through merit rather than privilege, while his army was tied by bonds of affection rather than by self interest or obligation. For readers with radical sympathies, such as William Blake, the appeal of *Ossian* was not merely stylistic and indeed, the free style of the verse seemed a reflection of the free society of Ancient Britain.

Unlike the urban society of Western Europe, Macpherson's Celts almost seemed part of the natural world. Their passions, unhindered by social conventions, were expressed freely, using metaphors drawn directly from their surroundings. Ossian's language, like his landscapes, seemed refreshingly different from the tired poetic diction of much mid-eighteenth-century poetry, which Wordsworth was to attack in the Preface to *Lyrical Ballads*. Instead of personified abstractions and latinate vocabulary, Ossian used simple words which could be grasped by anyone.

Despite their newness, *The Poems of Ossian* also seemed to offer a comforting sense of permanence: it was ancient poetry like the Bible or Homer and therefore seemed safe. Although Macpherson's work anticipated many of the concerns of the Romantic Movement, the words of a third-century poet could hardly seem revolutionary. The melancholy preoccupations of the Celtic bard himself attracted the sympathy of an eighteenth-century audience, but he still retained the stature of an Ancient. The combination of the subjective poet and the sage prophet was perfect for the Romantic Period, where the image of the poet as an isolated genius emerged again and again. As sole survivor of a greater world, Ossian commanded the perennial fascination with the exiled hero and the loss of paradise.

NOTES
1. *Poesie di Ossian figlio di Fingal*, tr. M. Cesarotti, (Padua 1763). For the different editions of *Ossian*, see G. F. Black, *Macpherson's Ossian and the Ossianic Controversy*, (New York 1926); J. J. Dunn, 'Macpherson's Ossian: A Supplementary Bibliography', *BNYPL*, lxxv, 1971, 467-73.

2. Gray to Mason, 7 August 1760, *The Correspondence of Thomas Gray*, II, 690.
3. Gray to Wharton, *c.* 20 June 1760, ibid, II, 680.
4. Morris to Lort, *c.* 1763, J. Saunders Lewis, *A School of Welsh Augustans*, (London 1924), 134.
5. Ibid.
6. Ibid.
7. Morris to Pegge, ibid, 133.
8. Warner (1703–1768), though not an Irishman, produced a *History of Ireland* in 1763.
9. C. O'Conor, *Dissertations on the History of Ireland*, (Dublin 1766), 27. See also Sylvester O'Halloran, *An Introduction to the Study of the History and Antiquities of Ireland*, (London 1772); Charlotte Brooke, *Reliques of Irish Poetry*, (Dublin 1789).
10. E. C. Mossner, *The Forgotten Hume*, (New York 1943), 89.
11. J. Wilkes, *The North Briton*, ii, 1762, 11–12.
12. Hume to Blair, 19 September 1763, *Letters*, I, 399.
13. Ibid, 400.
14. *Ossian*, 1765, II, 452–53. Several of the letters received by Blair were eventually included in the *Report*, 1805.
15. Dr John Macpherson to Blair, 27 November 1763, *Report*, App. 14.
16. See ADV MS 73.2.13/1 (Macfarlan to Blair, 1763) and ADV MS 73.2.13/2 (MacQueen to Blair, 1763).
17. *Ossian*, 1765, II, 457; cf ADV MS 73.2.13/6, Hugh Mackay to Blair, 22 December 1763: 'many of the Poems by Ossian, given to the Publick by Macpherson are true and genuine, and have lost a great deal of their value and beauty in the Translation'. See also D. Macleod on the 'inequality of Macpherson's genius to that of Ossian', *Report*, App. 29.
18. Ewan Macpherson to Highland Society, 11 September 1800, *Report*, App. 96.
19. MacQueen to Blair, 17 April 1764, *Report*, App. 36.
20. Macdonald to Bottiger, 1797, in A. Gillies, *A Hebridean in Goethe's Weimar*, (Oxford 1969), 64. Macdonald was born in N. Uist *c.* 1771 but travelled to Weimar in 1796, where he wrote a series of letters on the Ossianic question.
21. Blair to Hume, 1 July 1765, cited by Saunders, *James Macpherson*, 210.
22. J. H. Burton, *The Life and Correspondence of David Hume*, 2 vols, (Edinburgh 1846), I, 471. 'Of the Authenticity of Ossian's Poems' first appeared in Burton's *Life*, I, 471–480. See also Mossner, *The Forgotten Hume*, 83–102.
23. D. McNicol, *Remarks on Dr Samuel Johnson's Journey to the Hebrides*, (London 1779). Macpherson is believed to have had a hand in the work: see R. F. Metzdorf, 'M'Nicol, Macpherson and Johnson', *Eighteenth Century Studies in Honor of Donald F. Hyde*, ed. W. H. Bond (New York 1970), 45–61; J. D. Fleeman, introduction to Johnson's *Journey*, 1985.
24. T. F. Hill, 'New Lights on the Ossianic Controversy', *Gentleman's Magazine*, lii, 1782, 570–71; liii, 1783, 33–6; 140–44; 398–400; liv, 1783, 590–92; 662–65. See also 'Hill's Collection of Ossianic Poetry', *Celtic Magazine*, xii, 1882, 316–21.

25. Chalmers to Constable, 17 July 1805, T. Constable, *Archibald Constable and his Literary Correspondents. A Memorial*, 3 vols, (Edinburgh 1873), I, 41.
26. *Critical Review*, xii, 1761, 405.
27. Reported by Boswell, 8 February 1763, *London Journal*, 182.
28. Ibid. See also Boswell's own enthusiasm in a letter to Erskine, 17 December 1761, 'I will not anticipate your pleasure in reading the Highland bard; only take my word for it, he will make you feel that you have a soul', *Boswell's, Correspondence with* . . ., 37.
29. Stukeley, *Fingal*, December 1761, Bod MS Eng Misc.e. 383, 4.
30. Blair, *Lectures*, I, 60.
31. *Annual Register*, iv, 1761, 282.
32. S. H. Monk, *The Sublime: A Study of Critical Theories in Eighteenth-Century England*, (New York 1935), 133.
33. Blair, *Lectures*, I, 60–61.
34. Blair, *A Critical Dissertation* . . ., 2.
35. Ibid, 11. Cf. Sheridan, 'We could not imagine that such sentiments of delicacy as well as generosity could have existed in the breasts of rude, uncultivated people', Boswell, *London Journal*, 182.
36. A. Gerard, *An Essay on Genius*, (London 1774), 408.
37. H. Home, Lord Kames, *Sketches of the History of Man*, 2 vols, (Edinburgh 1774), I, 292; later published as 'Critical Observations on the Poems of Ossian', *The Poems of Ossian*, (Edinburgh 1797), II, 285–314).
38. Kames to Mrs Montagu, 22 May 1771. The 'improvements' included a chronological arrangement of the poems and a preface introducing characters and explaining the events, Tytler, *Memoirs . . . of Kames*, II, 90.
39. *Fingal*, 10–11, cf. *Ossian*, 1773, I, 231.
40. R. Fiske, *Scotland in Music: A European Enthusiasm*, (Cambridge 1983), 33.
41. Jefferson to C. Macpherson, 25 February 1773, quoted by Frederic I. Carpenter, 'The Vogue of Ossian in America', *American Literature*, ii, 1930–31, 405–17. On the spread of Ossianism abroad, see Paul Van Tieghem, *Ossian en France*, 2 vols (Paris 1917); Isidoro Montiel, *Ossian en Espana*, (Barcelona 1974); A. Hook, 'Ossian and America', and P. Dukes, 'Ossian and Russia', *SLN*, iii, 1973, 23–7, 17–23; S. M. Gilardino, *La Scuola Romantica: la Tradizione Ossianica nella Poesia dell' Alfieri, del Foscolo a del Leopardi*, (Ravenna 1982); Y. D. Levin, *Ossian v Russkoy Literature* (Leningrad 1982).
42. Blake, 'Annotations to Wordsworth', 822. On Ossian's influence on Blake, see M. R. Lowery, *Windows of the Morning* (London 1940). For the influence on the Romantics in general, see J. J. Dunn, 'The Role of Macpherson's Ossian in the Development of British Romanticism' (unpublished doctoral dissertation, Duke University, 1966).
43. See J. J. Dunn, 'Coleridge's Debt to Macpherson', *SSL*, vii, 1969, 76–89.
44. See J. R. Moore, 'Wordworth's Unacknowledged Debt to Macpherson's Ossian', *PMLA*, 1925, 362–78.
45. See J. J. Dunn, op. cit.; R. Flower, *Byron and Ossian*, (Nottingham 1928).

Epilogue

> I breakfasted with Macpherson, the translator of *Fingal*, a man of great genius and an honest Scotch Highlander. It did my heart good to hear the spirit with which he talked. 'The Highlanders,' said he, 'are hospitable and love society. They are very hardy, and can endure the inconveniences of life very well. Yet they are very fond of London when they get to it, and indulge as much in its pleasures as any body. Let me,' said he, 'have something in perfection: either the noble rudeness of barbarous manners or the highest relish of polished society. There is no medium. In a little town you have the advantage of neither'.
>
> James Boswell, *London Journal*, 1762–1763

But what of the Sublime Savage himself? While allies such as Hugh Blair and John Clark were to spend years fighting to defend his credibility, Macpherson's own interests shifted from matters Celtic. As soon as *Fingal* had been published in December 1761, Macpherson's financial difficulties evaporated, along with any 'reserve' he might once have had. Suddenly the awkward young Highlander was a well-known figure in the capital, being toasted as a great poet by literary ladies and sought after as a drinking companion by the gentlemen. Any prejudices against urban civilisation or the Sassenachs seem to have vanished miraculously as Macpherson's eyes were opened to the compensations London offered ('I hate John Bull, but I love his daughters' – 14 May 1763). Once away from the restraining influences of university or the watchful eyes of family and friends, Macpherson was determined to make the most of life in the city.

Apart from a riotous social life, Macpherson also seems to have had a talent for meeting the right people. He had been introduced to the Earl of Bute soon after he arrived in England, and by 1763 he was taking his first steps out of a poetic career and into public service. Macpherson was offered a job in America as Surveyor General and Secretary to the new Governor of Florida. So as the Ossianic controversy began to rage after the publication of *Temora*, Macpherson moved off the scene for two years.

When Macpherson returned to Britain after visiting America and the West Indies, his life was to remain focused on London rather than the North. He moved into a house with the flamboyant Scottish writer/soldier, Alexander Dow, and continued to lead a full life, both socially and professionally. Although he was persuaded by his old colleagues in Edinburgh to revise *Ossian*, write an *Introduction to the History of Great Britain and Ireland*, and translate *The Iliad* in Ossianic language, his real interests were now political. Using his pen and his personal charm, Macpherson obtained work as a political journalist for the North Government, which led to an important commission in Paris in 1774. Macpherson's work on the Carte papers was published in 1775, as *Original Papers, containing the Secret History of Great Britain from the Restoration to the Accession of the House of Hanover, with Memoirs of James II*, and in the same year, he published a sequel to David Hume's *History of Great Britain*. James Macpherson was a now well-established historian, commanding sums of £3000 from William Strahan, the publisher, so the attack published by Johnson in the same year was little more than an irritation. Indeed, Macpherson seems to have largely lost interest in *Ossian* by this stage, and despite the spasmodic demands for the publication of the Gaelic originals, he continued to pursue his political interests. In addition to his historical and political writings, Macpherson was closely involved with the East India Company and had acquired a lucrative position as the London agent for the Nabob of Arcot. By 1780, he achieved his ultimate ambition when he became a Member of Parliament for Camelford in Cornwall.

In the space of twenty years, James Macpherson had changed from being a penniless Highland schoolmaster to being a wealthy, famous writer, with a seat in the House of Commons. It is perhaps not surprising that a certain touch of smugness can be detected in the face that stares out of the fine, colourful portraits by Reynolds and Romney. By the 1780s, Macpherson had money, fame and power; he had a town house in Westminster, a villa on Putney Common, a wide circle of friends, a string of mistresses and four illegitimate children. What more could anyone want? And yet, in the middle of all this, Macpherson still retained a sentimental yearning for the Highlands.

Many of Macpherson's close friends were Scots, while his attitude to political and business concerns was still influenced by the Clan spirit. His main correspondent in India, for example, was Sir John Macpherson, the son of the Celtic historian Dr John Macpherson, who had become Governor General of India. Their letters are full of references to fellow clansmen such as Lachlan Macpherson of Strathmashie's son who, by that stage, had become an officer in the Indian Army. James Macpherson was constantly being pressed to use his influence to further the careers of young Highlanders, and he still used Gaelic to convey any confidential information. It is no wonder

Epilogue 183

that he should decide in the late 1780s that the only thing he still needed to acquire was an estate in the Highlands.

As soon as the opportunity arose, James Macpherson purchased three estates in Badenoch and commissioned Robert Adam to build him a house. In the last years of his life, Macpherson travelled North regularly to stay at Belleville, the elegant Georgian mansion overlooking the countryside where he had grown up. Rather than adopt the pose of a recluse, Macpherson appears to have led as lively a social life in Badenoch as in London, throwing parties which often lasted well into the small hours. He was also a popular landlord, employing a large number of local men and paying them high wages for their work. When he died at Belleville in February 1796, his death resembled that of a Highland laird, being mourned by his men in Gaelic elegies, which still survive as evidence of the affection Macpherson seems to have attracted throughout his life. It is nevertheless characteristic that Macpherson had no wish to be buried in the Kirk where he had been baptised. His death was as flamboyant as his life, and he left explicit instructions in his will that his body should be moved South for a grand burial in Westminster Abbey. Even in death, Macpherson was divided between his romantic loyalty to the Highlands and his natural attraction to the wealth and splendour of the South.

Surviving Gaelic Manuscripts collected by James Macpherson

National Library of Scotland: ADV MS 72.1.37, 72.1.38, 72.1.39,
72.1.40, 72.1.41, 72.1.42,
72.1.43, 72.1.44, 72.1.45,
72.1.46, 72.1.48, 72.1.49,
72.1.50, 72.2.1, 72.2.2,
73.2.20 (part)
National Museum of Antiquities, Edinburgh MCR 39
Scottish Record Office RH 13/40
Trinity College Dublin MS 1698 (H.6.22)
Royal Irish Academy, Dublin, MSS 744 (Av2) ffi–?ii57–80
209–210;
751 (E iv 1), ff 10A–50V
778 (E i 3)
1234 (C i 2)
1237 (D i 1), Nos I and VI

I am indebted to Mr Ronald Black of the University of Edinburgh for this list of manuscripts.

Works by James Macpherson, including the major editions of Ossian

1755	'To a Friend, mourning the Death of Miss . . .' *Scots Magazine*, xvii, 249
1758	*The Highlander* (Edinburgh)
1758	'On the Death of Marshal Keith', *Scots Magazine*, xx, 550
1760	*Fragments of Ancient Poetry, collected in the Highlands of Scotland, and translated from the Galic or Erse Language* (Edinburgh)
1760	*Fragments of Ancient Poetry*, 2nd edn, facsimile (Edinburgh 1970)
1762	*Fingal, an Ancient Epic Poem in Six Books: together with Several Other Poems composed by Ossian, the Son of Fingal*
1763	*Temora, an Ancient Epic Poem in Eight Books: together with Several Other Poems composed by Ossian, the Son of Fingal*
1763	*Poesie di Ossian figlio di Fingal antico poeta Celtico ultimamente scoperte e tradotte in prosa inglese da Jacopo Macpherson, e da quella trasportate in verso italiano dall'Ab. Melchior Cesarotti* (Padua)
1765	*The Works of Ossian, the Son of Fingal. Translated from the Galic Language by James Macpherson*, 2 vols
1771	*An Introduction to the History of Great Britain and Ireland*
1772	—— 2nd edn
1773	—— 3rd edn
1773	*The Iliad of Homer, translated by James Macpherson*
1773	*The Poems of Ossian. Translated by James Macpherson. esq.*, new edn, 2 vols

1775	*Original Papers, containing the Secret History of Great Britain from the Restoration to the Accession of the House of Hanover, with Memoirs of James II*, 2 vols
1775	*The History of Great Britain from the Restoration to the Accession of the House of Hanover*, 2 vols
1776	*The Rights of Great Britain asserted against the Claims of America*
1779	*The History and Management of the East India Company, from its Origin in 1600 to the Present Times*
1779	*A Short History of the Opposition during the last Session*
1795	*Morison's edition of the Poems of Ossian, the Son of Fingal*, 2 vols, (Perth)
1796–7	*The Poems of Ossian, the Son of Fingal*, (Cameron and Murdoch's edn), 2 vols, (Glasgow)
1797	*The Poems of Ossian*, 2 vols (Edinburgh)
1799	*The Poems of Ossian* (Imray's edn), 2 vols (Glasgow)
1802	*Works of James Macpherson* (Edinburgh)
1805	*The Poems of Ossian translated by James Macpherson*, 3 vols
1805	*The Poems of Ossian, &c, containing the Poetical Works of James Macpherson, Esq. in prose and rhyme: with notes and illustrations by Malcolm Laing, Esq.*, 2 vols, (Edinburgh)
1807	*The Poems of Ossian, in the original Gaelic, with a literal translation into Latin, by the late Robert Macfarlan, AM. Together with a Dissertation on the authenticity of the poems, by Sir John Sinclair, Bart. And a translation from the Italian of the Abbe Cesarotti's Dissertation on the controversy respecting the authenticity of Ossian, with notes and a supplemental essay, by John M'Arthur, LL.D.*, 3 vols
1818	*Dana Oisein mhic Fhinn, air an cur amach airson maith coitcheannta muinntir na Gaeltachd* (Edinburgh)
1822	*The Poems of Ossian, translated by James Macpherson, Esq, Authenticated, illustrated, and explained by Hugh Campbell, Esq.*, 2 vols
1870	*The Poems of Ossian in the original Gaelic with a literal translation into English and a dissertation on the authenticity of the poems by the Rev. Archibald Clerk. Together with the English translation by Macpherson*, 2 vols (Edinburgh & London)

Works

1888	*The Poems of Ossian, translated by James Macpherson*. With an introduction, historical and critical, by George Eyre-Todd.
1896	*The Poems of Ossian, translated by James Macpherson*, with notes and with an introduction by William Sharp (Edinburgh)
1966	*Fragments of Ancient Poetry*, ed John J. Dunn (Los Angeles)
1971	*The Poems of Ossian* (Facsimile of Laing's edn), with an introduction by John MacQueen, 2 vols (Edinburgh)

Index

Note. J. M. is used as an abbreviation for James Macpherson.

Aberdeen University, 20, 24–37, 44, 86, 153
Addison, Joseph, 65, 143
America, 181–2
Annual Register, 174
authenticity of J. M.'s work, 1–4, 79–85, 99, 124–6, 137, 163, 165–71

Badenoch (J. M.'s home district),
  childhood in, 12, 14–5, 17, 19–20
  adult life in, 40–1, 61, 66, 123, 128, 183
  death in, 6, 183
Balavil House (Belleville), 6–7, 48, 183
bards,
  in J. M.'s work, 92–3, 96, 105–6, 110, 142–5, 155–7
  in Scottish Society, 13, 100, 111, 164
  see also oral tradition, MacMhuirich Family
Beattie, James, 26, letter, 59n, 'Ode to Peace', 74, 'Epistle to Blacklock', 144
Belleville (Balavil House), 6–7, 48, 183
Benbecula, 117, 120, 121
Berkeley, George, Bishop of Cloyne, 29, 30
Bible, 1, 89–92, 102–3, 106, 107, 135, 174, 177, 178
birth, 7
Blacklock, Rev. Thomas, 144
  Collection of Original Poems, 42–3
Blackwell, Thomas, 26, 28–37, 65, 87, 155–6
  Enquiry into the Life and Writings of Homer, 28, 30, 31, 35, 54, 135, 153

Memoirs of the Court of Augustus, 29
Blair, Hugh,
  comments on J. M.'s work, 80, 107, 111, 128
  controversy over authenticity, 168–70
  Critical Dissertation on the Poems of Ossian, 172–5
  influence on J. M., 66, 78–9, 96–7, 115–6, 157
  preface to *Fragments*, 96–9, 135
Blake, William, 77, 177–8
Boleskine, 118
Book of the Dean of Lismore, The, 89, 90–1, 118, 142–3
Boswell, James, 7, 9, 53–4, 61–2, 171–2
Buchanan, G, *Rerum Scoticarum Historia*, 70, 152
Buonaparte, Napoleon, 2, 177
Burke, Edmund, *Philosophical Enquiry into the Sublime and the Beautiful*, 86, 174
Burt, Edward, 8, 15
  Letters from a Gentleman in the North of Scotland, 8, 10, 13
Bute, Earl of, 117, 134–5, 166–7, 181

Camelford, Member of Parliament for, 182
Campbell, J.F., 81, 119, 120, 125–7, 171
  Leabhar na Féinne, 3, 63, 126
  Popular Tales of the West Highlands, 13, 119
Carlyle, Alexander, 43, 78–9, 114, 157
Carte Papers, 182
Celtic heroes, *see* heroes
Cesarotti, Abbe, 163, 171

Index

Chalmers, Robert, 133
Churchill, Charles, *Prophecy of Famine, The*, 133, 163, 166–7
Clan system, 10–11, 12–13, 122
Clark, John, 66–7, 80–1
   Answer to Mr Shaw's Enquiry, 170
Cluny Castle, 18
Collins, William, 'Ode on the Popular Superstitions of the Highlands of Scotland', 62, 77, 79
critical appraisals of J. M.'s works, 64, 80–1, 96–9, 113–4, 124–8, 163–78
Critical Review, 167, 171
Culloden, 17–19
Cumberland, 'Butcher', 18

Dalrymple, David, 116
Dalrymple, Sir Hugh, 133, 134
death, 183
   burial, 6, 183
'Death of Oscur', 84–93, 104
'Death', 48–51, 85
Dermid, 14, 84–93
Dow, Colonel Alexander, 182
   Tragedy of Zingis, 43
Druids, 157
Dryden, John, 27, 72, 79, 84, 86, 137–9
Duncan, William, 28, 29, 34–5
   Caesar's Commentaries, 34, 35, 153

East India Company, 182
Edinburgh, 52, 57, 66, 97, 113, 115, 128, 133, 158, 168
Edinburgh Review, 39, 114
Erskine, Andrew, 1–2, 4, 171

Farquharson manuscript, 122
Ferguson, Adam, 77, 114, 157–9
   Essay on the History of Civil Society, 158
Fiana (Fein), 3, 15, 69, 84, 89, 105, 110, 165
Fingal, 14–15, 69, 83, 104, 110, 133–49
Fingal Reclaimed, Anon, 165–6
Fingal, 58, 68–9, 135, 151–60 *passim*
   authenticity, 125
   critical appraisal, 127, 148–9, 163, 167, 176–7
   parallels, 69–70, 136–9, 145–6, 154
   plot, 127–8, 135, 140–1, 146–7, 152
   style, 135–141, 149
   themes, 83, 142–3, 144, 147
Florida, USA, 181
fortia facta patrum, 13, 147
Fragments of Ancient Poetry, 24, 96–111, 114, 124
   authenticity, 84–5, 99
   critical appraisal, 113, 164
   style, 85, 90–3, 104, 108–9, 136
   themes, 101–2, 103–6, 107, 139–40, 146–7
Fraser, Thomas, 118

Gaelic language, 16–17, 32–3, 62–3, 77, 80–1
Gaelic Poetry, 2–3, 13–14, 62–7, 77–85, 89–90, 97, 103, 115, 116–128, 136, 142, 148, 169
Gallie, Rev. Andrew, 83, 121, 123–4, 128
'Garbh mac Stairn' Ballads, 85, 127, 136
genealogy, 10–14
Gentleman's Magazine, 42, 113, 170
Gerard, Alexander, 26–8, 36–7, 144, 175
   Plan of Education, 32
ghosts, 55–7, 102–3, 138–8, 146–7, 156
Gibbon, Edward, *The Decline and Fall of the Roman Empire*, 33, 161n
Goethe, Johann Wolfgang, *Die Lieden des jungen Werthers*, 2, 177
Grant, Anne, 7, 8–9, 11, 13–14, 83, 88
   Essays on the Superstitions of the Highlands, 55
Gray, Thomas, 27, 53, 78, 87, 92, 96, 144–5, 163–4

Hazlitt, William, 1, 111, 149, 177
heroes in Scottish legend and poetry,
   Dermid, 14, 84–93
   Fingal, 14–15, 69, 83, 104, 110, 133–49
   Oscur, 14, 84–93, 109, 146
   other, 15–16, 46–7, 68–71, 75, 102–5
Highland Society, The, 121, 122
   Report of Committee, 3, 63, 64, 125, 170–1
Highlander, The, 31, 61–75

critical appraisal, 80, 114
  style, 70–74, 92, 108
Highlands, the, 6–20
  culture, 47, 58, 61–2, 93, 153–5
  landscape, 8–10
  oral tradition of, 13–14, 81–2, 154–6, 160, 164
Hill, Thomas, 170
History of Great Britain, 133, 182
Home, John, 77–9, 80, 84, 114, 117–8, 134
  Douglas, 114, 157
  Fatal Discovery, The, 104, 118, 134
Homer, 1, 63, 64, 72–3, 97, 114, 115, 135, 138, 148, 149, 156, 175, 176–8
  see also Blackwell, Thomas, *Enquiry into . . . Homer*
Horace, 53, 136
Imitation 'To a Friend', 43–6, 49
Hume, David, 114, 115, 157, 166–8, 170, 174
  Treatise on Human Nature, 33
'Hunter, The', 52–8, 61, 68, 73–4

Iliad, J.M.'s translation of the, 85, 182
illegitimacy, 12
influences on J. M.'s work,
  biblical, 89–93, 102–3, 135
  Blackwell, Thomas, 28–33, 35–6
  classical education, 27–8, 34–5, 44–6, 53, 71–3, 135–43, 153–4
  culture of Scotland, 7–10, 12–16, 18–20, 47, 61–2
  philosophical, 30–4, 36, 50, 158–9
Introduction to the History of Great Britain and Ireland, 151–5, 157, 158–9, 182
Invertromie, 7

Jacobite Rebellion, 16, 17, 46–7, 61, 74
Johnson, Dr., 2, 25–6, 62, 81–2, 167, 170, 177
  Journey to the Western Isles, 2, 170

Kames, Lord, 59n, 167, 176
Keith, James, 46–7, 48
Kingussie, 6
King's College (Aberdeen), 26

Laing, Malcom, 2, 42–3, 48, 137, 177
landscape of the Highlands, 8–10

Lismore, The Book of the Dean of, 89, 90–1, 118, 142–3
London, life in, 7, 133–4, 181–2
Loudon, Earl of, 18
Lowth, Robert, 86–7, 89–91, 106
Lucan (Marcus Annaeus Lucanus), *Pharsalia*, 100–1

MacDonald of Clanranald, 117, 121–2, 124
MacDonald, Alexander, 62–3
MacDonald, Hugh, 15
Macdonald, James, 169
MacFarquhar, Colin, 119–20
Mackenzie, Henry, see Highland Society
Mackintosh of Borlum, 8
Maclaurin, Alexander, 15–16
Maclean, J.N.M., 4, 12
MacMhuirich, family, 117, 120, 121–2
MacNeill, Angus, 121
Macpherson of Blairgowrie, Allan, 12, 18–19
Macpherson of Cluny, Ewan, 11, 18, 19, 20, 40
Macpherson of Sleat, Dr. John, 117, 120, 152–3, 169
  Critical Dissertations on the Origin, Antiquities etc, 152–3
Macpherson of Strathmashie, Capt. John, 18
Macpherson of Strathmashie, Lachlan, 116–7, 120, 123–4, 128
Macpherson, Alexander, 118
Macpherson, Andrew (father of J.M), 11
Macpherson, Donald (friend of J. M.), 40–1, 67–8
Macpherson, Duncan, 19
Macpherson, Ewan (friend of J. M.), 120–1, 169
Macpherson, Ewan (J. M.'s grandfather), 11
Macpherson, Finlay, 14, 24
Macpherson, Helen (mother of J. M.), 11
Macpherson, James,
  birth, 7
  character, 7, 25, 27, 29, 50–2, 79
  childhood, 7, 14–15, 17, 19–20
  death, 6, 183
  family history, 11–12
  life in London, 7, 133–4, 181–2

portraits, 182
rise to fame, 78–80
statue, 6
travels, 11–12, 116–123, 182
university life, 20, 24–37, 44, 153
works: see under individual titles
see also influences, manuscripts, occupations, sources
Macpherson, Malcolm, 118–9
Macpherson, Sir John (Governor General of India), 6, 182
MacQueen, Donald, 118, 169
'Magnus Ballads', 68–70, 127
manuscripts, J. M.'s collection, 77–8, 160, 168–171
Book of the Dean of Lismore, 89, 90–1, 118, 142–3
collecting, 61, 66–7, 117–24
translating, 77–81, 86
Marischal College, 26, 28
Martin, Martin, *A Description of the Western Islands of Scotland*, 9
A Voyage to St Kilda, 9
writings, 10
Member of Parliament, 182
Milton, John, *Paradise Lost*, 27, 55–6, 73, 92, 137–8, 143
Moffat, 77–8
Morris, Lewis, 164, 168
Mull, 117

occupations, of J. M.,
journalism, 134, 182
Member of Parliament, 182
other, 134, 181–2
teaching, 40–1, 47–8, 61, 66
tutoring, 66–7, 105–6
'On the Death of Marshall Keith', 46–7, 48
oral tradition of the Highlands, 13–14, 81–2, 154–6, 160, 164
Original Papers . . ., 182
Oscur, 14, 84–93, 109, 146
Ossian, 14–15, 20, 89–90, 92–3, 105, 110, 135, 141–2, 144–5
Outer Hebrides, 117, 118
O'Conor, Charles, 165

parallelism, 64–5, 90–1, 69, 72, 153–4
Paris, 182
Poems of Ossian, The, 7, 14, 30, 33, 41, 44–6, 49, 75, 142, 147, 149, 163–178
authenticity, 2–3, 43, 79–85, 99, 123–6, 137, 163–8, 165–171

critical appraisal, 1–4, 48, 111, 164–8, 171–5, 178
style, 49, 52, 103–4
themes, 45–6, 49, 51, 74–5, 147
Poker Club, The, 114
Pope, Alexander, 27, 63, 72–3, 79, 114, 175
portraits, 182

Ramsay of Ochtertyre, J, 66, 132n, 133
Reid, Thomas, 26–32, 155
Report on Ossian, The (by the Highland Society), 3, 63, 64, 125, 170–1
Rising of 1715, *see* Jacobite Rebellion
Rousseau, Jean-Jaques, 24, 26, 38n, 41n, 178
Ruthven,
Barracks, 17–18, 19–20
J. M.'s life in, 40–1, 48, 61, 117
see also Badenoch

Saunders, Bailey, *The Life and Letters of J.M.*, 4, 40
Scots Magazine, The, 42–4, 63, 65, 74, 113
Seven Years' War, 74, 114
Shaw, William, 170
Sheridan, Thomas, 171–2
Skye, 117, 118, 120
Smollett, Tobias G.,
Briton, The, 167
Humphrey Clinker, 62, 167
sources of J. M.'s work, 68, 70, 82–4, 126–8, 152–3
SSPCK (Society in Scotland for propogating Christian Knowledge), 7, 16–7
Stern, Ludwig, 126
Sterne, Laurence, *Tristram Shandy*, 141–2
Stone, Jerome, 63–5, 127
'Albin and the Daughter of Mey', 64–5, 85, 86
Gaelic Collection, 63, 70, 127
'The Death of Fraoch', 64
Stuart, Charles Edward, 18–19
Stukeley, William, 172
sublimity, The Sublime 4, 64, 86, 87, 154, 172–4, 178

Tacitus, *Germania*, 154
Temora, 10–11, 15, 134

critical appraisal, 163–5, 168, 169
highland influence, 82, 151–3, 158–9
parallels, 139, 141
style, 97, 124–5
themes in J. M.'s works,
  biblical, 102–3, 107
  blindness, 110, 143–6
  death, 45–6, 47–50, 104–7, 146–7
  human nature, 159
  parent outliving child, 51, 106–7, 146
  patriotism, 57–8, 73–5
  religion, 107, 156–8
  romantic, 46, 52, 70–2
  sexual, 46, 105
  supernatural, 55–7, 102–3, 138–9, 146–7, 156
  see also heroes
Thomson, Derick, *Gaelic Sources of Macpherson's Ossian*, 3, 70, 126–7
'To a Friend mourning the Death of Miss . . .', 43–6, 48

Uist, 121

Virgil, 45, 53, 71, 72, 73, 86, 137–8, 147

Wade, General, 10, 17
Ware, Sir James, *De Hibernia*, 152
Warner, Ferdinando, 164–5
West Indies, 182
Wilkes, John,
  North Briton, The, 166–7
Wilkie, William, 114
  Epigoniad, The, 99–100, 114
Withers, Charles, *Gaelic in Scotland* 16
Wolfe, James, 19
Wordsworth, William, 77, 173, 177

Young, E, *Conjectures on Original Composition*, 141–2, 174
  Night Thoughts, 27, 48